THE SCHOOL STORY

Children's Literature Association Series

THE SCHOOL STORY

Young Adult Narratives in the Age of Neoliberalism

David Aitchison

University Press of Mississippi / Jackson

The University Press of Mississippi is the scholarly publishing agency of the Mississippi Institutions of Higher Learning: Alcorn State University, Delta State University, Jackson State University, Mississippi State University, Mississippi University for Women, Mississippi Valley State University, University of Mississippi, and University of Southern Mississippi.

www.upress.state.ms.us

The University Press of Mississippi is a member of the Association of University Presses.

Copyright © 2022 by University Press of Mississippi
All rights reserved

First printing 2022

∞

Library of Congress Cataloging-in-Publication Data

Names: Aitchison, David (David Carlyle), author.
Title: The school story : young adult narratives in the age of neoliberalism / David Aitchison.
Other titles: Children's Literature Association series.
Description: Jackson : University Press of Mississippi, 2022. | Series: Children's literature association series | Includes bibliographical references and index.
Identifiers: LCCN 2021046152 (print) | LCCN 2021046153 (ebook) | ISBN 9781496837622 (hardback) | ISBN 9781496837639 (trade paperback) | ISBN 9781496837653 (epub) | ISBN 9781496837646 (epub) | ISBN 9781496837677 (pdf) | ISBN 9781496837660 (pdf)
Subjects: LCSH: Schools—Fiction. | Children's literature—History and criticism. | Young adult literature—History and criticism. | Neoliberalism. | Education—Economic aspects. | Education—Social aspects. | Education—Political aspects. | Education—Aims and objectives.
Classification: LCC PS490 .A37 2022 (print) | LCC PS490 (ebook) | DDC 809.3/93557—dc23/eng/20211129
LC record available at https://lccn.loc.gov/2021046152
LC ebook record available at https://lccn.loc.gov/2021046153

British Library Cataloging-in-Publication Data available

CONTENTS

3   Introduction

19   **CHAPTER 1**
        Critics, Canon, and School Story Debate

69   **CHAPTER 2**
        Giving Education a Bad Name: Bookish Boys in Contemporary American School Stories

91   **CHAPTER 3**
        Darkness as Heuristic: Care and Development in Pathological School Fiction

123   **CHAPTER 4**
        Detention, Dis-ease, and Death: Contemporary School Experience in Popular World Cinema

153   **CHAPTER 5**
        Teenage Authors, Marketplace Consciousness, and the Deregulation of Childhood in the Age of Neoliberalism

183   Afterword

185   Acknowledgments

187   Index

THE SCHOOL STORY

INTRODUCTION

Simultaneously mundane in its everyday routines and sublime in its promise of improvement, the education facilitated by formal schooling, whether public or private, has come to play a definitive role for both the inner life of the individual and the vaster fabric of the social.[1] Like all institutions, school serves to shape, produce, and transmit certain fundamental values and principles, while presenting opportunities to disrupt or deconstruct others. As scholars of comparative and international education Colin Brock and Nafsika Alexiadou have observed, the dissemination of knowledge and skills carried out under the auspices of formal education has long served as a key mechanism for political, religious, and especially economic control: playing a critical role in the rise of the modern nation-state, in the numerous projects of colonization and empire building, in the major phases of urbanization, and in the upheavals of industrialization (5–8). For the same reasons, in the field of education studies inaugurated by John Locke's *Some Thoughts Concerning Education and of the Conduct of the Understanding* (1693) and Jean-Jacques Rousseau's *Émile, or On Education* (1762), it has long been an embattled institution: conceived variously as liberatory realm of play and inquiry, or consummate tyrannical enclosure; as locus of free thinking, or rote prison; as garden for spiritual cultivation, or training ground for skills building; as expansive route to well-roundedness, or narrow passage to disciplinary specialization. These and other rival possibilities suggest just how pluralistic school experience can be, because it is so unevenly motivated by philosophies of education, constructions of childhood, religious convictions, cultural politics, and marketplace imperatives, all forces that compete, clash, and overlap in various ways.

No wonder, then, that school is one of our most volatile realms of affect, making for intimately emotional engagements, highly critical reflections, and lasting impressions. My purpose in this book is to think about the work of writers, filmmakers, and critics who, investigating, imagining, or looking back on the school realm, help to shape dominant ideas of school. My primary subject is the school story, a genre that has received considerable scholarly attention in the fields of children's literature and social history. Early scholars such as W. R. Hicks, Isabel Quigly, and Jeffrey Richards, for example, explored the real-life institutions behind the classic English boys' boarding-school story; later generations of scholars including Beverly Lyon Clark, Rosemary Auchmuty, and Pat Pinsent diversified that archive to include American and Australian works, and to recuperate a long-neglected body of boarding-school stories for girls and by women; and understanding of the genre continues to broaden as scholars such as Allison Speicher and Amelia V. Katanski consider literary engagements with common schools (precursors to the American public school) and Indian boarding schools, respectively. Because they concentrate on the nineteenth and early twentieth centuries, however, most major studies of the school story have stopped short of exploring the ways in which writers and critics continue to reflect on the meaning and value of education in and for our time. My aim is to draw attention to that neglected contemporary turn in what has to be recognized as a complex period: marked on the one hand by new and impassioned interests in the progressive possibilities of education, with reformers such as James A. Banks championing diversity, inclusivity, equality, and empowerment; and on the other by the rise of conservatives hostile to what they see as a liberal bias in higher education[2] and neoliberal policy makers—such as Betsy DeVos, US Secretary of Education under President Trump—bent on dismantling public education by supporting charter and for-profit schools (which compete with traditional public schools), pressing for voucher systems (which allow students to pay for private education with public-school funds), and generally working to deregulate education (by loosening the federal government's regulations on accreditation and aid).[3] This is not to say flatly that neoliberalism is categorically—politically, economically, morally—bankrupt. On the contrary, it seems more accurate to say that the tenets of neoliberalism play a vital role for democracy: they raise critical talking points that help to work out exactly what we mean by individual freedoms and social responsibility—when asking, for example, whether the welfare state damages citizens' motivations to work and learn, whether government is capable of holding companies to the same strict standards as consumers, and whether power should rest with governments rather than the people. That said, it would be misleading to suggest that the neoliberal tendencies to privatize and financialize public goods including the provision of education are healthy for democracy when, put into practice, they serve to bolster rather than dismantle class and race hierarchies.

Whether in the realm of scholarly research or the more popular world of blogs and podcasts, it has become standard in discussions dealing with neoliberalism to acknowledge it as either a difficult term because of its wide range of reference or a contested term because it is used by different people to mean different things. A case in point is journalist-blogger Ezra Klein's podcast episode "Neoliberalism and Its Discontents," in which Klein interviews professor of political theory Wendy Brown and columnist-economist Noah Smith—respectively, one of the foremost leftist critics of neoliberalism, which she describes as a "governing rationality" in the process of "undoing" democracy (*Undoing the Demos: Neoliberalism's Stealth Revolution*, 2015); and a self-proclaimed "progressive" neoliberal, who argues for "left-leaning neoliberals" while cautioning against rigid market regulations ("'Neoliberal' Isn't a Dirty Word," 2019). Klein's podcast begins thus: "'Neoliberalism' is one of the most confusing phrases in political discourse today. The term is often used to describe the market fundamentalism of thinkers like Milton Friedman and Friedrich Hayek or politicians like Ronald Reagan and Margaret Thatcher. At the same time, critics often place more progressive figures like Bill Clinton, Barack Obama, and even Elizabeth Warren under the neoliberal banner. This raises an important question: what the hell is neoliberalism?" For Manfred Steger and Ravi Roy, "perhaps the best way to conceptualize neoliberalism is to think of it as three intertwined manifestations: (1) an ideology; (2) a mode of governance; (3) a policy package" (11). First, neoliberal ideology "puts the production and exchange of material goods at the heart of the human experience" (12). Second, neoliberal governmentality is "rooted in entrepreneurial values such as competitiveness, self-interest, and decentralization. It celebrates individual empowerment and the evolution of central state power to smaller localized units. Such a neoliberal mode of governance adopts the self-regulating free market as the model for proper government. Rather than operating along more traditional lines of pursuing the public good (rather than profits) by enhancing civil society and social justice, neoliberals call for the employment of governmental technologies that are taken from the world of business and commerce" (12). And third, neoliberal policies are expressed in what Steger and Roy call "the 'D-L-P Formula': (1) deregulation (of the economy); (2) liberalization (of trade and industry); and (3) privatization (of state-owned enterprises)," along with other measures including tax cuts for businesses and high earners and reduced social services and welfare provision (14).

Especially helpful for understanding how and why neoliberalism matters for a study of literature is Mitchum Huehls and Rachel Greenwald Smith's introduction to *Neoliberalism and Contemporary Literary Culture* (2017), where neoliberalism is treated as an economist ideology that has evolved through four historical phases: a first, economic phase beginning in the 1970s, marked by a series of deregulatory shocks set in motion by the Nixon administration, including abandoning the fixed currency of the gold standard, which resulted in suspending the extant international monetary system (the Bretton Woods system) in favor of a system of floating flat currency exchange much more amenable to free-market capitalism; a second, political-ideological stage, in which those free-market principles were integrated into the platforms and policies of the Thatcher and Reagan administrations, both of which implemented massive reforms in de-unionizing labor, privatizing industry, and deregulating commerce; a third sociocultural stage, in which the rationality of the market saturates the world of cultural production and consumption to a point at which it becomes common sense; and a fourth ontological stage, in which "this extension of market rationality to otherwise noneconomic domains of life shifts from a way of thinking—quantitative, efficient, pragmatic, and profitable—to a way of being. No longer just a set of ideological beliefs or deployable rationalities, neoliberalism becomes what we are, a mode of existence defined by individual self-responsibility, entrepreneurial action, and the maximization of human capital" (9). In their description of the sociocultural and ontological stages of neoliberalism, Huehls and Smith seem to be gesturing beyond Wendy Brown's theory of neoliberalism as "governing rationality," although the point she makes is that such a rationality is totalizing—not simply describing "the range of thought allowed by our politics" (Metcalf), but indexing conditions within which *everything* is economized:

> Human beings become market actors and nothing but, every field of activity is seen as a market, and every entity (whether public or private, whether person, business, or state) is governed as a firm. Importantly, this is not simply a matter of extending commodification and monetization everywhere—that's the old Marxist depiction of capital's transformation of everyday life. Neoliberalism construes even non–wealth generating spheres—such as learning, dating, or exercising—in market terms, submits them to market metrics, and governs them with market techniques and practices. Above all, it casts people as human capital who must constantly tend to their own present and future value. (Brown, qtd. in Shenk)

In spite of the tenets of neoliberalism that, as articulated in the founding work of Hayek (*The Road to Serfdom*, 1944) and Friedman (*Capitalism and Freedom*, 1962), make a case for economic and political freedoms, critics detect disturbingly unfree conditions in neoliberalism that not only undermine the principles of welfare and equality championed by modern liberals but also threaten the broader possibility of democracy itself.

Reminded by Brown and fellow scholars such as Henry Giroux (*Neoliberalism's War on Higher Education*, 2014) that democracy depends on the public provision of education, it seems appropriate to acknowledge, first, the intimate relationship between education and economics and, second, the extent to which the school story as a genre speaks to economic conditions—on the understanding that such conditions intersect with and inflect a vast range of experiences and identities distributed along lines of class, ability, gender, sex, race, ethnicity, nationality, and faith. Historically, formal education has been predominantly elitist in its function, privileging the wealthy over the poor, boys and men over girls and women, and white demographics over people of color; and, in spite of modern education acts and declarations of human rights, it continues to be deeply stratified at all levels (elementary, secondary, and higher), especially along class and race lines. But education has also emerged as a very particular field of neoliberal conflict in its own right: in part due to the antigovernment legacies of Thatcher and Reagan, who sought to cut state provisions for public education; in part due to free-market appropriations of the education sector; and in part due to more insidious neoliberal logics that have transformed the meaning and value of education from within the school system itself. As E. Wayne Ross and Rich Gibson note, "Education is a key target of the neoliberal project because of market size (e.g., global spending on education is more than $1 trillion), education's centrality to the economy, and its 'potential to challenge corporate globalization if education succeeds in producing critical citizens for a democratic society'" (Kuehn, qtd. in Ross and Gibson 4). For Ross and Gibson, major curricular reforms of recent decades such as the No Child Left Behind Act of 2001 in the United States work both to "commodify public education by reducing learning to bits of information and skills to be taught and tested" and to "marketize education through programs that promote privatization and user fees in place of free, public education"; meanwhile, as for-profit organizations take over the administration of educational services, "efforts are made to reduce educational costs, often through economies of scale. Closing school libraries, reducing the number of special needs teachers, increasing class size, expanding online learning programs are examples" (4). As for how such reforms affect students' understanding of what their education is for, Matt Hastings clarifies that the neoliberal project favors curriculums that "[frame] the purpose of education in terms of investments made in the development of students' human capital. What students should learn and the value of education is relative to their individual prospects for future earnings. This narrowed conception of education raises important questions about the purpose of education and the relationship between schools, democratic life, and state governance." Comparable debates surround the Common Core State Standards[4] in the USA, an education initiative that on the surface promises to raise achievement levels and prepare elementary and secondary students for productive, innovative lives—but is often framed in neoliberal terms of "open[ing] up this market so that innovators, businesses, can insert themselves at the testing level, at the curriculum development level, at the instructional level, in order to meet a 'uniform base of customers looking at using products that can help every kid learn and every teacher get better.' This neoliberal side of Common Core comes to us through private, not public, channels" (Shannon, Whitney, and Wilson 298, quoting Bill Gates). To the extent that school stories definitively draw attention to classrooms and buildings, textbooks and libraries, tests and report cards, teachers and administrators, we do well to recognize not only how the tenor of the genre has changed between the poles of its classic and contemporary forms but also how even the most benign stories, if attentive to actual school experiences, speak to critical developments in the history of education.

Though primarily interested in contemporary American school stories, this book takes on an archive of fiction and films from around the world. To begin with, because so many literary and educational conventions have crossed between Britain and America, I have in mind a broad Anglo-American tradition: one that begins with the private boarding-school novels of the mid- to late nineteenth century, peaks with the popular boys' and girls' weeklies of the early to mid-twentieth century, undergoes a paradigm shift in the mid- to late twentieth century when the form and fiction of school become more inclusive, and arrives in the twenty-first century at a much altered—ostensibly more democratic yet decisively more disturbed—understanding of school and school fiction. But an even broader background emerges in the history of education informing the classic school story if we acknowledge, with Brock and Alexiadou, that "very few countries outside Europe escaped the imprint of a colonially derived European model of education, and major examples that did, such as China and Japan, turned to Europe and North America as exemplars for major reforms of their educational provision in the late nineteenth century" (8). Recognizing the need for comparative studies of school systems and school experiences from around the world—especially when many of the same economic forces shaping education policy in the USA work not only internationally but also globally—compels me to move beyond the Anglo-Americanist archive into the world archive of contemporary school stories.

I take the school story to be a subgenre of children's literature, though not exclusively so. In fact, one distinct period for the school novel came when critics in the early twentieth century tried to sever ties with its popular juvenile readership and establish it as an adult literary form, only to have midcentury critics such as George Orwell argue that the juvenile audience was precisely what made it significant for the study of culture and society ("Boys' Weeklies,"

1940). Most of the works I discuss were written for children and young adults, serious works of fiction for teen audiences such as Laurie Halse Anderson's *Speak* (1999) and Faiza Guène's *Kiffe Kiffe Demain/Kiffe Kiffe Tomorrow* (2004), lighthearted middle-grade novels such as Andrew Clements's *Frindle* (1996) and Tommy Greenwald's *Charlie Joe Jackson's Guide to Not Reading* (2011), and the autobiography *I Am Malala* (2014) by Malala Yousafzai; or else they take children and young adults as their primary subjects—novels such as Sapphire's *Push* (1996) and films like *Cooties* (USA, 2015) and *Batoru Rowaiaru/Battle Royale* (Japan, 2000), which were restricted to adult audiences or prohibited outright by motion picture associations, but whose young protagonists and narrative arcs have strong appeal for teens. In fact, while the novel has been the mainstay form of the genre for the critics, the school story has received possibly its most striking expression in world cinema, with filmmakers from countries as far afield as Japan, Korea, England, Ireland, Canada, and the USA dramatically envisioning school as a locus of fear and horror. Of course, the genre has always—definitively—been preoccupied with the violent underside of school experience, exemplified in the seminal depictions of bullies and fistfights in works such as *Tom Brown's School Days* (1857). But since the 1970s, coinciding with the rise of neoliberal ideologies in the Americas, an altered understanding of that underside has emerged, with hyperbolic images of terror being attributed less to discrete situations and more to totalizing conditions motivated by aggressive, competitive individualism. Drawing attention to how the school story continues to thrive while crossing mediums, audiences, and cultures, I hope to encourage critical interest in a genre known well for its classic but hardly at all for its contemporary significance.

Influenced by the recent work of Caroline Levine (*Forms: Whole, Rhythm, Hierarchy, Network*, 2015), in this study I foreground certain formal choices brought to bear in school fiction and the ways in which these meet and speak to the formal structures governing actual school experience. The pluralistic, simultaneous, and competing forms theorized by Levine—bounded wholes, temporal rhythms, structured hierarchies, and evolving networks—seem right for grasping the complexities of school as a real-life institution historically marked by bitter conflicts over equality, diversity, and outcomes. So, I probe a school experience characterized by the shift and clash of multiple forms—institutional, cultural, social, academic, environmental—each with its own affordances, to think anew about the discourses, narratives, and logics that either open up or foreclose on the diverse identities and life stories of the young.

Acknowledging that theories of education have profound implications for the arrangement of society—and holding on to Levine's call for radical social change—attending to the politics of the school story is a major undertaking in this study. Influential here is the work of Julia Mickenberg (*Learning from the Left* 2006; with Philip Nel, "Radical Children's Literature Now!" 2011), Kimberly Reynolds ("Puffin and the Legacy of Progressive Publishing for Children in Britain," 2013; *Left Out*, 2016), and Beverly Lyon Clark (*The Afterlife of "Little Women,"* 2014; *Kiddie Lit*, 2003), whose histories and readings attest to the meaning and value of not only the aesthetic and rhetorical accomplishments in young fiction but also the political possibilities. Comparably important is the work of Constance Flanagan (*Teenage Citizens*, 2013; with Peter Levine, "Civic Engagement and the Transition to Adulthood," 2010), whose studies on teenage development and civic responsibility guide my interests in political constructions of student life. And just as influential is the work of scholars exploring contemporary intersections of children's literature, education history, and pedagogy: Elizabeth Marshall ("Monstrous Schoolteachers: Women Educators in Popular Cultural Texts," 2016), Karin Westman ("Blending Genres and Crossing Audiences: Harry Potter and the Future of Literary Fiction," 2011), Elisabeth Gruner ("Teach the Children: Education and Knowledge in Recent Children's Fantasy," 2009), and Lisa Hopkins ("Harry Potter and the Acquisition of Knowledge," 2003), to name a few. For me, Marshall, Westman, Gruner, and Hopkins represent a timely turn in a century-old school story debate to questions of student intellect, learning, and development, and of what it means to imagine or intervene in the school experience. Informed especially by Levine, my intention is to consider how broad concerns over literacy and education, in conjunction with more specific questions of class, ability, race, ethnicity, religion, and gender, afford opportunities to rethink how we might address the structural inequities of school experience in the early twenty-first century. Since I dedicate one chapter to prose narratives engaging with school experience authored and coauthored by teens, I am inclined to argue that these concerns over the meaning and value of education and its myriad representations in popular culture index living concerns not only for teachers and scholars but also for children and young adults.

Since its inception—whether we look to the tales of domestic academies exemplified by Sarah Fielding's *The Governess, or the Little Female Academy* (1749), or the novels of private boarding-school life popularized by *Tom Brown's School Days*—the school story has mostly assumed a mimetic function, purporting to account for (and sometimes even augment) the institution of school. This is true of even the most fantastic school stories, represented most recently and most notably by J. K. Rowling's *Harry Potter* series (1997–2016), whose otherwise magical adventures are grounded in familiar forays into classic boarding-school traditions. As such, it pays to be attentive to how the genre engages with actual issues of concern—from academic performance to character and intellectual development, from student-teacher relationships to the life prospects of both students and teachers, from discipline and punishments to rewards and opportunities—and to remember its educative possibilities. This seems especially important in an era when neoliberal policy makers are not only poised to weaken public education by rerouting funds for at-risk students into private schools but also increasingly skeptical of the meaning and value of higher education.

Informed by the conviction that a true democracy must legitimize the voices, languages, histories, and beliefs of all its groups, this project gives a diverse account of school experience and considers the genre of school story in much the same way that Banks considers the discrete learning environment: as a *microculture*, a cultural environment comprising dominant and subcultures replete with "norms, values, roles, stratifications, and goals like other cultural systems" (27). Hence my foray into texts and contexts, across genres and mediums, from Asia, Europe, and the Americas representing diverse identities in terms of class, race, ethnicity, ability, gender, and faith. Considered this way, school fiction offers surprising insights into key issues along lines of equity (the extent to which students from diverse cultures succeed academically), prejudice (the extent to which race, gender, class, and ability biases influence school experience), and empowerment (the extent to which peers and educators, along with structures and practices, encourage students from diverse groups to gain strength, confidence, and selfhood). Put another way, foregrounding stories that speak in various ways to the presence of neoliberalism in the lives of students around the world, I hope that this project will present opportunities to reflect on the power of fiction to rouse readers' political and pedagogical consciousness.

Because the neoliberalization of education carries a strain of anti-intellectualism long familiar to modern American culture (as if the democratization of education entailed a turn away from the life of the mind), and because the same is sometimes said about literature for the young (even the school story genre, named for the central role it gives to school experience, has mostly been discussed for its depictions of social rather than academic life), there is a need to look out for those rarer narratives that give expression to the intellectual lives of the young. Thus, though a substantial part of this book explores plain and painful critiques of school institutions, I also explore stories in which character development correlates positively with academic development. Even so, it needs to be stressed that such narratives are usually forged in the face of adversity: in the thick of struggles with racism and disability (*Push*), sexual assault and mental illness (*Speak*), sexism and poverty (*Kiffe Kiffe Demain*), and war and exile (*I Am Malala*), to say nothing of the quotidian pressures felt by students, parents, peers, and educators in their everyday lives. Situating readings of popular texts within broader concerns over education, curricula, and children's literature, I make a case for renewing our understanding of the school story as a vibrant form offering thought-provoking depictions of diverse schoolchildren as thinkers and learners.

Of my five chapters, the first provides a survey of critics' attempts to define and canonize the school story (primarily in the form of Anglo-American fiction), from the late nineteenth century to the present. The subsequent four chapters explore notable contemporary stories for print and screen engaging with the idea and practice of school in the late twentieth and early twenty-first centuries: feel-good American stories that seem to celebrate learning, literacy, and community, yet reductively conceive education as a means to selfish, acquisitive ends; gritty psychological stories from the USA that, though fraught to the point of pathological, speak hopefully about the possibilities of student development and care; horror and horror-comedy stories from around the world that comment critically on the totalizing forces that sometimes seem to define the school experience; and speculative stories from around the world by writers of school age imaginatively working through questions about the future that have become definitive for contemporary school experience. Building throughout on Levine's theories of form, in these last four chapters I foreground, respectively, power structures (hierarchy), institutional routines (rhythm), enclosed spaces (whole), and social relations (network), revealing the school story as a rich and complex site engaging critically with the meaning, value, and form of education in the age of neoliberalism.

Works of criticism aside, I draw my primary texts from an archive that not only already comprises a hefty back catalogue of titles and subgenres but also continues to pile up. It would be misleading to suggest that the handful of stories to which I give scrutiny could genuinely represent that archive as a whole. But I do take them to be representative of a particular moment in the history of that archive, one overdetermined by market forces and political interests working in distinctive ways on the idea and practice of education. In making my choices, it seemed important to engage with a range of narratives, characters, and cultural contexts, which, in addition to revealing the thriving diversity of the genre as a global phenomenon, also has the effect of showing how neoliberalism works through various logics informing age, class, race, ethnicity, nationality, gender, sexuality, and ability. All eight of my primary texts have staggered me in some way, whether for good or bad, in their depictions of students and teachers speaking to the meaning and value of learning and growth. Put another way, while varied in their narrative, aesthetic, and formal accomplishments, all eight share a certain rhetorical force that, for this reader, speaks profoundly to our times.

In my first chapter, "Critics, Canon, and School Story Debate," I survey critics' claims and commentaries on the genre of school story made between the late nineteenth and early twenty-first centuries. This chapter reads in two ways: as a single, chronological line of inquiry into a long and ongoing reception history, and as a sampling of stages when discrete turns of thought were brought to bear in fathoming the genre. The different periods discussed—late nineteenth century, early twentieth century, between the wars, mid- to late twentieth century, late twentieth century, turn of the century, and early twenty-first century—reveal a body of criticism and scholarship moving from flatly elitist, patriarchal, and sexist territory into a much more nuanced realm of feminist, postcolonial, and multicultural pluralism. The guiding assumption of this chapter is that, in reckoning the gamut of critical responses, we glean a field of literary and critical production testifying to social, cultural, and economic conditions, and that, in doing so, we are compelled to acknowledge a relative loss of interest in those same conditions informing the genre in and for our time. As such, this chapter makes a case for recuperating the school story as a living genre with a rich history, and for recognizing how contemporary school stories offer vital insights into the critical issues of our time.

After thinking broadly about critics' responses to school fiction, I go on to offer four studies exploring notable popular engagements with school experience in the late twentieth and early twenty-first centuries. Between the first and last of these chapters, I move from conventional to unconventional territory—from stories set within the familiar confines of classrooms to stories in which students in crisis all but leave their schools behind but do not give up thinking about them. In my second chapter, "Giving Education a Bad Name: Bookish Boys in Contemporary American School Stories," I look at feel-good school stories that seem to tout the merits of education. Concentrating on Andrew Clements's *Frindle* (1996) and Tommy Greenwald's *Charlie Joe Jackson's Guide to Not Reading* (2011), I discuss upbeat and mischievous protagonists who thrive on cheating, lying, and avoiding schoolwork but nevertheless figure as models of success. In both books, I read a common problem in terms of hierarchical forms, gauging how authors pit marketplace readiness against liberal education in a strict binary, as if the one prevails only at the expense of the other. Situating such works in ongoing debates over literacy, learning, class, and race in the USA, I argue that the school story raises critical questions about the role of formal education in preparing young people for civic and professional life in the twenty-first century.

In chapter 3, "Darkness as Heuristic: Care and Development in Pathological School Fiction," I consider what happens when the school story and what is currently known as the rape story converge in two popular but controversial works, Sapphire's *Push* and Laurie Halse Anderson's *Speak*. In response to children's book critic Meghan Cox Gurdon's criticism of "dark" and "pathological" teen fiction, I ask whether pathologies—instances of abuse and harm—in teen fiction might figure less as dangerous lures for careless readers and more as promising heuristics for gauging provisions of care and possibilities for development (for students and teachers alike) under neoliberalism. Tracing routines and patterns of growth in and out of school, both works invite us to recognize the rhythmic forms by which school institutions increasingly bolster neoliberal understandings of young adult and adult development.

Recognizing film as one of the most remarkable mediums for school stories in recent decades, in my fourth chapter, "Detention, Dis-ease, and Death: Contemporary School Experience in Popular World Cinema," I turn attention to two movie satires of public education in the neoliberal era: one, *Batoru Rowaiaru/Battle Royale*, a sentimental Japanese story of ninth graders kidnapped by the government and made to fight to the death; the other, *Cooties*, a madcap romp from the USA about teachers fleeing their zombie students. In both works, formal enclosures are put to work in punishing and totalizing ways, and, inflected with the conventions of horror and comedy, they come to figure as ciphers for neoliberal education's hallmark spaces of standardization and competitiveness.

In my fifth and final chapter, "Teenage Authors, Marketplace Consciousness, and the Deregulation of Childhood in the Age of Neoliberalism," I discuss contemporary authors who have written, sold, or published their work while still of school age, on the assumption that it matters how students themselves give voice to their desires to learn and grow in the neoliberal era. I read Malala Yousafzai's *I Am Malala: The Girl Who Stood up for Education and Was Shot by the Taliban* (young readers edition, coauthored with Patricia McCormick) and Faiza Guène's *Kiffe Kiffe Tomorrow* (English translation by Sarah Adams) as books that reflect unflinchingly on the teenage search for meaning and purpose in neoliberal contexts where commercialism intersects with racism, sexism, and ethno-nationalism. While neither of these books is a school story in the conventional sense, both root their narratives in crises brought on by global neoliberalism manifesting in the realm of education—crises that take the protagonists away from the everyday practices and routines of school but not from its structures of purpose and feeling. Foregrounding the social and character networks in Guène's story of the Moroccan immigrant projects in Paris and Yousafzai's story of Pakistan under Taliban occupation, I consider how such narratives renegotiate conventional child/citizen boundaries troubled by the market-oriented structures of global capitalism in the early twenty-first century.

Redefining the school story as a capacious form lending itself to a diverse understanding of school experience, while attending to the political and pedagogical implications of the genre, with this book I hope to enliven discussions about education and young identity and how these are constructed in popular culture and public discourse. The potential impact of these stories on child and teen readers is significant to the extent they negotiate a range of critical possibilities: children as consumers or producers of culture; the classroom as locus of education or platform for entrepreneurship; the child as dupe of the state or social revolutionary; teachers as mouthpieces of the state or radical reformers; teachers and students as allies or enemies; and school as site of personal reflection or public discourse. My understanding is that the school story, at its best, provides young readers with ways to think and feel critically about a realm of experience shared by many and yet still too often taken for granted because it is ubiquitous, quotidian, mundane. So, in much the same spirit as feminist scholars who recognize the particular value of girls' school stories for girl and women readers,[5] I want to make a more general claim on the school story as a whole, as a genre with the potential to help students and teachers think critically about the political and ethical implications of school experience in our contemporary age of neoliberalism.

NOTES

1. By "formal schooling," I mean a shared school experience in an institutional setting governed by trained pedagogues teaching to a standardized curriculum.

2. Drawing on survey results published by the nonpartisan Pew Research Center, recent news articles and opinion pieces attest to Republican and conservative skepticism over the value of college education. Joe Pinsker, writing for the *Atlantic*, reported that "at the beginning of the 2010s, 58 percent of Republicans believed that colleges and universities had a positive impact on the course of the country, according to the Pew Research Center. As the decade nears its close, that number has fallen precipitously: It now sits at 33 percent, with the majority of the drop occurring from 2015 to 2017. According to Pew, there seems to be little disagreement between political parties on the notion that a diploma helps one succeed in the world or that the cost of attaining one is too high. The complaints particular to Republicans, though, are ideological in nature: They are far more likely than Democrats to believe that higher education is shaping America for the worse because too many professors impose their politics on students and because colleges go too far in shielding students from things that might offend them." *Inside Higher Ed* contributor Andrew Kreighbaum confirms partisan bias, noting that "President Trump has questioned the value of community colleges and suggested universities 'restrict free thought.'" And, as Caroline Simon puts it, "If you're

an American conservative today, you might feel uncomfortable sending your children to colleges and universities, where nearly two-thirds of faculty identify as liberal or far-left"; or in the blunter terms of Candice Greaux's *Observer* article, "Conservatives Don't Hate Higher Education—They Hate That It's Liberal."

3. See, for example, Ross Barkan's "The Trump Administration Is Waging a Quiet War on Education" (2019): "The Trump/DeVos vision of American education? Unshackle the rich and let them turn a profit at the expense of working-class students."

4. Common Core State Standards (CCSS): US education initiative outlining grade-level knowledge in English language arts and mathematics for K–12 students, sponsored by the National Governors Association (comprising all US governors) and the Council of Chief State School Officers (nonpartisan organization of public officials heading departments of elementary and secondary education).

5. See, for example, Judith Humphrey, *The English Girls' School Story: Subversion and Challenge in a Traditional Conservative Literary Genre* (2009).

WORKS CITED

Banks, James A. "Multicultural Education: Dimensions and Paradigms." *The Routledge International Companion to Multicultural Education*, edited by James A. Banks, Routledge, 2009, pp. 9–32.

Barkan, Ross. "The Trump Administration Is Waging a Quiet War on Education." *Guardian*, 14 Jun. 2019, Guardian News and Media Limited, www.theguardian.com/commentisfree/2019/jun/14/trump-betsy-devos-education-quiet-war. Accessed 22 Dec. 2019.

Brock, Colin, and Nafsika Alexiadou. *Education Around the World: A Comparative Introduction*. Bloomsbury, 2013.

Brown, Wendy. *Undoing the Demos: Neoliberalism's Stealth Revolution*. Zone Books, 2015.

Friedman, Milton. *Capitalism and Freedom*. 1962. University of Chicago Press, 2002.

Giroux, Henry. *Neoliberalism's War on Higher Education*. Haymarket Books, 2014.

Greaux, Candice. "Conservatives Don't Hate Higher Education—They Hate That It's Liberal." *Observer*, 12 Jul. 2017, *Observer Media*, observer.com/2017/07/pew-report-conservatives-value-higher-education. Accessed 24 Dec. 2019.

Hastings, Matt. "Neoliberalism and Education." *Oxford Research Encyclopedia of Education*, May 2019, *Oxford University Press*. Accessed 27 Nov. 2019.

Hayek, Friedrich. *The Road to Serfdom*. 1944. University of Chicago Press, 2007.

Huehls, Mitchum, and Rachel Greenwald Smith. "Four Phases of Neoliberalism and Literature." *Neoliberalism and Contemporary Literature*, Johns Hopkins University Press, 2017, pp. 1–18.

Humphrey, Judith. *The English Girls' School Story: Subversion and Challenge in a Traditional Conservative Literary Genre*. University of Hertfordshire Press, 2009.

Klein, Ezra. "Neoliberalism and Its Discontents." *The Ezra Klein Show*, 24 Oct. 2019, *Stitcher*, www.stitcher.com/podcast/vox/the-ezra-klein-show/e/64811077. Accessed 22 Dec. 2019.

Kreighbaum, Andrew. "Persistent Partisan Breakdown on Higher Ed." *Inside Higher Ed*, 20 Aug. 2019, www.insidehighered.com/news/2019/08/20/majority-republicans-have-negative-view-higher-ed-pew-finds. Accessed 24 Dec. 2019.

Kuehn, L. "Responding to Globalization of Education in the Americas: Strategies to Support Public Education." *IDEA* conference, 1999, Quito, Ecuador. Paper.

Locke, John. *Some Thoughts Concerning Education and of the Conduct of the Understanding.* 1693. Edited by Ruth W. Grant and Nathan Tarcov, Hacket Publishing Company, 1996.

Metcalf, Stephen. "Neoliberalism: The Idea that Swallowed the World." *Guardian*, 4 Sep. 2017, *Guardian News and Media Limited*, www.theguardian.com/news/audio/2017/sep/04/neoliberalism-the-idea-that-swallowed-the-world-podcast. Accessed 22 Dec. 2019.

Pinsker, Joe. "Republicans Changed Their Mind about Higher Education Really Quickly." *Atlantic*, 21 Aug. 2019, *Atlantic Monthly Group*, www.theatlantic.com/education/archive/2019/08/republicans-conservatives-college/596497. Accessed 24 Dec. 2019.

Ross, E. Wayne, and Rich Gibson, editors. *Neoliberalism and Education Reform.* Hampton Press, Inc. 2006.

Rousseau, Jean-Jacques. *Émile, or On Education*. 1762. Translated by Allan Bloom, Basic Books, 1979.

Shannon, Patrick, Anne Elrod Whitney, and Maja Wilson. "The Framing of the Common Core State Standards." *Language Arts*, vol. 91, no. 4, 2014, pp. 295–302.

Shenk, Timothy. "What Exactly Is Neoliberalism?" *Booked*, 2 Apr. 2015, *Dissent Magazine*, www.dissentmagazine.org/blog/booked-3-what-exactly-is-neoliberalism-wendy-brown-undoing-the-demos. Accessed 23 Dec. 2019.

Simon, Caroline. "Conservatives' Rising Concern about the Value of College." *Forbes*, 12 Sep. 2017, *Forbes Media LLC*, www.forbes.com/sites/carolinesimon/2017/09/12/conservatives-contempt-for-college-on-the-rise/#5a5652eb0b1d. Accessed 24 Dec. 2019.

Smith, Noah. "'Neoliberal' Isn't a Dirty Word." *AP News*, 12 Mar. 2019, *Associated Press*, apnews.com/60bb402028ae405c9b8af8eabe593419. Accessed 23 Dec. 2019.

Steger, Manfred B., and Ravi K. Roy. *Neoliberalism: A Very Short Introduction.* Oxford University Press, 2010.

Universal Declaration of Human Rights. United Nations. www.un.org/en/universal-declaration-human-rights. Accessed 21 Dec. 2019.

CHAPTER 1

Critics, Canon, and School Story Debate

Earnest discussions of the school story as a genre date back to at least the late 1850s, when critics in quality British periodicals took the opportunity, while reviewing Thomas Hughes's *Tom Brown's Schooldays* (1857), to reflect on the character of the public-school system.[1] Phenomenally popular, Hughes's semiautobiographical novel soon established itself as the seminal tale of boys' boarding-school life replete with archetypal scenes of fagging (the system of younger students working as servants for older students), cribbing, bullying, rugged sports matches, and rough-and-tumble out-of-school adventures. Victorian critics detected a difference in moral purpose between *Tom Brown* and its close successor, Frederic Farrar's *Eric, or Little by Little* (1858), and, contrasting the two, compared them with earlier fictional reflections on school by authors such as Maria Edgeworth, Thomas Day, William Makepeace Thackeray, and Charles Dickens. So began substantive efforts to define the school story as a genre—by no means the earliest critical commentaries on school fiction, which was popular with not only British but also American audiences, but among the first to situate discrete texts within distinct literary traditions for the purpose of making genre claims. Today, scholars are more likely to deem Talbot Baines Reed (who wrote for the *Boy's Own Paper* established by the Religious Tract Society in 1879) more influential in popularizing the Victorian boys' school story than either Hughes or Farrar. At the time, however, Reed—unlike Hughes—was pegged as an author of juvenile fiction by critics who more or less ignored juvenile works, whether for boys or girls, except to disparage them. In taking *Tom Brown*—embodiment of budding masculinity, morality, and British imperialism—as the gold standard of school fiction, they made a point of valorizing patriarchal public-schoolboy stories for adult readers.

Not until after World War II and the publication of George Orwell's landmark critique of popular story papers, "Boys' Weeklies" (1940), did the British critics' hegemonic hold on the school story as a highbrow patriarchal form begin to loosen. Some, apparently, mistook this loosening for the collapse of the genre. But, with hindsight, the cries of collapse speak less of a flagging literature and more of a failure of nerve on the critics' part: reluctance to acknowledge newer fiction that was moving beyond the boys' public-school paradigm so redolent of the age of empire and, as such, denial of Britain's declining colonial and economic power. Claims that the genre was exhausted, after all, coincided with not a stoppage but a reorientation in literary production, with school stories for girls coming to outsell stories for boys, and not a closing down but an opening up of vistas as school stories in general registered the democratization of education: introducing modern comprehensive school settings, turning sympathetic attention to working-class characters, and reflecting the mandate of "school for all" that was giving birth to a new order of British schools. One might make a comparable claim about the long-held belief that America never had a school story tradition like Britain's, a claim counterfactual if it means that American school stories were neither written nor read widely, but somewhat accurate if it means that British critics mostly presumed a British archive, while early American critics tended to situate American school stories in domestic and regional, rather than school, literary traditions.[2]

Taking to heart only some of the lessons from that midcentury paradigm shift, critics (with exceptions) tended to follow one of two major routes: either they continued to consolidate the archive of classic boys' public-school stories, or they set about recuperating long-neglected and much-belittled girls' school stories. Despite the strict binary, diversification was key, evidenced in the recovery of the literary and social histories of school stories written by women, written for girls, and read by girls; in the new appreciation of popular culture for the evolution of the genre; in efforts to complicate or deconstruct the chauvinistic literary, political, and social assumptions reified by earlier critics; in the growing recognition of school fiction from other countries, primarily America; and in the maturation of a scholarly field more and more conscious of its methodologies, theoretical frameworks, and critical implications. Since the turn of the millennium, while classic British boys' and girls' stories continue to draw attention, fresh critical paradigms have led children's literature scholars to foreground the pedagogical, curricular, and civic implications of contemporary school fiction, while studies in American and Native American traditions have opened the field to strikingly new texts, forms, and contexts including those related to the common school (precursor to the American public school) and the Indian boarding school (established to strip Native

American children of their tribal identities and force their assimilation into Euro-American civilization).

In what follows, I survey major works of criticism on school fiction in English from the 1850s to present—review essays, book chapters, and monographs that I have singled out for their (often competing) claims on the school story as a genre. Conscious that much has been said about the school story before the democratic turn in public education, but very little about it after that turn, I cast that long backward glance as a way of preparing to think through contemporary school fiction in the age of neoliberalism. Put another way, if we are currently living neoliberalism's ontological stage—when the "extension of market rationality" ("quantitative, efficient, pragmatic, and profitable" forms of thinking) has transformed into a way of being, "a mode of existence defined by individual self-responsibility, entrepreneurial action, and the maximization of human capital"—and if the neoliberal assault on democracy comes hand in hand with the undoing of public education, then it seems right to ask if the school story and its critics help us in any way to understand these developments.[3]

While this chapter as a whole comprises a single, chronological line of inquiry into the reception history of an eclectic genre, individual sections are framed to draw attention to changes in the dominant modes of thought by which critics have imposed order on the field—modes at times hierarchical and binary, at others more pluralistic. My intentions are to grasp the ways in which critics have debated the archive, especially in terms of which particular texts, authors, and experiences have been deemed worthy of discussion (in other words, noting how the making and breaking of the canon carries an ethics or politics, intentional or not, serving to influence beyond an appreciation of literariness the public's understanding of the role of education in the making or breaking of democratic imaginaries); to explore the intersection of critical conversations, school stories, and real-life issues of educational concern (noting how the documentary possibilities of fiction compete with the imaginary to disclose actual practices and fuel debate on education reform); and to consider the extent to which the critics have engaged with and responded to cultural change from the mid-nineteenth century to the early twenty-first, whether indicated in their sense of the literature, their own methodologies, or the historical conditions (noting in particular the tendency to cast the school story as a historical rather than a living form and, so doing, to lose sight of its cultural and critical affordances in and for our time). If, as contemporary critics of neoliberalism such as Wendy Brown and Henry Giroux tell us, democracy depends on the public provision of education, then I propose reading the school story debate for what it reveals of the democratic imaginary between the British Empire of the nineteenth century and the American empire of the twenty-first.

Late Nineteenth Century: Masculine and Feminine Forms

Victorian critics of school fiction gauged literary merit in terms of verisimilitude, morality, and a strict gender hierarchy, setting out to distinguish what they praised as truthful, uplifting, and masculine works from unrealistic, pernicious, and feminine ones. Representative are two early reviews of *Tom Brown's Schooldays* from the *Edinburgh Review* (1858) and *Blackwood's Edinburgh Magazine* (1861). Though cognizant of the novel's effects on boy readers, both essays resist situating *Tom Brown* wholly within a tradition for the young. For the *Edinburgh Review*, for example, Hughes's portrait of school life seems to follow the model of children's stories set by Maria Edgeworth's "The Barring Out" (1796) and Thomas Day's *The History of Sandford and Merton* (1783), while the social commentaries are more in tune with the adult fiction of William Makepeace Thackeray ("Tom Brown's Schooldays," *Edinburgh Review* 180). Describing a story for boys with a moral for adults, the review suggests a complex readership for whom gender matters. That is, while Hughes is certainly reprimanded for erasing the academic side of school experience, Edgeworth is disqualified outright for writing as a woman without firsthand experience of public-school life: "The author [Hughes] has succeeded in an attempt in which Miss Edgeworth failed. The Weak point of such stories as 'Barring out,' 'Eton Montem,' 'Frank,' and others in which schoolboys and their doings are put upon the scene, is that they were written by a woman who could only guess at the real character of that most curious phase of society, life at a public school" (172). This presumption that fiction must be informed by autobiography rather than imagination makes for a counterintuitive bias: though Hughes is guilty of misrepresenting Rugby's schoolmaster Thomas Arnold, attributing to him the doctrine of "muscular Christianity" properly belonging to Charles Kingsley, it is Hughes who is said to offer the more "honest" glimpse of schoolboy life by inviting critical but affirmative reflections on the public-school system.

Early attempts to define the genre favored reassuring representations of the public-school system that articulated boys' school experience as a healthy intersection of masculinity, morality, and life preparedness.[4] By way of contrast, *Blackwood's* lambasted predictable and moralizing "feminine volumes" by authors such as Edgeworth that boy readers would dismiss as "rot" and "bosh" ("School and College Life" 133). Again, Hughes is chastised for giving a "false impression" of headmasters (this time, for implying that Arnold's predecessors, because they did not draw the same public attention, were somehow lesser educators), but still *Tom Brown* is held up as exemplary for its veracity. To make the point, the reviewer situates the novel within a body of contemporaneous works—William Edward Heygate's *Godfrey Davenant* (1847), Edward Monro's

Basil, the Schoolboy, or, the Heir of Arundel (1854), Charlotte M. Yonge's *The Daisy Chain, or Aspirations* (1856), and Farrar's *Eric, or Little by Little*—all grouped under the category of "scholastic novels." Though all are praised, the authors are not found equal in merit: Farrar is "painful" and "repulsive" and, for depicting the vices of the school system, compared to "lower class visitors who show off their hideous sores, proudly, like martyrs" (137). Heygate and Monro, meanwhile, are not realistic enough (144). Only Yonge's story of a girls' grammar school is stamped with approval: "If a boy were to borrow it from his sister's library, he'll be delighted" (145). Though intended as a compliment, valuing the girls' story because boys find it readable suggests a gender-segregated understanding of the relation between literature and life—an understanding corroborated when, comparing Farrar and Hughes, it is argued that "Mr Farrar's books are decidedly of the weaker sex altogether. *Tom Brown*, whether at Rugby or Oxford, is the masculine, and *Eric* and *Julian Home* the feminine, of school and college life" (139–40). So, the masculine success of Hughes contrasts with the feminine failure of Farrar, a binary parsed elsewhere in the article as the victory of "reality" over "unreality," and of "prose" over "poetry" (140).

Late Victorian critics' interest in truthful and in moral representations of school life (which did not necessarily overlap) led to firmer calls for school fiction that might improve schoolboys across the public-school spectrum from the most to the least exclusive institutions. Toward the end of the century, Hughes still dominated the critical imagination with *Tom Brown's Schooldays* held to be, "still, after forty years, the only picture of school life in which schoolboys believe, and probably no schoolboy ever read it without becoming in some measure at once a more reflective and a manlier lad" ("Thomas Hughes" 11). According to Edward Salmon in *Juvenile Literature as It Is* (1888), "School stories may discharge a very important function in assisting boys to overcome the trials and resist the temptations of school-life. 'Tom Brown's Schooldays' is unquestionably entitled to the first place among this class of stories" (74). In even stronger terms, as one critic in London's weekly *Spectator* (1899) put it, "Hughes, more than any other man, made the modern schoolboy": he "convinced schoolboys that it was possible to be manly, and truthful, and pure, and even religious, and yet remain healthy schoolboys still with muscles in their frames longing for exercise, and ferment in their hearts" ("The Influence of Tom Brown" 17). In this manner, the exemplary school story was reckoned by its capacity to encourage the muscular Christianity that Hughes had attributed to Arnold, the doctrine of brave and cheerful Christian virtue expressed through strenuous physical activity, especially on the playing fields of schools like Rugby. But this moral imperative was also leading critics to look beyond the narrow realm of the most elite institutions. Wondering "whether any one will ever arise to do for Board-schools,⁵ especially those of the great cities, what Mr. Hughes did for Rugby and its rivals," and arguing that "it is tone, not knowledge, that we now want in board schools," the same *Spectator* critic exclaimed that "tracts are no good; We want stories that the children will read of their own motion, and, reading, get a higher view of what their own tone should be"—stories that would make "lying," "gambling," and "bad language" shameful to all schoolboys (18).

But even when fin-de-siècle critics set aside moral concerns, they still found the literature of the time wanting in its capacity to treat boyhood seriously and render the schoolboy character convincingly. "Is there no first-rate school-story," asked one critic, "a story, that is, which contains a really good study of schoolboy character?" ("The Schoolboy of Fiction" 9). The author describes a boys' genre riddled with "the quaintest of caricatures" from "the bad schoolboy" to "the prig," either given to an "exceedingly improbable . . . amount of incident" or told from a "wholly . . . humorous or satirical point of view" (9). A novel such as F. Anstey's fantasy of father and son swapping bodies, *Vice Versa* (1882), might be entertaining, so the argument goes, but it fails to convey "half the 'sense' of school-life that makes 'Tom Brown' as alive today as in the days of the old 'Pig and Whistle' [the boys' name for the Oxford coach], and in some respects as true a picture of the life of any school as it was true of Rugby in the time of Arnold. 'Tom Brown' is, indeed, one of the very few attempts that have been made to write seriously of schools as they are" (9). For this critic, the only contemporary writer who comes close to Hughes in "his knowledge of boyhood" is Rudyard Kipling, "difficult as it may be to some people to accept whole-heartedly his portrait of Stalky and his companions" (9). Referring to Kipling's military prep school novel, *Stalky & Co.* (1899), the author alludes to the not only anti-sentimental but distinctly brutal sensibilities of a book that divided the critics. As then governor of New York Theodore Roosevelt put it, in a 1900 essay on the character of the American boy, *Stalky* was "a story which ought never to have been written, for there is hardly a single form of meanness which it does not seem to extol, or of school mismanagement which it does not seem to applaud" (573). Roosevelt's rejection of *Stalky & Co.* suggests a real fear of school fiction's rhetorical force, of its potential to corrupt the character of not only the child but also the nation. Notably, in spite of *Stalky*'s moral shortcomings, the *Spectator* author asserts the book's value as a study of character. Doing so, he signals a culture of criticism coming around to sifting out literary merit from moral purpose, a move in turn preparing the way for critics to make merit-based distinctions between school stories for juveniles (conventionally adhering to strict, often evangelical, moral codes) and for adults (increasingly unsettling the moral codes).

It is less clear whether early critics entertained comparable concerns for schoolgirls in fiction, since they were inclined to relegate their commentaries on girls' stories to the curt review rather than the developed essay, a compact form that doubly sidelined girls' authors by dispensing with them quickly and passing judgement without explication. There is less evidence of early critics sorting the archive as they did with boys' fiction to distinguish, say, between "juvenile" and "literary" works, or to celebrate actual school experience with the insider knowledge brought to bear on the stories of the boys' schools such as Eton or Harrow. Historically, of course, girls had been excluded from the public and preparatory systems in both Britain and the USA, a condition informing the development of the literary school story: stories of girls in actual schools lag behind those of boys for the simple reason that boys were admitted in numbers to formal schools centuries before girls were. That said, the original story of girls' education predates the boys' school story by at least more than a century, if reckoned by the 1749 publication of Sarah Fielding's *The Governess, or, The Little Female Academy*. For the genre purists, however, Fielding's intimate circle of girls loosely tutored in a private household suggests a different archive from that of *Tom Brown's Schooldays* with its throng of boys straining to navigate a fixed curriculum in the vaster space of the formal school environment. In the course of the eighteenth century, girls and young women on both sides of the Atlantic were given increasing opportunities (beyond private academies and seminaries) for formal education, at first by way of coeducational amendments to existing schools, and later in all-women's institutions. Still, as noted by Felicia Lamb (*Locked-up Daughters: A Parents' Look at Girls' Education and Schools*, 1968) and Gillian Avery (*Childhood's Pattern: A Study of the Heroes and Heroines of Children's Fiction 1770–1950*, 1975), at the turn of the twentieth century the meaning and value of educational emancipation for women was in no way settled.

As American reviews from the early twentieth century show, stories for girls, whether set in finishing schools, normal schools, or women's colleges, were read—perhaps even more so than the boys' stories were—for their insights into girls' character; but where the guiding star for navigating the boys' story was a positive masculine ideal, that for the girls' story was a negative feminine or feminist stereotype. In other words, early reviews of girls' school stories seem to reveal less about the stories and more about their reviewers. Thus, in one *New York Times* piece on boarding-school stories, Rita Anthony Baker's *Frolics at Fairmount* (1910) is dismissed as "a very fluffy, frilly festive story, recounting a continuous round of impossibly good times, engineered by some very unconvincing schoolgirls"; meanwhile, in Elsie Singmaster's *When Sarah Went to School* (1910), "the usual fluffs and frills which ornament most stories about schoolgirls are happily subordinate to graver matters," making for "convincing, capital reading for girls" ("Boarding School Stories" 17). Implicit in this sliding scale from the "usual," "impossibly good" stories to unusually "graver" stories is an ambiguous aesthetic, possibly praising a capacity for gravitas, but just as possibly judging style, verisimilitude, rhetorical purpose, or gender hierarchy. Gender bias certainly informs the opinion that "a student of conditions might find in these accounts of the unending round of good times, the subordination of serious study and the freedom from domestic duties generally an answer to a vital part of the 'woman question' of today" (17). Such a slanted comment invites readers to correlate the poor quality of girls' school fiction with the historical upsurge in girls' schools, as if to say that the logical end of women's emancipation is frivolity and idleness. Comparable bias informs another *New York Times* piece singling out Raymond Jacberns's *A Discontented Schoolgirl* (1907) as an "excellent" book and "a good story of English school life," but not before declaring that "books for girls are not as exciting as those for boys, and they do not average up as well in the long run. Books of adventure stand for courage, manliness, and self-defense, and are usually more or less worth while, but the girls' books, if not really well written, are apt to be poor stuff, the virtues of the heroines and contrasting unpleasant characters of other book children being equally unpleasant" ("Reading for Girls" 765).

Even ostensibly impartial reviewers could lose their sense of purpose because of an inclination to patronize girls' authors. Hence a *Spectator* reviewer commenting on L. T. Meade's *A Sweet Girl Graduate* (1891) begins by noting that "this story is better worth reading than nine tenths of the tales that are published," its subject "fresh, for it describes life in one of the two Colleges where the higher education of women has been followed more or less seriously and more successfully than anywhere else" ("A Sweet Girl Graduate," *Spectator* 275–76). But in the lines that follow, presuming that Meade is falsely representing actual college settings, the review collapses into pedantry as it goes about correcting allegedly inexact details: "It is Newnham rather than Girton that appears to be intended, but Mrs. Meade has by an oversight given the names (fictitious, of course) of *four* halls . . . whereas there are in the real Newnham only three. Electric light, electric bells, and a chapel belong to the ideal rather than to the real. And certain details of manners are . . . not exact" (276). To set the record straight, Meade responded in a letter published one week later, noting that, "in writing the story, it was my wish to describe a College which could not be exactly identified with any of these in existence" (302). Though fragmentary, such contributions to the school story debate from Victorian and Edwardian critics attest to an enduring readiness to set aside, rather than understand or appreciate, girls' school fiction. In the passage from Edgeworth to Meade, from the late eighteenth century to the late nineteenth, and from the Anglo-Irish side of the Atlantic to the American, not much seems to have changed: despite the distance in time and space, mainstream critics continued to appeal irrationally to a documentarian principle to diminish school fiction by women authors.

Early Twentieth Century: Classic and Critical Forms

The turn of the twentieth century marked a watershed for the boys' school story: taking their lead from increasingly critical depictions of school experience in the fiction, reviewers began to distinguish the classic world of school life from the "modern," a distinction that, for some, evinced a turn away from sheltered innocence toward worldly pessimism. Such a movement is certainly suggested in two of the earliest book-length studies of school experience to include chapters on fictional representations, Harold Child's *The Public Schools from Within* (1906) and Ian Hay's *The Lighter Side of School Life* (1914). Striking a revisionist note, Child attempts to recuperate Farrar from past neglect, which he attributes to earlier critics unfairly judging the moralism of *Eric* and *St. Winifred's* (1862) against that of the more influential *Tom Brown's Schooldays*: Child makes the point that Farrar's moralism, represented in the vice-ridden decline and demise of Eric, was consciously "intended, we presume, to counteract the muscular element" embodied by Tom Brown. Going on to survey past and present writers, Child distinguishes between the "feeling which lay hidden in boyhood" and the feeling "dug up in maturity," his point being that in favoring the latter over the former, recent authors such as Kipling had gone astray, the result being a work like *Stalky & Co.* that "should be scrupulously kept from the hands of all under nineteen" (299). Still, it is important to remember that, as Isabel Quigly relates in *The Heirs of Tom Brown* (1982), Kipling, though of a different moral order from Hughes, played a comparable role in rationalizing ideals that were foundational for the British Empire in its peak years of territorial and economic expansion.

Kipling figures prominently for Hay, too, when describing a "revolution" in the writing and reception of school fiction: "Whereas school stories were formerly written to be read by schoolboys, they are now written to be read— and are read with avidity—by grown-up persons," on the strength of which he concludes that "school stories are much better written than they were" (151). Surveying "ancient" and "modern" titles, Hay moves from "immortal giant" Tom Brown ("the real thing"), alongside "depressing companion" Eric (who "does not ring true") (155), to Stalky, who "hits the sentimentalists hard" (164). Although acknowledging the class of school story "written primarily for boys"—exemplified by Talbot Baines Reed's *The Master of the Shell* (1901) and Desmond Coke's *The Bending of a Twig* (1906)—Hay is smitten with the adult appeal of the Kipling paradigm, in which "limelight has been shifted from the boy to the master, with the result that school life is now presented in a more true and corporate manner" (151). In sum, "school stories have become less romantic, less sentimental, more coldly psychological. They are tinged with adult worldliness, and, too often, with adult pessimism" (151). Pointing out how Kipling "has drawn masters as they have never been drawn before—the portraits may be cruel, biased, not sufficiently representative; but how they live!" (164)—Hay choreographs a number of critical moves consolidated in the decades to come: taking the boys' school story to be *the* school story; defining the genre as an adult archive constelled with juvenile texts discussed as adult works; characterizing the genre as inherently critical in its assay of modern public-school experience; and exploring the genre's understanding of teaching as a profession, as well as its capacity to distinguish between individual teachers and the education system as a whole.

The serious reading of boys' school fiction for its commentaries on the teaching profession peaked in winter of 1917–18 in an exchange of letters to the *Spectator*—mostly written by schoolmasters—sparked by Alec Waugh's *The Loom of Youth*. Published in July of that year and, by November, already in its sixth printing, Waugh's semiautobiographical novel gained notoriety for its depictions of cribbing, bad language, and intimations of homosexuality in the public-school setting. But what provoked the first article, signed by "A Mere Schoolmaster," was Waugh's vision of masters as not merely inept guardians but representatives of an entire school system that was morally bankrupt. Claiming that "the school story, formerly a tale written to amuse schoolboys, has been adopted recently as the chief weapon in the armoury of those who assail the Public School system," the author describes a consciously ideological realm of cultural production. Whereas earlier critics had worried about the novelist's power to misrepresent the public-school system, or to dwell on its less noble elements, this one balks at the potential intentionally to deconstruct that system (8). "Fiction," he says, "is a subtle and elusive form of criticism," for "when the fiction-critics have persuaded all good men to stay out of the profession they will have successfully wrecked education" (8). Aware that Waugh was only nineteen when *The Loom of Youth* was published, the Schoolmaster argues that "the young are arrogant and undiscriminating critics," describes Waugh as an "erratic youth" who missed his chance of having "some sound sense and sound principle . . . knocked into his head," and dismisses the novel as "a very young man's book" (9). In the letters to the *Spectator* that followed between November 1917 and January 1918, the correspondents—including schoolmasters (some anonymous, mostly minus their affiliations, though two identified as assistant-masters from Charterhouse and Winchester colleges), a schoolboy, one British Army officer, one peer of the realm, the schoolmaster of the first article, and Waugh himself—fell into factions: on one side, those who condemned the novel as a work of "amazingly self-centered ignorance" that could hardly speak for the whole public-school system; and on the other (not including Waugh), those who, if not entirely convinced by the novel, recognized enough truth in it that "schoolmasters may learn something from it" (Yet Another Schoolmaster 15).

At a time when boys' school story critics were trying to dissociate with the juvenile audience, one of the most nuanced defenses of Waugh in the *Spectator* debate was apparently put forward by a schoolboy (under the pseudonym of "A Mere Schoolboy"). "Speaking for myself," he explains, "I do not consider the book sordid, 'crude and unsavory.' The actual facts which it so faithfully describes are unpleasant, to put it mildly, so it could hardly be a pleasant book. One should not read it for pleasure, any more than one should read Lord Bryce's account of German atrocities for pleasure; but we read it for profit" (A Mere Schoolboy 675). Though he goes on to say of Waugh, "What a healthy and beautiful mind the author has. He is no mere cynical satirist and caricaturist, but a writer with a proper sense of gratitude and a proper gift of self-expression" (675), the boy argues not for the aesthetics but the ethics of the school story: removed from the realm of satire, caricature, and sensationalism, and aligned with the documentary literature of government commissions, the value of the genre here hinges on its potential for disclosing and calling to account.

Bearing in mind that Waugh wrote *The Loom of Youth* as an officer in training, and that its publication coincided with his being sent to France as a machine-gun second lieutenant, the Great War of 1914–18 aptly continued to inform the *Spectator* debate—notably so when the Earl of Dartmouth (Humphry Legge) tallied the public-schoolboys who had recently lost their lives or received wounds serving "their country's cause," to make the point that "it does not seem quite the best time to choose to throw stones at a system, whatever its faults may be, that has produced so splendid a record" (Dartmouth 768). Two weeks later, Waugh replied to decry Dartmouth's glib patriotism, arguing that "everywhere systems (that were before the war objects of criticism) are trying to cement their shaking walls with human blood" (Waugh 36). Asserting that "we that live owe it to them not to use their spilt blood as cement for a jerry-built civilization. Because of them it is for us to straighten the twisted prop and rebuild the fragile wall" (36), Waugh implies a comparable role for the writer of school fiction as one who takes part in the straightening and rebuilding of civilization, a project not only critical (of imperialism's apologists) but also purposefully constructive. And in doing so, he represents an impulse to defend the boys' public-school story for adults as a definitively moral genre—a genre finding its purpose in questioning rather than blindly championing the public-school ethos. Put another way, the value of the school story here lies not in its ability to showcase the moral behavior of exemplary individuals that might be imitated by actual schoolboys, but in its capacity to disclose the immoral conditions of school environments and cultural logics that ought to be corrected by educators, policy makers, and civic leaders. If, as Quigly argues, the public schools were the training grounds for the British Empire's future civil servants, then the school story in the opening decades of the twentieth century—at least as represented by Waugh—sets an early precedent for recognizing the teenage writer of school fiction as a serious theorist and critic of the social, a skeptic of both the dominant forms of education in the homeland and the inhumane global "systems" they underwrite.

The war itself began to enter the plots of school stories, often to the regret of critics lamenting not the generic crossovers fused with espionage and intrigue but the tendency of authors to exploit and encourage ethno-nationalism. One problem with ethno-nationalism was that it not only divided nations but also encouraged girls to break with conventional gender roles. That is, school stories incorporating war plots tended to bypass the high, thoughtful moralism for which Waugh was celebrated, opting instead for the crude, divisive strokes of the "cynical satirist and caricaturist" with which he had been contrasted. Exploring the theme of "the war schoolgirl" in new stories such as E. E. Cowper's *Maids of the "Mermaid,"* Dorothea Moore's *Head of the Lower School*, E. L. Haverfield's *The Happy Comrade*, Doris A. Pocock's *Judy Sees It Through*, and Brenda Girvin's *Jenny Wren* (all 1919), one *Nation* reviewer detected common "touches of hate" with a potential to recast the ideal of girlhood: "We find that charming person, the British schoolgirl, being taught in her storybooks, this Christmas, that no forgiveness is possible for an enemy that is German—or rather, Hun, for he is rarely referred to by any other name—that, even when the war is over, Huns still plot to destroy English civilians by foul means, and that our late enemies are, one and all, devoid of every virtue or humane characteristic" ("The War Schoolgirl" 364). Recounting a plotline from Haverfield's *The Happy Comrade*, in which a French Girl Guide, during a German attack, "appears to have killed three out of five Germans with a hand grenade and then finished off the remaining two with a revolver" (366), the reviewer seems to resist a potent image of young, female agency. Yet the point is also made that "the spy story is infinitely preferable to the old namby-pamby tale that used to be thought particularly suitable to girls, but generally drove them to their brothers' books" (364), a criticism not of the girls but of the "old-fashioned girls' book"—insufficient as an object in its own right, but nevertheless remembered as one "in which there was no war, and no inducement to hate somebody else's country in order to love one's own, to be bloodthirsty in order to be brave" (366). In closing, the reviewer notes that while "it is a great thing for the readers of girls' books ... that the admission of women to the fighting Services gave them so much new material for tales of adventure," the opinion is expressed that "really, by this time, we should have thought sex distinctions in fiction might cease and good stories find their own market, unlabelled among girls and boys alike" (366). Such sentiment suggests a progressivism not typical of a debate given to crystalizing gender differences. It is not clear, however, whether dispensing with those differences meant subsuming girl characters in a realm of literary conventions already aligned with boyhood and masculinity, or imagining a new, ungendered or alternatively gendered paradigm.

By the 1920s, the war plot had become just one of many formulas, stereotypes, and clichés said to be weighing down the girls' school story; and while the war continued to inform school fiction for girls, for reviewers the best stories were those that introduced "modern" elements that unsettled conventional mores. Hence one 1924 *New Statesman* reviewer of Susan Coolidge's much earlier novel *What Katy Did at School* (1873) argued that it is the character of "mischievous angel" Rose Red who "will reconcile many children who would otherwise find the good example of Katy rather overpowering" (Y.Y. 405). Describing "a girl who was at once as mischievous as the bad girls and as virtuous as the good ones," the reviewer recalls Kipling, who "gave us a mixture of much the same kind in *Stalky & Co*—schoolboys who were honourable lawbreakers, scamps of whom the angels would not disapprove too strongly. What charms us in characters of this kind is that they carry their virtue so easily. We like to see virtue moving through life with as free a gait as vice" (405). For the modern critic, the appeal in Coolidge's Rose Red lies in her departure from Victorian ideals, daringly suggesting that what makes a girl's virtue worthy of attention is its proximity to, rather than its isolation from, vice. Related concerns inform a 1927 *Spectator* piece, which observes that, "on the whole, the school girl of fiction is becoming a more natural person; she is not continually fighting flames, falling down precipices, or leaping in one term from top to bottom of the school" (T. 995). Praising recent works by Ann Macdonald, Christine Chaundler, Elinor Brent-Dyer, Josephine Elder, Dorita Fairlie Bruce, Angela Brazil, and May Baldwin, the reviewer singles out Elder's *Thomasina Toddy* (1927) to applaud "a delightful character, who speaks and behaves quite naturally and has a high disposition: this is high praise for a school girl of fiction" (995). Other reviewers attest to a comparably welcome sense of change, distinguishing between the mass of schoolgirl stories that are "much the same as they have always been" ("For

Girls of All Ages" 863) or "so much of a muchness" and rarer stories "showing modern symptoms" ("Some Changes in School-Girl Fiction" 901). Whether at the level of language (introducing new slang), characterization (introducing "mentally less anaemic" characters), or settings (describing "out of the ordinary schools"), the breaking with convention by Bruce and Brent-Dyer, along with Elsie J. Oxenham, Margaret Ironside, and Deborah Tindall, led critics in the late 1920s to validate rather than vilify the girls' school story ("For Girls of All Ages" 861). Indeed, though still considered the lesser sibling of the boys' story, that the girls' story could be spoken of in the same breath as *Stalky & Co.*—as a point of comparison rather than contrast—shows the willingness of some critics to move beyond strictly gendered readings.

Between the Wars: Adult and Adolescent Forms

The sense that the form and function of the school story had altered irrevocably became commonplace for scholars between the world wars; as W. R. Hicks, on the subject of boys' school fiction, summed up, "The public school novel began by being very narrative and laudatory and became analytical and critical" (39). In the very first book-length study of the genre, *The School in English and German Fiction* (1933), Hicks offered a comparative analysis that was fresh but untimely: its publication coincided with the rise to power of the Nazis in Germany and the movement toward the Second World War, a period with diminishing opportunities to appreciate the shared interests of authors and educators in England and Germany. Still, the enduring value of Hicks's book comes down to his working with an international rather than a national analytic. Comparing and contrasting literary and school traditions at home and abroad, he concludes that the English boys' school story followed an idiosyncratic course, becoming less a representative and more an idyllic form: emblematic of a cloistered, private, and upper-class experience removed from the modern world of state secondary schools where the majority of children were by the 1930s receiving their education. For Hicks, English representations of school before the twentieth century were either fragmentary ("scraps") or "casual," and "the novelist's increasing interest in the school system has followed closely the expansion of our school system; it has coincided both with the interest taken by the nation in its schooling and with the increasing tendency to use the novel as a medium of social criticism" (9). Edgeworth receives an honorable mention for "The Barring Out," as does Dickens for his fiction attacks "on the evils of the cheap private school" (11), but *Tom Brown's Schooldays* is still the fulcrum—hailed not as the first school novel, but the one that suggested to the popular audience the moral possibilities of public-school life (19)—while *Stalky & Co.* stands out as "the first novel by a famous author to be devoted entirely to life at school," a fact "suggest[ing] that at last the school was acquiring literary status" (21). Hicks describes two waves of modern school fiction after Kipling: a first, from 1900 to 1910, marked by singular works on boarding-school experience such as Horace Annesley Vachell's *The Hill* (1905), Coke's *The Bending of a Twig*, and Alice and Claude C. Askew's *The Etonian* (1906); and a second, from 1910 to 1930, diversifying in interests and attitudes—giving new attention to day schools, as in Compton Mackenzie's *Sinister Street* (1913), and masters, as in Hugh Walpole's *Mr. Perrin and Mr. Traill* (1911); and making more room for bitter realism, as in Arnold Lunn's *The Harrovian* (1913), or social criticism, as in H. G. Wells's *Joan and Peter* (1918). Thinking expansively, Hicks offered one of the first taxonomies of the boys' school story based on thematic engagements with "intellectual training," "athleticism," "conformity and tradition," "the prefect system," "religion and morals," and "master and boy," most of which had been broached by earlier reviewers, but never for the purpose of staking out a genre as such.

What needs to be stressed is the extent to which early-to-mid-twentieth-century critics purposefully shifted discussions of the archive away from the genre's juvenile beginnings, in part by claiming Hughes as the progenitor of a school story tradition for adults rather than boys, and in part by simply disregarding the majority of school stories published at the time (especially in the popular weekly press). As Hicks phrased it, "In the nature of things, a book written mainly for boys cannot be judged by literary standards, and from one point of view *Tom Brown* must be classified with juvenile literature, which was already in existence. But seen from a different angle, that of its influence, it is of serious importance—for it is the ancestor of all the public school novels that have been written since" (20). Treating the genre seriously, says Hicks, means picking and choosing what defines it as a genre: juvenile literature is not "literary," but since the seminal school story is just that, a juvenile book, we turn a blind eye to its juvenile qualities and think instead of its cultural accomplishments as a harbinger of ideas. Comparable adult chauvinism informs Adrian Alington's reflections on modern school fiction in "School Stories—Old and New" (1936), an article in which, surveying the movement between *Tom Brown's Schooldays* and *The Loom of Youth*, he discounts "the many books which have been written primarily for boys to read" because he "can consider only those works which are seriously intended as studies of school life" (415). Qualifying his disregard for the juvenile demographic, Alington argues that "a marked change comes over the school story ... For the first time the grim word 'adolescence' begins to make itself felt" (420). Explaining that "the modern school story is almost entirely the work of . . . often very young men," who are "too young probably to have achieved a sense of proportion or to exercise the first duty of the novelist, which is selection" (421), Alington evinces both distaste for and mistrust of the schoolchild. In keeping with his critical forebears, Alington grasps the genre in polarizing terms; but where earlier critics fixated on the differences between male and female authors, boys' and girls' stories, or laudatory and critical attitudes, he draws the line between the adolescent and the adult—between the juvenile and the serious, or the juvenile and the literary. As if suffering from a crisis in identity or stage development, the genre is parsed as one beset from within (novels burdened with youthful preoccupations) and from without (authors suffering from lack of experience), and the schoolchild emerges as a figure palatable only when filtered through the narrative of the mature, nostalgic alum.

Such attempts to play down the juvenile readership on which the boys' school story had been built, sequestering *Tom Brown* as a seminal work for an adult literary tradition, throw into relief the intervention made by George Orwell in his 1940 essay "Boys' Weeklies," published in the small but influential arts and literature review *Horizon*. Orwell stands out for two reasons. First, he redirected critical attention toward the popular realm of story papers for young readers, in which the boys' school story had burgeoned in the hands of Reed writing for the *Boy's Own Paper* (1879–1967)—issued by the Religious Tract Society for the purpose of "providing healthy boy literature to counteract the vastly increasing circulation of illustrated and other papers and tales of a bad tendency" ("Minutes of the General Committee of the Religious Tract Society," 1878, qtd. in Cox 18). Second, Orwell tackled head-on the politics of a school story aesthetic marred, in his words, by "snobbishness and gutter patriotism" (126). Discussing ten two-penny weeklies owned by Amalgamated Press and D. C. Thomson & Co., he focuses on two leading titles, *The Gem* (1907–1939) and *The Magnet* (1908–1940), giving particular attention to the *Billy Bunter/Greyfriars School* stories of Frank Richards (pseudonym of Charles Hamilton). Orwell notes that the salient features of these stories have little to do with learning: "They are the clean-fun, knock-about type of story, with interest centring round horseplay, practical jokes, ragging roasters, fights, canings, football, cricket and food" (95). Unlike Alington, Orwell insists that juvenile literature, especially in the form of the weekly story paper, truly matters. "Here," he argues, "is the stuff that is read somewhere between the ages of twelve and eighteen by a very large proportion, perhaps an actual majority, of English boys, including many who will never read anything else except newspapers" (124). Reasoning that the "imaginative background" acquired by most people in such reading is carried into adult life, he argues that the popular school story represented by

Richards encouraged an antiquated, class-skewed vision of the school system out of touch with social and cultural reality in the early to mid-twentieth century. For such fiction, says Orwell, "The clock has stopped at 1910" (119).

Frank Richards's response, which appeared two months later in the same magazine, only confirmed many of Orwell's suspicions, maintaining that what young readers needed was neither literary realism nor critical thinking, but a plain kind of entertainment underpinned by chauvinistic assumptions such as "noblemen generally are better fellows than commoners" and "foreigners are funny" (488). Together, Richards and Orwell leave us to infer that the critical turn did not make it into the production of boys' story papers, where the imperialist ethno-nationalism valorized by Kipling and decried by Waugh lived on well past midcentury (*Billy Bunter*, for example, continued in comic strip form until the 1980s). Insisting that the boys' weeklies not only represented popular culture but also laid bare "what the mass of the English people really feels and thinks" (90), Orwell made a definitive claim for the enduring significance of both the school story and the young audience. Making a rare assay of the mass audience, Orwell more than any of his critical predecessors sensed the socioeconomic stakes and implications in the writing, reading, and reviewing of school fiction. Unlike Waugh, however, Orwell asserts not the critical possibilities of a genre ready to disclose the hidden order of things but the ideological effects of a genre working to distract readers from their lived reality—and this in a time of not only marked economic and territorial decline for the British Empire (relative to the industrial and commercial rise of Germany and the USA), but also of war on a world scale, all indexing a global economy and political geography in radical flux.

The early 1940s proved a ripe time for reflecting on politics, aesthetics, and public schools in England, with Orwell's essay followed soon after by Edward C. Mack's authoritative *Public Schools and British Opinion Since 1860: The Relationship Between Contemporary Ideas and the Evolution of an English Institution* (1941). While accounting for the actual school system, Mack traces a body of autobiographical narratives and popular fiction coming to play a central role in the controversy over public-school education. He describes, in the wake of *Tom Brown's Schooldays*, a flood of late Victorian "romantic-conservative" memoirs and reminiscences unanimously valorizing the public schools, along with "the great period of the rise of juvenile literature about schools," including "the greatest and most influential product of the period, the *Boy's Own Paper*" (148). "This magazine," argues Mack, "and the books and magazines it inspired helped to an incalculable extent, through their influence on the rising generation who 'read thousands of them, and whooped for their heroes,' to keep alive the public school legend and therefore to influence in an indirect but important way the course of public school history"—an influence Mack attributes to R. Hope Moncrieff and Talbot Baines Reed's reworking of the formula of *Tom Brown* with "the deadly seriousness and the overstrained idealism left out" (148). Kipling, too, is pivotal for Mack, dispensing with "the preachings of *Tom Brown's Schooldays* and *Eric*, their melodramatic sentimentality . . . [and their] occasional stiffness and formality" (193), and opening up the adult school story to not only a modern, realist aesthetic but also a politically charged critical consciousness. After Kipling, Mack identifies "the coming of age of public school fiction" in the hands of Lionel Portman, Vachell, William De Morgan, G. F. Bradby, and Coke. But that maturation, for Mack, is complicated more or less immediately by novels such as Wells's *Joan and Peter*, Ronald Gurner's *The Day Boy* (1924), and Elizabeth Banks's *School for John and Mary* (1924), all of which contrast the public schools with progressive or state secondary schools to exhibit "a very characteristic and significant development of the twenties, indicating, as it does, that many people no longer felt the public school to be something apart, but . . . a branch of the educational system which needed to justify itself against other types of school" (330). Notably, by Mack's account, Reed is just as influential as Hughes and Kipling, all three implicated in shaping, as writers, the popular understanding of modern education. Equally important is the glimpse Mack gives of the genre as a field of class conflict, not merely acknowledging tensions between public-school and comprehensive worldviews, but bearing witness to a radical reconfiguration of social and economic power: the genre registers the public school, elite bastion of empire, losing its privileged status to be regarded as just one, relatively outdated, form of education among others. Whereas Orwell accused writers of public-school fiction of touting an antiquated view of education and empire, Mack suggested not only that the public schools themselves were living by similarly stopped clocks but that the genre on the whole as it diversified had begun to play a vital role in raising comparable awareness.

Midcentury: Imperial and Democratic Forms

Possibly the most remarkable aspect of the postwar moment—when the school story was newly appraised as a field of class conflict in an era of democratic reforms—is the extent to which it marks a growing divergence in how scholars defined the archive. While some sought to broaden the archive—to include stories for and about girls, stories with working-class characters, stories of day and state schools, and stories for popular audiences—others remained preoccupied with the classic public- and private-school novels and, in doing so, manufactured a narrative of the genre faltering with the age of empire.

Absent in Mack's study, but striking in Orwell's, is a nascent interest in the gendered nature of the school story; although Orwell says little about school fiction written explicitly for girls, he acknowledges that girls read the same weeklies as boys and opens the conversation to discussing story papers for women. Following that lead, former *Boy's Own* writer Geoffrey Trease dedicated a chapter in *Tales Out of School* (1948) to gauging the merits of the "girls' school story": having "lagged many years behind" the boys' story (due to the lag in real-world education), girls' school fiction was taking off just as boys' was declining (128)—another decline correlating with historical conditions. The same period in which the classic British boys' public-school experience began to be regarded as outmoded, as the expression of a bygone age of empire no longer relevant in the midcentury climate of decolonization, came with profound educational reforms that exponentially increased girls' chances of secondary and higher education. Trease's interests, however, are at best academic: though eager to note the popularity of the girls' school story—exemplified by Enid Blyton's *The Naughtiest Girl in School* (1940)—he fixates on "the low level of writing in this field" (128), ranking it alongside lowbrow boys' fiction. As he describes girls' fiction, "Its Talbot Baines Reed was Angela Brazil . . . Its Kipling has yet to come" (128). But in spite of that tacit homage to Kipling, Trease is still very much snagged on Hughes. Hence his closing claims that "juvenile [school] fiction is conspicuously insensible to the changes of the last few decades," and "though Arnold's revolution at Rugby quickly produced the classic *Tom Brown*, the other outstanding changes in education during the past hundred years find no notable reflection in stories" (137). A comparable claim was made soon after by Frank Eyre in *20th Century Children's Books* (1953) when reflecting on the "virtual extinction" of the school story (50). To his credit, Eyre gives equal space in his short survey to both boys' and girls' novels, albeit to dismiss both: he lambasts Kipling for paving the way for modern writers to "tag some new plot ideas onto the old pattern" (51), and he cites Brazil, Brent-Dyer, Bruce, and Oxenham to say that "none of them bears much relation to present-day school life" (52).

By the early 1960s, however, a handful of critics detecting postwar cultural forces in school fiction began—rightly—to describe the school story as a genre living beyond the Victorian and Edwardian boarding-school paradigm: here, cautiously negotiating classic and modern works; there, more daringly dispensing with the classics altogether. Among the cautious works of criticism, Margery Fisher's *Intent Upon Reading: A Critical Appraisal of Modern Fiction for Children* (1962) distinguished between the timeless works of writers such as Reed, who led the way with model stories; the "fossilized" works of writers such as Brazil, Brent-Dyer, and Oxenham who, in following formulas, let the real world pass them by; and the works of new writers such as Antonia Forest and William Mayne, who were allegedly revitalizing the genre. Among the more daring, L. Spolton's "The Secondary School in Post-War Fiction" (1963) testified to not an exhaustion but a proliferation of midcentury boys' school novels, to be understood in terms of three contexts: an evolving literary scene in which representations of children had first emerged from the didactic-pedagogical tradition set in motion by Rousseau's *Émile* (hence, the literary presence of children in general is said to be indebted to the school story genre); burgeoning academic fields, in which childhood studies had shifted attention from sentimental presumptions about childhood innocence to psychoanalytical conceptions of stage development; and reforms in British education, chiefly the 1944 Education Act, which replaced the all-age elementary period (ages five to fourteen) with a two-stage division between primary (ages five to eleven) and secondary (ages eleven to fifteen) levels, while establishing a secondary school system more accessible for girls and working-class students. According to Spolton, following the act, the creation of "over two and a half thousand secondary modern schools [in Britain], newly promoted from senior elementary," gave rise to significant pedagogical problems. Going on to argue that "in fiction it is the failures which have attracted more attention than the successes," Spolton claims that writers of school fiction disproportionately dwelt on the problems. At the same time, big-screen adaptations of works such as Michael Croft's *Spare the Rod* (1954) and E. R. Braithwaite's *To Sir with Love* (1959) helped consolidate those negative conceptions of school experience in the cultural imaginary.

So, the critical tradition once led by Waugh was still dominant a half-century on, though now the fiction-critics were speaking out against the modern and grammar schools rather than the elite boarding schools. This is the central observation of M. Mathieson and M. T. Whiteside's "The Secondary Modern School in Fiction" (1971), an article (like Spolton's) recognizing the school story as a genre transformed as it engaged with "the three problems of post-war Britain, education, adolescence, and working-class culture" (285). Surveying stories about idealist teachers frustrated in their attempts to turn around impoverished pupils' lives—from Croft's *Spare the Rod*, Edward Blishen's *Roaring Boys* (1955), and John Townsend's *The Young Devils* (1958) to Braithwaite's *To Sir With Love*, Glyn Jones's *The Learning Lark* (1960), and James Barlow's *Term of Trial* (1961)—Mathieson and Whiteside discuss a body of school fiction marked by "angry protest against a variety of evils in working class life and the inadequacy of the schools' attempts to educate slum children" (285).

But while Fisher and Spolton were disclosing a substantial, living tradition of state- and day- school fiction, the retrograde conception of the field was reinstated in three influential works: Marcus Crouch's *Treasure Seekers and Borrowers: Children's Books in Britain, 1900–1960* (1962), John Reed's *Old School Ties: The Public Schools in British Literature* (1964), and John Rowe Townsend's *Written for Children* (1965), all of which took school fiction to be synonymous with public-school fiction, pinned down the definitive works in the nineteenth and early twentieth centuries, and asserted that girls' books lagged irremediably behind boys' books. Crouch's era-by-era account of children's literature paints a dismal picture of the genre after midcentury, pinpointing the 1920s as "the age of the school story," albeit one with "no significant developments; the boys' story followed the pattern set by T. B. Reed forty years earlier, while hardly anything in the girls' story had escaped the prior attentions of Angela Brazil" (40–41). Of the prolific boys' stories, he singles out Gunby Hadath's *Carey of Cobhouse* (1928) and Hylton Cleaver's *Harley First XV* (1922) as the best; and of the girls' stories, he praises Elinor Brent-Dyer's *The School at the Chalet* (1925), Dorita Fairlie Bruce's *Nancy* and *Dimsie* series, and Josephine Elder's *Evelyn Finds Herself* (1929) for showing "a little of the influence not of the traditional school-story but of the 'adult' school novels of Hugh Walpole and others" (41). "Such books," says Crouch of the girls' books, "stand out so brightly from the grey mass of school-stories that it is tempting to exaggerate their excellences. They are in fact the shallowest of steps towards Elfrida Vipont, but at least they lead upwards" (41). These relative merits are further explained when Crouch describes Vipont's contribution: Vipont, "while attempting no such thing, pushed outwards the boundaries of the school story" with *The Lark in the Morn* (1948) and *The Lark on the Wing* (1950)—two books that were "radiant" but "lacked distinction of style; their merits were not literary, but they were so firmly based in understanding and faith that they rose far above the level to which they superficially belonged" (105). In classic backhanded style, Crouch writes off the entire archive of girls' school stories, identifying a spirited rather than a literary endeavor and describing accomplishments incidental rather than intentional.

Far more successful is the tradition described by John Reed, which departs from the field of children's literature to figure Charles Dickens as the seminal author in an increasingly leftist school story arc for adults, with Thackeray, George Meredith, Kipling, Samuel Butler, Wells, Walpole, and Waugh producing "serious" works of "protest" that "cried out against the great swindle" of public-school education (43). With a comparable sense of the political stakes, Townsend returned to the children's archive to figure Hughes as the progenitor of a conservative tradition of boys' stories, a legacy continued by Farrar and Tablot Baines Reed only to be killed by Kipling. By the turn of the twentieth century, argues Townsend, "it was growing difficult for an intelligent writer to produce a school story for boys. Kipling had damaged the genre by making it appear naïve; the 1914 war almost finished it off. After that, the best school stories were to be found in adult literature" (66). By way of qualification, in his second school chapter, he explains: "No author of the first rank was writing school stories for boys or girls in the 1920s and 1930s" (129), and "in spite of . . . signs of adaptation to the times, the boys' school story has never really got going again since the last war" (130). Although he concedes that "there has been far more life on the feminine side" (130), represented by Antonia Forest's *Autumn Term* (1948) and *End of Term* (1958)—"far and away the best girls'-school stories I know" (131), Townsend's final judgment is that the children's school story existed only as a "battered literary form" (135). The bad faith of this moment should not be underestimated: for it was this ageist, sexist, classist, and above all counterfactual verdict of doom and gloom touted by Crouch, Reed, and Townsend that was quickly taken up as a tenet of the genre—in spite of fairer and far more accurate claims to the contrary by Fisher, Spolton, Mathieson, and Whiteside. And to the extent that the ensuing critical tradition followed the former rather than the latter, we do well to consider what was lost in affirming that the school story is best remembered as a boys' story and not a girls'; that the school story could not cross over from the public school to the comprehensive; that the school story spoke only of a narrow realm of privilege and not a broad section of the social; and that the school story is best remembered as an imperial and not a democratic form.

Mid- to Late Twentieth Century: Middlebrow and Marginalized Forms

Battered or not, the school story enjoyed a renaissance in criticism, which began with scholars giving dedicated attention to the long-neglected girls' school story. Foundational were two book chapters looking historically at landmark developments in girls' school fiction: Felicia Lamb's "In School Stories" (from *Locked-up Daughters: A Parents' Look at Girls' Education and Schools*, 1968) and Gillian Avery's "'Modern Girls' and Schoolgirls 1880–1940" (from *Childhood's Pattern: A Study of the Heroes and Heroines of Children's Fiction 1770–1950*, 1975). For Avery, the trajectory of the schoolgirl story paralleled a broad shift in cultural mores beginning in the late nineteenth century. In early boarding-school novels such as Juliana Horatia Ewing's *Six to Sixteen* (1875), "school was a thing to escape *from*, not as it became later, an escape in itself"—eventually the locus of a "frivolous world," as Charlotte Yonge termed it, at odds with the Victorian ideal of ladylike domesticity (200). In spite of dominant discourses prioritizing home duties for girls, school stories began to represent "modern" alternatives—education beyond the home sphere, economic independence, and a professional career—with works including Ellinor Davenport Adams's *Miss Secretary Ethel* (1898) and Mrs. George de Horne Vaizey's *A College Girl* (1913) dramatizing the various affordances of dependence and independence. Although not spelling out the cause-and-effect relationship, Avery claims that school fiction allowed girls "chafing to escape from home" to do so "vicariously" (204). Like the Girl Guide movement, the school story in the 1920s and 1930s, exemplified by May Wynne's *Peter the New Girl* (1936), offered an image of "organization, strenuous group activities, an appearance of self-government, and institutions which demanded *esprit de corps*" (207).

While it is tempting to read in these changes a narrative of liberation, seeing the schoolgirl escape the trappings of the domestic ideal, Lamb's essay invites a more skeptical interpretation, suggesting that schools in the later period played a comparable role in containing and controlling girls' desires. She sets out with the general observation that early twentieth-century schoolgirl stories "almost all have the same plot" involving a spoilt, shy, and unpopular girl, initially at odds with the "jolly rabble" of peers but eventually accepted into the school community (68). Representative of the early authors is Angela Brazil, whose novel *Monitress Merle* (1922) foregrounded an affectionate relationship between headmistress and pupil; characteristically, "there are no inhibitions about love between females" (71). Describing a sea change in the genre, marked by the rise of Enid Blyton, Lamb—apparently speaking of both schools and school stories—notes how "this attitude, that strong and sometimes demonstrative passions between girls or for older girls and young teachers were a natural and harmless stage of development, was not allowed to last long . . . the time honoured crush or pash came under suspicion . . . [and] close friendships were automatically broken up" (71). Although she goes on to note new contributions from Brent-Dyer and Delia Huddy, Lamb insists that something was lost in the movement from Brazil to Blyton, something reckoned by the eventual "uniformity" of characters and "dullness" of presentation (72). Avery suggests a comparable loss. Noting the athletic image of the schoolgirl embodying the "zeal for games dominat[ing] the girls' stories between the wars," she claims that "the adolescent emotions that [in earlier periods had been] spilt out over evangelical experience, charitable works, filial pieties, and sentimental friendship, have now been directed towards school" (217–18)—an effect of administrations purposefully seeking to reorient girls' sensual and emotional energies. Together, Avery and Lamb draw attention to the ways in which the girls' school story encoded competing appeals to its readers, fluctuating in its potential to offer visions of belonging, promise, and liberation.

A broader survey of girls' school stories came with Mary Cadogan and Patricia Craig's *You're a Brick, Angela! A New Look at Girls' Fiction from 1839 to 1975* (1976), which dedicated five of its nineteen chapters to scrutinizing school novels and school weeklies for girls. On the one hand, the task was to detail the popular school stories that had captured the imaginations of girl readers in the early decades of the twentieth century—in the novels of Brazil, Oxenham, Bruce, and Brent-Dyer, and in the pages of Amalgamated's two-penny weeklies *The School Friend/The Schoolgirl* (1919–1940), *Schoolgirls' Weekly* (1922–1939), and *The Schoolgirls' Own* (1922–1940). Conspicuously, in their discussion of the novels (especially Brazil's), Cadogan and Craig describe a body of work that they find laughably naïve and formulaic. More affirmative is their discussion of the weeklies, to which they attribute strong and successful gender politics: "They projected a new image of responsible but lively girlhood, in which pompous adults—and assertive boys—were thoroughly debunked. Editorial policy demanded that the heroine of every story should be active in her own interests and not simply, as in many earlier books, a victim of events; femininity although not forgotten was enlivened by adventure and enquiry. Girl readers began to consider not only fictional heroines but themselves as initiators rather than shuttlecocks of fate, or backers-up of men" (230). Yet, as Cadogan and Craig spell out, "the whole girls' enterprise [in the weeklies] was conceived, created and sustained by men"—by writers such as Frank Richards and Horace Phillips who shared the pen name "Hilda Richards" (230). As such, Cadogan and Craig make an unsettled foray into the girls' school story archive, treating authors such as Brazil as prolific but essentially redundant, while attributing to men posing as women the most coherent, progressive fantasies for girl readers dreaming of domestic and professional freedoms.

Though the archive continued to diversify as scholars addressed changes in culture and education, in the 1980s, girls' school fiction was still a sticking point for major critics. This is especially true of Quigly's *The Heirs of Tom Brown: The English School Story*, a work capacious and generous in its account of boys' school fiction but at pains to denigrate the girls'. Pointing out that girls' books had "never achieved the status of the boys' books," Quigly claims that, among the girls' authors, "there was no one anywhere near the level of Kipling or Wodehouse, or even of Reed, Walpole or Turley. Like every other form of fiction, girls' school stories have a sociological interest, telling us a great deal about their time and its attitudes; but it is very hard to consider them as more than (occasionally charming) kitsch" (212). Putting Brazil's novels in the spotlight, Quigly insists that, "although they have a good deal of presence and fire, they are inescapably silly, childish and insubstantial"; and "what is limiting and wrong and absurd is not the set-up of the stories but the outlook that produced them, the total lack of irony that can say: '"I still can't quite, quite believe it—it's too absolutely, perfectly, deliciously scrumshus!' bleated Gwen hysterically," and expect the reader to take it quite straight" (218). Making short shrift of Brazil, Quigly gives her fullest attention to demarcating a classic lineage of boys' fiction in a clear dramatic arc: the genre's emergence in Hughes and Farrar, popularization in Reed, idiosyncratic encounter with Kipling, maturation in P. G. Wodehouse, and ultimate demise in Richards, author of the "pop school story" churned out by the weeklies. Like Townsend, she defines the genre by its close association with the public schools, and paramount is the matter of tone: the genre, she argues, lived by virtue of a certain seriousness (the plausibility of the public-school system in the age of empire), and it died by dissolving into the farce represented by Billy Bunter (originally in *The Magnet*, 1908–1940) and St. Trinians (originally in Ronald Searle's comic strip, 1946–1952, and early film adaptations, 1954–1966). Like the earliest critics, Quigly is invested in the historical reality behind the fiction, defining a genre that peaked in an era when the English public-school system was complicit in preparing a certain class of boys for administrative service on behalf of the British Empire. Hence her claim that once the empire lost its hold, both ideologically at home and economically abroad, the school story was effectively dead: though the form could be sustained, she argued, the spirit was gone.

As authoritative as Quigly's contribution seemed, subsequent scholars were compelled to challenge the archive as she saw it. Thus, P. W. Musgrave's *From Brown to Bunter: The Life and Death of the School Story* (1985), though tracing a comparable constellation of major authors (Hughes, Farrar, Reed, Kipling, and Waugh) and reiterating the death-of-the-genre thesis, demonstrated more sensitivity to children's literary traditions for grasping the genre. Criticizing Quigly for not differentiating between stories for boys and for adults (249), Musgrave describes a genre premised on the young audience. He notes that *Tom Brown* had precursors in school stories for children but not for adults; that the "full development" of the genre came with Reed's contributions to the *Boy's Own Paper*, especially *The Fifth Form at St. Dominic's* (1881); and that adult school stories only emerged in what he terms the late period of diversification, 1890–1940, when the increasing presence of formulaic stories for boys emptied the genre of moral meaning and literary merit. Refuting the "revolutionary" status of *Tom Brown*, Musgrave queries the very idea of genre, asserting that it is not an essentialist concept—a claim seemingly put into practice when he shows how the school story accommodated drastic transformations as it moved between Hughes, Farrar, Reed, Kipling, Waugh, and Richards. In doing so, however, he leaves unanswered the question of how the genre could have died along with the public-school paradigm rather than moving into the new territory of comprehensive and secondary-modern school fiction. That is, like others before him, Musgrave does in fact presume an essential generic identity intimately caught up in boys' public-school experience, presupposing a form that might be carried across different schools within a single elite system, but not across different school systems segregated by class lines.

Characteristic of a decade in which cultural studies and reception theories were newly priming scholars to unpack the ideological assumptions of literature and criticism alike, feminist critics in the 1980s began to reorient discussion of the school story to foreground representations of girls' school experience. Published in the same year as Musgrave's book, Gill Frith's "'The Time of Your Life': The Meaning of the School Story" (1985) undertook an influential study of the girls' school story and its relation to "ideologies of female subjectivity" (113). Critical for Frith is a sense of the girls' story shifting, historically, in its understanding of girls' education. She takes the precursor of the modern story to be the college novels of L. T. Meade, such as *A Sweet Girl Graduate* and *The Girls of St. Wode's* (1898), works "feminist in their impulse," in which "there is a persistent *celebration* of women's newly found access to knowledge, in which . . . the pleasure of learning for its own sake is always balanced by an emphasis on its *usefulness*, on the necessary relationship between the knowledge acquired in the college and its currency in the outside world" (128). But a turning point comes in the early twentieth century, when novels such as Clemence Dane's *Regiment of Women* (1915) show ambivalence, if not outright opposition to, feminism. Thereafter, the genre increasingly understands school as a locus of fun rather than learning, "a *refuge* from the real world, an *escape* from knowledge" (130)—dramatically at odds with the escape necessitated by the much earlier boarding-school novels described by Avery. Yet, rather than suggest a simple linear decline, Frith describes a body of stories that, still popular in the 1980s, retained a "residue of their original feminist impetus, in that they offer a positive and active identity for girls" (131). More to the point, that residual feminism afforded a normal picture of female strength and potential at odds with the constructions of girlhood dominant in late twentieth-century girls' weeklies such as D. C. Thomson's *Jackie* (1964–1993), in which girlhood was constructed as a problem—in which "to be assertive, physically active, daring, ambitious is . . . a source of tension" (121). Frith's interest in *Jackie* makes it clear that scholars in the Reagan-Thatcher years did not find it difficult to give critical attention to contemporaneous primary texts. And yet, when they set their sights on school fiction, it typically compelled a turn away from the present—from an era bruised and bloodied by the breaking of the unions, the valorization of individualism, and the political and ideological bolstering of neoliberal economics—back to narratives predating both the democratization of education and the rise of neoliberalism.

Interests in popular culture, influenced by the nexus of cultural studies, communication studies, and critical theory, continued to lead scholars in the late 1980s to question the kinds of works deemed to be representative of, or definitive for, the genre of school story. In *Happiest Days: The Public Schools in English Fiction* (1988), Jeffrey Richards returned to the boy's public-school story with a brief apology for his exclusive interests when he describes the girls' school story as "a universe of its own," one that "has already received perceptive analysis in Mary Cadogan and Patricia Craig" (Acknowledgements). Although a small detail, it suggests a suspicion that he was knowingly perpetuating gender bias in his survey of the boys-only school story. Like Quigly, Richards recognizes the fundamental role of narrative attitudes in grasping the genre, though he comes to the opposite conclusion: that certain popular forces did not so much corrupt as invigorate the public-school story. Discerning three distinct attitudes among writers of school fiction, "the conformist, which endorses the dominant ideology, the alternative, which proposes changes, and the oppositional, which proposes rejection and abolition" (8), Richards makes the point that such stances were distributed unevenly across works of high and popular culture. That is, "popular culture seems on the whole to have been strongly sympathetic to the public schools," while "high culture has contained a greater portion of condemnation and dissent" (8). What's more, the fiction critics had in fact occupied a "narrow intellectual world . . . of high-society literary salons and low-circulation magazines, rarely reaching out to or affecting the perceptions of the wider public" (17). Accusing Quigly and Musgrave of snobbishly disregarding "the middle-brow best-sellers," Richards redraws the lineage of the boys' school story to figure Frank Richards as its legitimate culmination: "[Frank] Richards stands in direct line of descent from Thomas Hughes's *Tom Brown's Schooldays* through Talbot Baines Reed and the *Boy's Own Paper*, and brings the public school story to its mythic apotheosis" (276). Richards also reminds us that, while the British Empire had had its day, the public-school system not only continued to thrive in the late twentieth century but enjoyed strong popular support, a fact he attributes to the work of those timeless characters such as Billy Bunter that Quigly found so distasteful. Hence the closing claim that "it may well be found that Mr Chips [from *Goodbye, Mr. Chips*, novella by James Hilton, 1934; film, 1939] along with Tom Brown, the Greyfriars Remove, Stalky and Co., Rupert Ray and Edgar Doe [from Ernest Raymond's *Tell England*, 1922], and the fifth form at St Dominic's have done as much as anything else to preserve the public schools. That is the power of popular culture" (300).

To their credit, the scholars of this period began to redress the gender bias and class chauvinism that had for so long skewed the critics' vision of the school story. Yet it remains true that the major studies of school fiction in the 1970s and 1980s, though up to date in their theoretical approaches, continued to set their sights on fiction of defunct school settings. Keeping in mind that these same decades saw the rise to power of Thatcher in the UK (secretary of state for education and science, 1970–1974; leader of the Conservative Party, 1975–1990; and prime minister, 1979–1990) and Reagan in the USA (governor of California, 1967–1975, and president, 1981–1989), it seems remarkable that there was no comparable interest in school fiction speaking in and of the time—that is, during the years in which the neoliberal assault on education began. As *Guardian* columnist Peter Wilby notes, speaking of the British education scene, "From the mid-1980s . . . ministers behaved as though education were an ailing, near-bankrupt industry. Their role was to challenge, even denigrate, the views of 'insiders,' to demand value for money, to impose performance management, to root out endemic 'failure' and to insist on what they saw as customer satisfaction. This attitude continued through Labour as well as Tory governments. Future historians may see the years 1997–2010, which seemed ones of frenetic activity at the time, as just a pause in a revolution begun by Thatcher." Meanwhile on the other side of the Atlantic, as Gary Clabaugh documents, "in campaigning for the presidency, Mr. Reagan called for the total elimination of the U.S. Department of Education, severe curtailment of bilingual education, and massive cutbacks in the federal role in education. Upon his election he tried to do that and more"—and this following his tenure as governor of California, remembered for his "calling for an end to free tuition for state college and university students . . . annually demanding 20 percent across-the-board cuts in higher education funding . . . repeatedly slashing construction funds for state campuses . . . engineering the firing of Clark Kerr, the highly respected president of the University of California . . . [and] declaring that the state 'should not subsidize intellectual curiosity'" (256–57). We can only imagine what shape or tenor the genre would have assumed if the critics had given serious and dedicated attention to, say, Robert Cormier's *The Chocolate War* (1974)—a school story of institutional abuse, mob mentality, and nonconformity, all revolving around a deviously orchestrated chocolate sale—as a seminal work in a living literature about school experience and young identity informed by marketplace consciousness.

Late Twentieth Century: Revisionist and Interventionist Forms

The masculine paradigms taken for granted by Quigly, Musgrave, and Richards came under pressure at the turn of the 1990s in two chapter studies rethinking the gendered ideals on which boys' and girls' school stories ostensibly rested: Judith Rowbotham's "Education for Model Maidens" (in *Good Girls Make Good*

Wives: Guidance for Girls in Victorian Fiction, 1989) and Claudia Nelson's "The Angel in the School" (in *Boys Will Be Girls: The Feminine Ethic and British Children's Fiction, 1857-1917*, 1991). Though mostly interested in the historical circumstances of education for girls in the Victorian period, primarily reading girls' school fiction as evidence of real conditions, Rowbotham drew attention to the ways in which discrete works—such as Meade's *A World of Girls* (1886), *Red Rose and Tiger Lily* (1894), and *A Madcap* (1904)—revealed dominant understandings of the purpose and value of girls' education. Noting that "estimation of character for both sexes is established as one of the fundamental elements of the spirit of the age" (103), she argues that, while the broad purpose of education for males and females certainly differed on account of gender-based expectations, the foundational character training expected of both was "essentially genderless" in many aspects (100–101). A collapse of gender distinctions of a different kind is signaled by Nelson's argument that "the Victorian school story for boys, set in a world largely devoid of family ties and indeed of women, developed into the male analogue of the Victorian domestic novel for girls" (57), a claim describing a deeply gendered literary tradition, though not in the way usually presumed. Unpacking the core morals at play in the more or less familiar sequence of *Tom Brown's Schooldays*, *Eric*, *Vice-Versa*, *Stalky & Co.*, *Mike*, and *The Loom of Youth*, Nelson makes three provocative points. First, that the major distinction between *Eric* and *Tom Brown* "is not one of didactic purpose so much as of authorial personality" (61), which is to say that "both agree on the ideal ["the role of team sports in building character and unselfishness"]—but Hughes looks on the positive, Farrar on the negative side of the means proposed" (62). Second, that there is no substantive difference in the core values between the early works of Hughes and Farrar and the later works of Kipling, Wodehouse, and Waugh—that "beneath the sophisticated veneer of antitraditional novels from *Stalky & Co.* to *Mike and Psmith* to *The Loom of Youth* are buried many of the same ideals that lie on the surface of Farrar's *Eric*" (59). And third, that in all these texts, the schoolboy code comprises the same qualities embodied in the Victorian domestic ideal of the angel in the house: the valorizing of purity, self-sacrifice, and enforced obedience in the context of a community single-sexed but marked nevertheless by a gendered hierarchy in its fagging system (the tradition of younger boys performing chores and household duties for older boys), and a culture of athleticism "that instilled womanly virtues in a manly world" (64–67). The real difference, argues Nelson, is that later authors such as Kipling rejected "not so much the ideals behind the pious model schoolboy as the conventions that have come to mark him" (81), meaning that "schools still mold character, but in Kipling's world they are not permitted to advertise the fact" (83). In a real sense, Nelson unsettled the gamut of criticism before her, almost all of which took the gender-segregated world of school at its face value, as if schoolboys of fiction and fact alike lived in a thoroughly masculine world of only male and manly ideals.

One significant critical contradiction continued to inform the scholarship in the 1990s: on one hand, a growing insistence that the school story canon had to be updated because it had left out major texts, registers, and experiences; and on the other, a stubborn clinging to the classic school story, at the expense of the modern, as the locus of meaning and value. It was a decade marked on either side by bibliographies and encyclopedias: two smaller works dedicated to boys' stories (Kirkpatrick, 1990; Watson, 1992), and a hefty two-volume work divided between boys' and girls' stories (Kirkpatrick, 2000; Sims and Clare, 2000). Robert J. Kirkpatrick, in *Bullies, Beaks and Flannelled Fools: An Annotated Bibliography of Boys' School Fiction, 1742–1990* (1990), identified the period from 1880 to 1940 as the heyday of the boys' school story, figuring Hughes as the possible progenitor of the popular form, though attributing its "birth" to Reed and the *Boy's Own Paper* (2). Like Richards, Kirkpatrick sets aside the girls' story as "in a league of its own," and makes a rare acknowledgement that the genre, not entirely English, also had German, Commonwealth, European, American, and Russian exponents. Focusing on British and Irish stories (minus girls' and primary-school stories), Kirkpatrick offers a quantitative rationale for identifying school stories proper: "The school occupies at least one-third of each novel, although in the vast majority of cases it is either the whole novel or at least half" (4). Again like Richards, Kirkpatrick makes much of popular culture, claiming that "the school story genre perhaps owes more to [the periodical serials], as being the true progenitors of the popular school story, than has previously been recognized" (19). Unlike Richards, he acknowledges the growing diversity of fictional schools after midcentury: he identifies Croft's *Spare the Rod*, Braithwaite's *To Sir With Love*, and John Wiles's *The Asphalt Playground* (1958) with a "small but important body of work set in secondary modern schools . . . that contributed in no small way to the public perception of secondary education"; and he makes mention of the comprehensive setting of Phil Redmond's *Grange Hill* television show (1978–2008) and novel spin-offs (1979–1988), along with a range of grammar, elementary, seminary, naval training, approved, and borstal (young offenders' institution) school stories (2). Still, as his title suggests, he associates the spirit of the genre with the classic public-school story. Benjamin Watson's *English Schoolboy Stories: An Annotated Bibliography of Hardcover Fiction* (1992) also attests to the continuing production of school stories, claiming that "schoolboy novels are still written and still widely read in the 1990s, both by a popular audience and by serious scholars of social history, education, adolescent psychology, and English literature" (ix), though he makes no mention of the modern turn represented by Croft, Braithwaite, Wiles, or Redmond.

In this same period, when most studies were consolidating the boys' archive, a new understanding of the value of popular culture for the genre emerged in the first book-length feminist study of the girls' school story, Rosemary Auchmuty's *A World of Girls: The Appeal of the Girls' School Story* (1992). Conscious of the ideological implications of the critical tradition behind her, Auchmuty opens with the statement that "literary critics have never concealed their contempt for the school story," explaining how "the school story was condemned, together with other forms of popular fiction ... as badly written, full of stereotyped characters and plots, and produced to a formula which made discrimination impossible and 'true critical values' irrelevant" (9)—the same criteria by which the school story critics, in turn, had summed up girls' school fiction. But more than merely drawing attention to a lopsided field of criticism, Auchmuty argues that the critics had concocted a narrative of decline for the genre at odds with historical reality: "While it is true that some school story authors, popular in their day, are no longer read, the school story as an artefact did not die the death its critics thought it deserved" (10). Focusing on the lives and works of Oxenham, Bruce, Brent-Dyer, and Blyton, she describes a body of girls' school-series fiction that never lost its popular appeal. Writing against arbiters such as Crouch, as well as Cadogan and Craig, Auchmuty questions the convention of making value judgments based on critics' rather than readers' tastes, an approach eliding the ways in which girls' school stories resonated—culturally, psychologically, and politically—with girl and women readers. Making a case for a historical rather than a literary critical reading, Auchmuty argues "that the decline of the girls' school story after the Second World War removed a potential source of strength for girls, and that its renewed popularity in the 1980s and 1990s points to a continuing need for a separate literature for girls and women which presents positive role models for their sex which are free from domination and control by men" (18). Hence, the value of the girls' story comes down to its capacity for representing "a world where authority figures as well as colleagues and comrades are female, where the action is carried on by girls and women, and decisions are made by them ... Women's emotional and social energies are directed towards other women, and women's friendships are seen as positive, not destructive or competitive, and sufficient unto themselves. School stories offer female readers positive role models to set against a reality which is often restrictive or hostile to them" (7). As she elaborates in her companion work, *A World of Women: Growing Up in the Girls' School Story* (1999), Auchmuty is interested in authors whose series books gave readers the chance to see characters grow into adulthood, enforcing the general idea that Oxenham's *Abbey* series (1914–1959), Bruce's *Dimsie* series (1921–1941), Brent-Dyer's *Chalet School* series (1923–1970), and Blyton's *St. Clare's* series (1941–1945) mattered—and continue to matter—because of the ways in which they invite readers to think developmentally about the lives of girls and women.

While it is true that feminist analysis in the last decade of the twentieth century was becoming the dominant framework for rethinking the school story, actual feminist analytics ranged widely in their understandings of both gender and genre. Making a dramatic departure from Frith's and Auchmuty's studies was Beverly Lyon Clark's *Regendering the School Story* (1996), a transatlantic deconstruction of the traditionally gender-segregated canon. Claiming that the school story never cohered as a genre for Americans the way it did for the British, a condition she attributes to a weaker boarding-school culture and a more democratic, coeducational school system, Clark nevertheless identifies a number of American texts, which she reads alongside British works from before, during, and after the Victorian school story's heyday—to recuperate works marginalized in the making of the canon, and to explore how various works and authors helped to shape, or lay bare the contradictions within, dominant ways of thinking about gender. Concentrating on what she calls "crossgendered" school stories, in which men wrote about girls and women wrote about boys, Clark articulates a sense of unease comparable to that informing Auchmuty's work—albeit with a different understanding of the boundaries between male and female worlds. Which is to say that Clark is more interested in moments when the binaries are undone—when works, authors, and canon are cross-gendered, regendered, and reshaped. Drawing on theorists such as Jacques Derrida and Hélène Cixous, Clark—like Auchmuty—foregrounds the matter of marginality, describing a kind of story doubly marginalized—first, within the broader genre of school story, and second, in the vaster realm of children's literature—on the understanding that such marginal texts speak to cultural contradictions vital for grasping the genre. Representative are two readings in particular: of *Tom Brown's Schooldays* as a work that "crystallized gender segregation ... decreasing the importance of domestic and religious influence" and "ma[king] it more difficult for women to write about boys' schools and also, curiously, for men to write about girls' schools" (103); and of Louisa May Alcott's *Little Men: Life at Plumfield with Jo's Boys* (1871), with which "Alcott is ... enabled to evade the essentializing of male and female, making possible a new gender dialectic, illuminating what had been repressed in the canonical story, its denial of the feminine" (176). True to her conceptual framework, Clark offers an archive of stories rarely discussed by the critics, including E. J. May's *Louis' School Days: A Story for Boys* (1850), Ellen Wood's *Orville College: A Tale* (1867), and Edward Everett Hale's *Mrs. Merriam's Scholars: A Story of the "Original Ten"* (1878), though their inclusion does not always rest on inherent qualities (as, for example, in Kirkpatrick's quantitative reckoning), for some are, by her own admission, only "marginally" school stories.

With the turn of the millennium, scholarship on the girls' school story returned to more familiar ground, with a classic-political rather than a critical-theoretical feminism renewing the sense of the gender divide informing both the fiction and the criticism. This is the spirit of Sue Sims and Hilary Clare's *The Encyclopaedia of Girls' School Stories* (2000), which includes a prefatory essay by Auchmuty on school story criticism. Sims's introduction takes on the combined task of recognizing the girls' story as a response to the historical circumstances of real-life education for girls (and, as such, no mere imitation of the boys' school story); outlining major authors, works, themes, and innovations in girls' school fiction; defending the girls' story from what she calls snobbish detractors; and clarifying its enduring popularity with readers. Sims accounts for the girls' story as a "full blown" form emerging in the late nineteenth century when, following the 1868 report of the Taunton Commission, new national provisions for secondary education brought high school and public school within reach of more girls than ever before. She describes an early period of moral, religious, and temperate works giving way, under the influence of Coolidge's *What Katy Did at School*, to a new era of implied rather than didactic moralism, often injected with (sometimes madcap) humor (6). She figures the 1920s and 1930s as the peak period, albeit one quickly exhausted—in part because actual school had lost the glamor of privilege it once had (12). Midcentury is described as a fraught moment of competing forces: with Brent-Dyer, Oxenham, and Bruce carrying on the traditional form; with new irony and greater realism taking hold in the works of Nancy Breary and Antonia Forest, respectively; and increasing mergers with other genres including pony fiction, ballet fiction, spy fiction, and crime fiction (12).

But if the girls' story declined, says Sims, it had more to do with librarians and publishers, rather than the popular audience, giving up on the genre—though she also argues that the changing nature of the school story, with its increasing interest in comprehensive and coeducational settings, led it away from its genre classification (16). This alleged decline in girls' fiction is elaborated further in Auchmuty's essay on "The Critical Response," which works through the ways in which "girls school stories have been ignored, dismissed, ridiculed or despised by adult critics, whether teachers, librarians, or literary scholars" (19). Auchmuty thus expands our understanding of the critical field, taking in not only the narrower realm of scholarly journals and literary reviews, but also the broader world of literature and literacy provision in schools and libraries. In doing so, she raises the key question of why it has been the feminist scholars, more than any others, who have treated the girls' school story as a genre worthy of serious inquiry—a question with a dual intent: to acknowledge the extent to which traditional gender bias has figured the girls' school story as relatively worthless compared to the boys'; and to acknowledge that the substance of girls' school stories rests on the ways in which they speak to that bias. Representing probably the most confrontational moment in the long history of the school story debate, Auchmuty calls out early scholars Eyre, Townsend, and Crouch for making "literary judgments [that] rest squarely on personal value systems, which in turn are part of wider public ideologies" (24), along with later scholars Musgrave, Richards, and especially Quigly for unrivalled disrespect, inaccuracy, and misogyny.

In comparison, it is tempting to think of Kirkpatrick's companion *Encyclopaedia of Boys' School Stories* (2000) as speaking from a relatively settled position, as if making not so much a critical intervention as a nuanced refinement of the familiar history of the boys' genre. Thus, *Tom Brown's Schooldays*, while no longer the absolute point of origin for Kirkpatrick, is the story that popularizes the public school for Victorian audiences. Reed is still a synthesis of earlier threads: periodicals for boys, respectable and sensational alike; evangelical fictions; and the Tom Brown model of moral fiction spiced with sports, fagging, and fights. Kipling is, again, the turning point introducing a darker potential. The genre still waxes in the early twentieth century, declines around the middle, and lives on in the late twentieth century in a smattering of more realistic stories set in state rather than public schools. And it is because this developmental narrative sounds so familiar that it is easy to miss Kirkpatrick's main point when he turns attention to the critics' construction of the field. Of all the major studies—by Eyre, Townsend, Trease, Hicks, Richards, Mack, Quigly, and Musgrave—"disappointingly . . . none of these studies have explored the backbone of the genre, the vast body of work by boys' writers which was, by its longevity and popularity, the driving force behind school fiction" (10). In a way, then, Kirkpatrick picks up where Orwell left off, though he comes to a different conclusion about the value of the boys' school story: to Orwell's point that the school story looked exclusively at public-school experience through the eyes of public schoolboys, Kirkpatrick asks, "And why not?" (5). Either way, Kirkpatrick insists wholly in the spirit of Orwell that understanding the genre is synonymous with understanding its young audience.

Turn of the Century: Pedagogical and Political Forms

In the decades on either side of the millennial turn, the children's literary studies establishment began to treat the school story more and more as worthy of respect, evidenced in the burgeoning of dedicated book chapters and encyclopedia entries—including Samuel F. Pickering Jr.'s chapter "School Stories" in *Moral Instruction and Fiction for Children, 1749–1820* (1993); Bobbie Wells, Maureen Nimon, and Connie Parker's entry "School Stories" in *The Cambridge Guide to Children's Books in English* (2001); Sheila Ray's essay "School Stories" in *International Companion Encyclopedia of Children's Literature* (2004); Declan Kiberd's chapter "School Stories" in *Studies in Children's Literature, 1500–2000* (2004); Pat Pinsent's chapter "Theories of Genre and Gender: Change and Continuity in the School Story" in *Modern Children's Literature: An Introduction* (2005); Auchmuty's entry "School Stories" in *The Oxford Encyclopedia of Children's Literature* (2006); M. O. Grenby's chapter "The School Story" in *Children's Literature* (2008); Mavis Reimer's chapter "Traditions of the School Story" in *The Cambridge Companion to Children's Literature* (2009); and Pinsent's entry "School Stories" in *The Routledge Companion to Children's Literature* (2010). Though varying in their preoccupations and approaches, taken together these surveys suggest far-reaching efforts to diversify the archive. First, they explore the ways in which early school stories from the eighteenth century, including Fielding's *The Governess* and Dorothy Kilner's *Anecdotes of a Boarding School* (1795), differentiated between boys and girls to inculcate gendered lessons in control, discipline, and morality. Second, they assert the need to give equal attention to girls' and boys' school stories as traditions responding to separate trajectories in real-life education. Third, they acknowledge that American, African American, and Canadian (as well as Australian, New Zealand, and African) authors, though allegedly not achieving recognizably national genres, yielded classic school stories in such works as Alcott's *Little Men* (1871) and Frances Hodgson Burnett's *A Little Princess* (1905), Mildred Taylor's *Roll of Thunder, Hear My Cry* (1976), and Gordon Kormon's Bruno and Boots/Macdonald Hall series (1978–1991). Fourth, they recognize that the genre continued beyond the boarding-school paradigm, developed complexly in works such as Cormier's *The Chocolate War* and Rosemary Wells's *The Fog Comes on Little Pig Feet* (1972), and underwent revival in popular culture and in fantasy crossovers including Jill Murphy's *The Worst Witch* (1974), Phillip Pullman's *His Dark Materials* trilogy (1995–2000), and J. K. Rowling's *Harry Potter and the Philosopher's Stone* (1997). And fifth, they articulate new, more inclusive definitions for a genre increasingly understood to be eclectic in its representations of school experience—best summed up in Grenby's "three basic criteria" for the school story: "It is set almost entirely in school; it takes the relationships between the scholars and their teachers as its primary focus; and it contains attitudes and adventures which are unique to school life" (90).

In these same decades, scholars in cultural studies began to consider the contemporary diffusion of British and American school stories in popular fiction, television drama, and especially cinema. Contributions including Sandra Weber and Claudia Mitchell's *That's Funny, You Don't Look Like a Teacher! Interrogating Images and Identity in Popular Culture* (1995); Mary M. Dalton's *The Hollywood Curriculum: Teachers in the Movies* (1999); Pamela Bolotin Joseph and Gaile E. Burnaford's *Images of Schoolteachers in America* (2001); Roy Fisher, Ann Harris, and Christine Jarvis's *Education in Popular Culture: Telling Tales on Teachers and Learners* (2008); and Edward Janak and Denise Blum's *The Pedagogy of Pop: Theoretical and Practical Strategies for Success* (2013) all helped in the building of a contemporary archive. Eclectic by nature, these studies cover a wide range of texts—from humorous animated shows such as *The Simpsons* (1989–present) and *South Park* (1997–present) that occasionally have something to say about education to school stories proper for the big screen including *Educating Rita* (1983), *Dangerous Minds* (1995), and *Pay It Forward* (2000). Admittedly, the purpose is rarely to discuss the form of the school story as such; rather, emphasis is on the ways in which representations of teachers, students, learners, pedagogy, and curriculum channel broader cultural discourses about education. Even so, in foregrounding potent, influential, and often acclaimed school fictions addressing modern school contexts too often overlooked by scholars of school fiction, Weber and Mitchell; Dalton; Bolotin and Burnaford; Fisher, Harris, and Jarvis; and Janak and Blum clarify the centrality of the cultural studies legacy in understanding the ongoing evolution of school fiction.

Although critics have, from time to time, shown interest in how the school story represents academic life—despairing, for example, of authors' lack of interest in intellectual pursuits (a complaint originally leveled at Hughes by Victorian critics)—mainstream discussions of school fiction in the twenty-first century came round to affirmatively foregrounding themes of learning and development. Key to this new sense of the genre was Rowling's *Harry Potter* series (1997–2007), whose fantasy take on the traditional boarding-school setting encouraged scholars to see Rowling as a more pedagogically mindful cousin to Hughes and Blyton. In book chapters and journal articles including Pat Pinsent's "The Education of a Wizard: Harry Potter and His Predecessors" and David Steege's "Harry Potter, Tom Brown, and the British School Story" (both in *The Ivory Tower and Harry Potter: Perspectives on a Literary Phenomenon*, 2002); Lisa Hopkins's "Harry Potter and the Acquisition of Knowledge" and Karen Manners Smith's "Harry Potter's Schooldays: J. K. Rowling and the British Boarding School Novel" (both in *Reading Harry Potter: Critical Essays*, 2003); Elisabeth Rose Gruner's "Teach the Children: Education and Knowledge in Recent Children's Fantasy" (*Children's Literature* 37, 2009); and Karin E. Westman's "Blending Genres and Crossing Audiences: Harry Potter and the Future of Literary Fiction" (*The Oxford Handbook of Children's Literature*, 2011), the classic school story was credited with a foundational role for understanding one of the most influential contemporary children's literary phenomena.

The broad consensus has been that the *Harry Potter* books constitute a healthy representation of schoolchildren thriving on reading, inquiring, and learning. Hence Hopkins's description of the series valorizing the "epistemological processes" of "knowledge, intuition, and deduction," while "Harry Potter himself legitimizes the good behavior associated with learning in school" (33). Comparing and contrasting *Harry Potter* with Terry Pratchett's Tiffany Aching novels (from his *Discworld* series) and Philip Pullman's *His Dark Materials* trilogy (1995–2000), Gruner identifies distinct processes of education in all three sets, in which the central elements of mentors, books and stories, and peers support a philosophy of "unschooling" or self-directed learning (220). Making the firmest connections with classic boys' and girls' school fiction, Westman argues that, "in contrast to the physical and spiritual knowledge of *Tom Brown's Schooldays*, the educational world of Harry Potter emphasizes the value of academic inquiry for intellectual growth, usually achieved through a pedagogy of collaborative exchange. In contrast to the moral certitude of Blyton's school stories, Rowling's school story recognizes and even rewards ambiguity as part of the educational endeavor. With this wider critical lens of 'school story' in hand we can see Rowling's series as a contribution to an evolving cultural narrative about the intersection of education and politics and recognize her complex representations of teaching and learning for individual moral growth" (97). In these and other commentaries, critics brought the school story debate around not only to an unequivocal celebration of the scholastic possibilities of the genre, but also to a strict assertion that such possibilities are definitive for the unrivaled success of works such as *Harry Potter*: on the one hand, identifying a highly individualistic learning experience, one dependent on students' idiosyncratically negotiating institutional demands, pursuing their own lines of inquiry, and, in the process, successfully breaking with convention; and, on the other hand, articulating such learning processes in the language of student development, describing stories of "critical thinking based on inquiry," "self-directed learning," "formulating research questions and identifying sources," "collaborative learning," and "identity development." Put another way, when Hopkins concludes that *Harry Potter* demonstrates how it is "admirable and necessary to work hard, read books, and spend long hours in the library, because the things you learn there may just save the world" (33), she implies a convergence of dramatic, pedagogical, and critical interests, describing a genre satisfying not only the young audience with a blend of fantasy, adventure, and character-driven stories of young identity formation, but also the teacher-scholar-critics conscious of learning outcomes and intellectual growth.

The *Harry Potter* scholarship reveals a curious moment for both school and the school story in the twenty-first century, laying bare the ways in which education has come to figure variously as victim of, instrument of, and weapon against neoliberalism. When children's literature scholars speak of education as a fundamental of healthy learning and growth for both individual and society, they channel the kind of learning conventionally at the core of the liberal arts curriculum—epitomized, above all, in the college writing classroom, where students undertake engaged lines of inquiry into issues of public concern in ways that encourage independent thinking, cohort collaboration, and service to the class community (if not a broader social community). As students and teachers of writing and research methods know, that kind of learning carries with it a powerful ethics, one that begins with the fair and honest use of sources (typically parsed as engaging with and responding to the voices of others) and ends with acknowledging the social consequences of research and rhetoric (parsed as answering the question of who stands to gain or suffer from specific arguments, innovations, and practices in, across, and beyond disciplines). For good reason, as Wendy Brown spells out in *Undoing the Demos* (2015), the twentieth-century extension of liberal arts education "from the elite to the many was nothing short of a radical democratic event, one in which all became potentially eligible for the life of freedom long reserved for the few"; that is, "the ideal of democracy was being realized in a new way insofar as the demos was being prepared through education for a life of freedom, understood as both individual sovereignty (choosing and pursuing one's ends) and participation in collective self-rule" (185). Hence Brown's concern when neoliberalism—or, rather, "neoliberal rationality"—"hollows out" education, when it "formulates everything, everywhere, in terms of capital investment and appreciation" so that: "knowledge, thought, and training are valued and desired almost exclusively for their contribution to capital enhancement"; "subjects, including citizen subjects, are configured by the market metrics of our time as self-investing human capital"; and "democracies are conceived as requiring technically skilled human capital, not education participants in public life and common rule" (176–77). And in transforming the ideals of liberal arts education into a culture of "best practices," neoliberal rationality has a knack for making education less about the democratic ideal and more about the entrepreneurial, a notion compelling us to question whether characters like Harry Potter genuinely evince the former and not the latter.

Implicit in the critics' interest in pedagogically purposeful school fiction is a belief in the potential for responsibility and growth in childhood, a concern for attitudes and behaviors considered foundational for not only succeeding in, but also contributing to, the adult community. Whereas most scholars in this area have looked to representations of children's intellectual and cognitive development, some have set their sights on the civic implications. Hence Jenny Holt's *Public School Literature, Civic Education and the Politics of Male Adolescence* (2008), a return to the traditional boys' public-school story to trace the intertwined discourses of adolescence and citizenship as they evolved in the late nineteenth and early twentieth centuries. Working through core texts from Hughes, Farrar, Anstey, Vachell, Howard Sturgis, Kipling, Lunn, and Waugh, Holt reads classic boys' public-school fiction for the ways in which it carried civic values. She argues that such stories, though typically telling of elite characters destined for state leadership, were not only intended for a largely working-class audience but also played a part in grooming working-class readers for lives of obedience—a claim not too far out of step with Orwell, but one that suggests a darker underside to the early archive. According to Holt, the public-school story emerged around the same time as the sociological concept of adolescence; as it evolved, it became a vehicle for defining and influencing ideas of both adolescence and citizenship. As she argues, "the nineteenth and twentieth century establishment tried to demarcate normal and devious adolescent behavior through public school literature" (10), with the "public school experience of adolescence held up to working class children as the optimal way to experience youth"—a positioning of class identities and roles maintained until the 1950s by publishers supplying state schools with classics such as *Tom Brown's Schooldays* (3).

Holt's understanding of boys' school fiction as a mouthpiece for establishment values is worth comparing to Judith Humphrey's study of girls' school fiction in *The English Girls' School Story: Subversion and Challenge in a Traditional Conservative Literary Genre* (2009). Like Frith, Humphrey acknowledges that the girls' story is in many respects a reactionary form, replicating patriarchal ideals in plots articulating women's life accomplishments in terms of marriage, exaggerated fecundity, and career abandonment (244). But such texts, she argues, are only superficially conformist, simultaneously carrying more subversive "images of liberation" and depicting girls and women dispensing with masculine authority (1). Humphrey defines the girls' archive by its preoccupations with six liberating images of women that challenged disempowering patriarchal discourses: the "intellectual woman," the "active woman," the "questioning woman," the "strong woman," the "God-woman," and the "woman-loving woman" (5–8), all refuting commonplace assumptions that women were naturally unfit for asserting themselves outside the home sphere. Humphrey speaks of stories "working in the fault-lines between ideologies, articulating one mode of being, but embodying quite another. The surface of the text appears to support the constructs of society, yet the emotional experience of reading the text indicates that the emphases in fact fall quite differently" (49). Like Auchmuty, Humphrey is shifting discussion away from subjective tastes toward a serious understanding of what it means for women readers to have encountered those images. Lives, she says, are at stake—when such texts "allow women to reclaim their selfhood and to reject the damaging lies they have been told about themselves by so many of the discourses of society" (248). Together, Humphrey and Holt make a case for recognizing the school story as a profoundly political genre, to some extent a one-sided affair overdetermining class and gender hierarchies, but also riddled with contradictions to the point of affording alternative structures of identification and belonging.

Early Twenty-First Century: Postcolonial and Americanist Forms

While British texts and contexts have dominated critical conversations on the school story, a genre often described as quintessentially English, Americanist scholars have begun to present wholly new archives and paradigms for grasping the possible meanings and values of school fiction: Amelia V. Katanski's *Learning to Write "Indian": The Boarding-school Experience and American Indian Literature* (2005), Alexander Pitofsky's *American Boarding School Fiction, 1928–1981: A Critical Study* (2014), and Allison Speicher's *Schooling Readers: Reading Common Schools in Nineteenth-Century American Fiction* (2016). Unlike most studies of school stories, Katanski's turns attention to school experience informed primarily by race consciousness. To be sure, critics have long recognized white chauvinism to be a characteristic of the British boys' and girls' school fiction written in the age of empire, though the tendency has been to foreground the class and gender paradigms informing the dominant institutions of education. Race, however, more firmly comes to the fore when the subject is narratives of Indian boarding schools, federally supported institutions mandated in the late nineteenth century to expedite Native American assimilation: by removing Native children from their tribal communities, stripping them of their traditional language, culture, and religion, and immersing them in the Euro-American curriculum. Explaining how the Indian boarding-school system, modeled on the prototypical Carlisle Indian Industrial School of 1879, operated according to a "controlling pedagogy" designed to "monitor and restrict representations of Indianness so that students would affirm their assimilative project and embrace a sense of tribal culture as inferior and 'savage'" (7), Katanski explores the work of former students including Francis La Flesche (*The Middle Five: Indian Boys at School*, 1900) and Zitkála-Šá ("Indian Teacher Among Indians" and "School Days of an Indian Girl," both 1900); early-to-mid-twentieth-century writers such as Darcy McNickle (*The Surrounded*, 1936, and *Runner in the Sun: A Story of Indian Maize*, 1954); and contemporary writers such as N. Scott Momaday (*The Indolent Boys*, 1992) and Leslie Marmon Silko (*Gardens in the Dunes*, 1999). Noting how the schools themselves had their own literary outlets in anti-tribal magazines, Katanski explores heterogeneous Native narratives that draw on tribal, pan-tribal, and Anglo-American traditions to establish a "process of literary reinvention of the representational tools of assimilation, staking a claim to continued tribal identity and connection to land, history, and language through the telling of boarding school stories" (6). All in, identifying a tradition of school stories responding to experiences far removed from the domestic, private, and public contexts described in conventional British and American school fiction, Katanski opened up a strikingly new realm of inquiry for the school story debate of particular relevance for scholars in American studies.

In the wake of Katanski, Pitofsky's study returned to a more mainstream archive of American authors not only white but—as he himself notes—"male, Protestant, and privileged" (6). Setting his sights on the 1950s and 1960s, he identifies a body of modern American novels akin in spirit to F. Scott Fitzgerald's "The Freshest Boy" (1928), an angst-ridden story of prep school that departed from the usual antics and moral lessons of classic British and American school fiction. Working through J. D. Salinger's *The Catcher in the Rye* (1951), John Knowles's *A Separate Peace* (1959), Louis Auchinloss's *The Rector of Justin* (1964), James Kirkwood's *Good Times/Bad Times* (1968), and Richard Yates's *A Good School* (1978), Pitofsky describes a tradition of "mournful" but popular narratives of exclusive American boarding schools, counterparts to the elite British public schools. Together these texts challenge what Pitofsky calls the "prep-school myth," showing that, regardless of wealth and privilege, the students' experiences in such schools were marred by "cruelty, bigotry, snobbery, and suffering" (171). Like Humphrey, Pitofsky in his closing remarks detects a certain political ambivalence, a capacity in these works for being both "left-leaning" (suggesting "there is something specious about the Eastern old-money establishment") and "conservative" (suggesting "low and middle-income Americans should not monopolize our sympathy") (167). "Both arguments have merit," he explains, "but ultimately political messages are beside the point, because these works portray boarding school as a sphere in which partisan views are rarely mentioned. It may seem odd to label works that highlight class and gender issues as politically neutral, but how else can we label novels and short stories set in the 1940s, '50s, and '60s that are virtually silent about the Cold War, civil rights, and women's rights?" (167–68). I would argue by pointing out, in the spirit of Theodor Adorno ("Commitment," 1962), that maintaining silence in times of crisis is anything but neutral.

What Pitofsky does for American literature of the twentieth century, Allison Speicher does for American literature of the nineteenth century; in spite of critics' recurring claims that America never had its own school story genre, she recovers a substantial body of "common school" narratives: stories set in the early precursors of the modern public schools ("public" in the American sense of supported by public funds) written between the 1830s and 1880s, when reformers were pressing for a unified system of mass education to secure social cohesion in the face of increasing urbanization, industrialization, and immigration. "Fiction," argues Speicher, "allowed authors, wittingly or unwittingly, to expose the contradictions at the heart of the reform program ... common school narratives presented a challenge to the thinking of reformers and to their ability to set the terms of the public conversation regarding schooling" (11). Speicher draws on stories from the South, the Midwest, the North, and the West, mostly in the form of cheap magazine fiction but also sentimental, local-color, regional, and reform novels, to make a case for hailing American school fiction in much the same way British critics hailed *Tom Brown's Schooldays*: for profoundly influencing popular debates over the nature and purpose of education—chiefly by particularizing the "vision of what schooling did, could, or should look like" (4). Discussing a variety of works including Caroline Kirkland's "The Schoolmaster's Progress" (1846), Edward Eggleston's *The Hoosier Schoolmaster* (1871), and Hale's *Mrs. Merriam's Scholars*, Speicher identifies four recurring plot points definitive for the common-school literary tradition: "school exhibitions and spelling bees, school violence, student-teacher romance, and teacher-student adoption" (17), which allowed authors to explore concerns about curriculum, social class, school government, teacher-community relations, national belonging, schooling for girls, and female sexuality and subjectivity. In many ways a landmark study, *Schooling Readers* firmly establishes the school story in Americanist terms, revealing a substantial archive of popular American narratives immersed in representing, and implicated in reforming, distinctively American school experiences. Together, Speicher, Pitofsky, and Katanski have transformed the school story debate, at times conservatively, at others more radically, by introducing diverse texts speaking to demographics, experiences, institutions, pedagogies, ethics, and politics hitherto beyond the ken of school story critics.

Conclusion

The above studies draw attention to the ways in which writers and critics of school stories have worked to establish, enforce, or refute dominant attitudes toward education—mostly by privileging certain types of school, certain school experiences, and certain school demographics over others. As already noted, whether laudatory or critical, the school stories that have mostly preoccupied the critics for the last century and a half have been those exploring the private, independent, British boarding-school paradigm of the late nineteenth and early to mid-twentieth century. And yet it is also true that, considered as a single, broad field, the criticism reveals a constant vying for more nuanced representation. As such, it suggests an ongoing need to grasp the social and cultural significance of the school story in its capacity to speak to school experience at its most promising and its most damaging. Offering disparate images of schools and schoolchildren, school stories even in their slightest forms yield a shared understanding of education as a process weighted with far-reaching presumptions and raising a range of critical questions: who is deserving of formal education; who and what merits success in school; who will be prepared to lead and govern, and who to follow and serve; what does it mean for culture and society if schools are founded as private or public institutions, independent or part of a centralized system, day or boarding, single sex or coeducational; what does it mean for the one and the many when learning communities are segregated along age, gender, class, or race lines; what happens when educators and administrators intervene in the bodily growth, emotional development, and sexual identity of students; should learning outcomes be academic, vocational, athletic, moral, religious, or civic; should curricula be dogmatic, doctrinaire, or experimental; should graduates be groomed for conservatively preserving the status quo, intervening in the name of progressive reform, or more radically revolutionizing the social?

If the sources are to be trusted, the historical lesson is that, in times of crisis, school stories do indeed influence critical, political, and popular understandings of the nature and purpose of school: by particularizing certain school scenarios and so crystalizing concerns over student behavior, teacher practices, institutional structures, and curricula and their theories of value; and, at exceptional moments—usually in times of crisis—by compelling policy makers and the general public to act on legislative and cultural change. This, after all, was *Tom Brown's* legacy, remembered by subsequent critics as *the* artefact, more than any other of its time, that swayed public opinion in favor of the great public schools as bastions of morality. One might also make the inverse claim about a more modern novel such as *The Chocolate War*, a book that continues to draw censure for its fatalistic vision of the Catholic boys' school as a locus of systemic abuse. With the benefit of hindsight afforded here, it is not difficult to detect the vaster forces operating in and around the institution of school, to see distinct cultural logics, ideologies, and economic imperatives—here period-bound, there enduring; here stable, there shifting—informing both the talking points and the efforts of authors and critics alike as they attempt to articulate the meaning and value of school. It seems unwise, in such light, to take for granted the ways in which real-world conditions, fiction, and criticism converge as sites of ethico-political contestation—perhaps most obviously on the question of gender segregation, but just as pressingly on questions of class chauvinism, ethno-nationalism, and racialization. We do well, too, to acknowledge how the popular school story debate began in an age of empire, with critics valorizing a patriotic-moralistic ethos of civic education that tended not to speak of market imperatives (even though the British Empire, at its peak, dominated a global realm of industry and commerce), and continues in an age of neoliberalism, when educators are increasingly distressed (if not imperiled) by the ongoing alignment of public education with entrepreneurial ideals that fuse competitive individualism with free-market principles. What scholars such as Holt make clear is that the body of work conventionally presumed to represent the school story in its heyday rose and fell along a distinct ideological trajectory, one bent on shaping a nexus of youth, masculinity, and citizenship, with both local and global implications. As such, it makes sense to question the values at work when influential critics at midcentury began to announce not the transfiguration but the death of the genre—in spite of the fact that school stories continued to be written, read, and enjoyed by popular audiences—to write its obituary as a genre category; and, by the same token, to question the values at work when critics at the turn of the millennium began to announce the rejuvenation of the genre on the strength of a singular school story—*Harry Potter*—a story phenomenally popular yet conspicuously escapist in its return to a classic boarding-school paradigm with a fantasy twist.

Let us acknowledge that the genre, like any genre, is a construct: not a natural deposit of raw ore unambiguously announcing itself, but material channeled by critics diverging widely in their understandings of not only what is worthy of attention but also how that attention should be given—variously looking inward on the form, through the form to the world depicted, or even past the form to conditions only tentatively suggested by the texts. For most of the last century and a half, the dominant tendency among scholars has been to work with a hegemonic association of the unqualified term "school story" to mean "traditional school story," "English school story," "public-school story," "boarding-school story," and, above, all, "boys' school story." Even after the successful recuperation of the long-neglected girls' school story, the unqualified "school story" still seems to suggest a genre firmly behind us, best (though not exclusively) represented by a single period of production in which serious stories of boys boarding at elite English schools held the critics', along with the market's, attention. To let that slippage go by is tacitly to perpetuate the snobbery challenged by Orwell, implying that the school story in the age of comprehensive education indefatigably collapses as a genre category, as if the definitive elements—of schoolchildren interacting with educators and administrators in an institutional setting—simply do not transpose from the exclusive realm of privileged education to the diverse realm of democratic education. What the critics at midcentury actually announced was not so much the death of a popular form of school fiction but their refusal, if not inability, to discuss the modern school as an institution serving the establishment in ways comparably influential to, if politically different from, those of the private school system.

Put another way, while feminist scholars successfully and democratically challenged the patriarchal grip on the archive, that need to recover and explore the separate world of girls' education also served to return emphatically to stories and conditions of yesteryear—in much the same way that most scholars of boys' school stories have done. This is not to disparage historicism (far from it), but to acknowledge that the field, as a whole, could make more room for texts and contexts speaking to late twentieth and early twenty-first-century conditions in and across schools. To be sure, the best critics, no matter their period or niche, afford insights that are portable; this is my experience of reading, among others, Nelson, Katanski, and Holt, all of whom look to early contexts but, in doing so, disclose operations of discourses, politics, and aesthetics that resonate profoundly beyond the close readings of discrete texts to speak to us in the here and now. But if representations, interpretations, and negotiations of education really underpin our critical-methodological purpose, then it is imperative that we grasp the contemporary school story in our age of neoliberalism—a time, especially in America but also beyond, marked by dramatically shifting racial and ethnic demographics in elementary and high schools; consternation over literacy levels, persistence, and retention; heated debates over curriculum, state standards, and learning outcomes; battles over the funding and regulation of public schools, private charter schools, and teachers' unions; and unprecedented expressions of school violence in sexual assaults and mass shootings. Mindful of the educational, literary, and critical traditions behind us, it seems timely to consider, now—in the chapters that follow—what the school story in the age of neoliberalism has to say.

NOTES

1. Public in the British sense of (mostly) boarding schools conceived in the late medieval period as "grammar schools for the education of the poor" but transformed following the post-Renaissance rise of the middle classes into "private establishments for the education of the rich and privileged" (Reed 4). Hughes's alma mater, Rugby, was counted among the great public boarding schools of England along with Charterhouse, Eton, Harrow, Shrewsbury, Westminster, and Winchester.

2. A generalization based on early periodical reviews of prominent titles such as Catharine Sedgwick's *A New-England Tale* (1822), Warren Burton's *The District School as It Was* (1852), and Edward Eggleston's *The Hoosier Schoolmaster* (1871).

3. According to Mitchum Huehls and Rachel Greenwald Smith, the latest of four stages: after a mid-twentieth-century rise to power of free-market advocates, who believed in classical liberalism's core principles of "civil liberty and economic freedom" while disavowing "social liberalism's core values of equality and justice"; after the privatization and deregulation of industry consolidated politically and ideologically under the Margaret Thatcher and Ronald Reagan administrations in the early 1980s; and after a point at which culture in its various forms becomes saturated by an "economic calculus committed to efficient profit maximization")—a stage when the "extension of market rationality"—"quantitative, efficient, pragmatic, and profitable" forms of thinking—has transformed into a way of being, "a mode of existence defined by individual self-responsibility, entrepreneurial action, and the maximization of human capital" (4–9).

4. More accurately, early efforts seem bent on tempering earlier conceptions of the great public schools as dens of depravity—represented by one schoolmaster's observation from 1806 that "the youth of Eton are dissipated gentlemen; those at Westminster dissipated with a little of the blackguard; and those at St. Paul's the most depraved of all" (in Richards [1988] 10, quoting from Ogilvie 125)

5. "A school under the management of a School-board, as established by the Elementary Education Act of 1870. Also attributive, as in board-school mistress, board-school education, etc." ("Board-school, n.").

WORKS CITED

Adorno, Theodor. "Commitment." *Aesthetics and Politics*, by Theodor Adorno, Walter Benjamin, Ernst Bloch, Bertolt Brecht, and Georg Lukács, Verso, 1977, pp. 177–95.

Alington, Adrian. "School Stories—Old and New." *English: Journal of the English Association*, vol. 1, no. 5, 1936, pp. 414–26, *ProQuest*. Accessed 1 Jan. 2018.

Auchmuty, Rosemary. *A World of Girls: The Appeal of the Girls' School Story*. Women's Press, 1995.

Auchmuty, Rosemary. *A World of Women: Growing Up in the Girls' School Story*. Women's Press, 1999.

Auchmuty, Rosemary. "School Stories." *The Oxford Encyclopedia of Children's Literature*, edited by Jack Zipes, Oxford University Press, 2006, *Oxford Reference*. Accessed 13 Aug. 2018.

Avery, Gillian. "'Modern Girls' and Schoolgirls 1880–1940." *Childhood's Pattern: A Study of the Heroes and Heroines of Children's Fiction 1770–1950*, Hodder and Stoughton, 1975, pp. 199–218.
"Boarding School Stories." *New York Times*, 4 Dec. 1910, p. LI17, *ProQuest*. Accessed 13 Aug. 2018.
"Board-school, n." *OED Online*, March 2019, *Oxford University Press*, oed.com/view/Entry/20744. Accessed 10 May 2019.
Child, Harold. "The Public School in Fiction." *The Public Schools from Within*, Sampson Low, Marston & Company, 1906, pp. 293–300.
Clabaugh, Gary K. "The Educational Legacy of Ronald Reagan." *Educational Horizons*, vol. 82, no. 4, 2004, pp. 256–59, *JSTOR*, jstor.org/stable/42926508. Accessed 19 May 2018.
Clark, Beverly Lyon. *Regendering the School Story*. Routledge, 1996.
Cox, Jack. *Take A Cold Tub, Sir! The Story of the Boy's Own Paper*. Lutterworth Press, 1982.
Crouch, Marcus. *Treasure Seekers and Borrowers: Children's Books in Britain, 1900–1960*. Library Association, 1962.
Dalton, Mary M. *The Hollywood Curriculum: Teachers in the Movies*. Peter Lang, 1999.
Dartmouth. "The Public School in Fiction [To the editor of the 'Spectator']." *The Spectator*, no. 4670, 29 Dec. 1917, p. 768, *ProQuest*. Accessed 8 Feb. 2018.
Fisher, Margery. *Intent Upon Reading: A Critical Appraisal of Modern Fiction for Children*. Franklin Watts, 1962.
Fisher, Roy, Ann Harris, and Christine Jarvis. *Education in Popular Culture: Telling Tales on Teachers and Learners*. Routledge, 2008.
"For Girls of all Ages." *The Spectator*, vol. 141, no. 5241, 8 Dec. 1928, pp. 861–63, *ProQuest*. Accessed 14 Aug. 2018.
Frith, Gill. "'The Time of Your Life': The Meaning of the School Story." *Language, Gender and Childhood*, edited by Carolyn Steedman, Cathy Urwin, and Valerie Walkerdine, Routledge & Kegan Paul, 1985, pp. 113–36.
Grenby, M. O. "The School Story." *Children's Literature*, Edinburgh University Press, 2008, pp. 87–116.
Gruner, Elisabeth Rose. "Teach the Children: Education and Knowledge in Recent Children's Fantasy." *Children's Literature*, vol. 37, 2009, pp. 216–35.
Hay, Ian. "School Stories." *The Lighter Side of School Life*, T. N. Foulis, 1914, pp. 149–73.
Hicks, W. R. *The School in English and German Fiction*. Soncino Press, 1933.
Holt, Jenny. *Public School Literature, Civic Education and the Politics of Male Adolescence*. Ashgate, 2008.
Hopkins, Lisa. "Harry Potter and the Acquisition of Knowledge." *Reading Harry Potter: Critical Essays*, edited by Giselle Liza Anatol, Praeger, 2003, pp. 25–34.
Huehls, Mitchum, and Rachel Greenwald Smith. "Four Phases of Neoliberalism and Literature." *Neoliberalism and Contemporary Literature*, Johns Hopkins University Press, 2017, pp. 1–18.
Humphrey, Judith. *The English Girls' School Story: Subversion and Challenge in a Traditional Conservative Literary Genre*. University of Hertfordshire Press, 2009.
"The Influence of 'Tom Brown.'" *The Spectator*, 1 Jul. 1899, pp. 17–18, *The Spectator Archive*. Accessed 8 Feb. 2018.
Janak, Edward, and Denise Blum, editors. *The Pedagogy of Pop: Theoretical and Practical Strategies for Success*. Lexington Books, 2013.
Joseph, Pamela Bolotin, and Gaile E. Burnaford, editors. *Images of Schoolteachers in America*, 2nd ed. Lawrence Erlbaum Associates, 2001.

Katanski, Amelia V. *Learning to Write "Indian": The Boarding-school Experience and American Indian Literature.* University of Oklahoma Press, 2005.

Kiberd, Declan. "School Stories." *Studies in Children's Literature, 1500–2000,* edited by Celia Keenan and Mary Shine Thompson, Four Courts Press, 2004, pp. 54–69.

Kirkpatrick, Robert J. *Bullies, Beaks and Flannelled Fools: An Annotated Bibliography of Boys' School Fiction, 1742–1990.* Robert J. Kirkpatrick, 1990.

Kirkpatrick, Robert J., editor. *The Encyclopaedia of Boys' School Stories,* Ashgate, 2000.

Lamb, Felicia. "In School Stories." *Locked-up Daughters: A Parents' Look at Girls' Education and Schools,* by Felicia Lamb and Helen Pickthorn, Hodder and Stoughton, 1968, pp. 68–74.

Mack, Edward Clarence. *Public Schools and British Opinion Since 1860: The Relationship Between Contemporary Ideas and the Evolution of an English Institution.* Columbia University Press, 1941.

Mathieson, M., and M. T. Whiteside. "The Secondary Modern School in Fiction." *British Journal of Educational Studies* vol. 19, no. 3, 1971, pp. 283–93, *JSTOR.* Accessed 1 Jun. 2018.

Meade, L. T. "'A Sweet Girl Graduate' [To the editor of the 'Spectator']." *The Spectator,* vol. 68, no. 3332, 27 Feb. 1892, p. 302, *ProQuest.* Accessed 13 Aug. 2018.

A Mere Schoolboy. "The Public School in Fiction [To the editor of the 'Spectator']." *The Spectator,* no. 4667, 8 Dec. 1917, p. 675, *ProQuest.* Accessed 8 Feb. 2018.

A Mere Schoolmaster. "The Public School in Fiction" [To the editor of the 'Spectator']." *The Spectator,* no. 4663, 10 Nov. 1917, pp. 516–17, *The Spectator Archive.* Accessed 8 Feb. 2018.

Musgrave, P. W. *From Brown to Bunter: The Life and Death of the School Story.* Routledge & Kegan Paul, 1985.

Nelson, Claudia. "The Angel in the School." *Boys Will Be Girls: The Feminine Ethic and British Children's Fiction, 1857–1917,* Rutgers University Press, 1991, pp. 56–86.

Ogilvie, Vivian. *The English Public School.* Batsford, 1957.

Orwell, George. "Boys' Weeklies." *Inside the Whale and Other Essays,* Victor Gollancz, 1940, pp. 89–128.

Pickering, Samuel F., Jr. "School Stories." *Moral Instruction and Fiction for Children, 1749–1820,* University of Georgia Press, 1993, pp. 31–57.

Pinsent, Pat. "The Education of a Wizard: Harry Potter and His Predecessors." *The Ivory Tower and Harry Potter: Perspectives on a Literary Phenomenon,* edited by Lana A. Whited, University of Missouri Press, 2002, pp. 27–50.

Pinsent, Pat. "Theories of Genre and Gender: Change and Continuity in the School Story." *Modern Children's Literature: An Introduction,* edited by Kimberley Reynolds, Palgrave Macmillan, 2005, pp. 8–22.

Pitofsky, Alexander. *American Boarding School Fiction, 1928–1981: A Critical Study.* McFarland, 2014.

Quigly, Isabel. *The Heirs of Tom Brown: The English School Story.* Chatto & Windus, 1982.

Ray, Sheila. "School Stories." *International Companion Encyclopedia of Children's Literature,* edited by Peter Hunt, Routledge, 2004, pp. 467–80.

"Reading for Girls." *New York Times,* 30 Nov. 1907, p. BR765, *ProQuest.* Accessed 13 Aug. 2018.

Reed, John. *Old School Ties: The Public Schools in British Literature.* Syracuse University Press, 1964.

Reimer, Mavis. "Traditions of the School Story." *The Cambridge Companion to Children's Literature,* edited by M. O. Grenby and Andrea Immel, Cambridge University Press, 2009, pp. 209–25.

Richards, Frank. "Frank Richards Replies to George Orwell." *George Orwell: An Age Like This, 1920–1940*, vol. 1, edited by Sonia Orwell and Ian Angus, David R. Godine, 2000, pp. 485–93.
Richards, Jeffrey. *Happiest Days: The Public Schools in English Fiction*. Manchester University Press, 1988.
Roosevelt, Theodore. "What We Can Expect of the American Boy." *St Nicholas*, vol. 27, no. 7, pp. 571–74, *HathiTrust*. Accessed 8 Feb. 2018.
Rowbotham, Judith. "Education for Model Maidens." *Good Girls Make Good Wives: Guidance for Girls in Victorian Fiction*, Blackwell, 1989, pp. 99–140.
Salmon, Edward. "School Stories." *Juvenile Literature as It Is*, Henry J. Drane, 1888, pp. 83–101.
"School and College Life: Its Romance and Reality." *Blackwood's Edinburgh Magazine*, vol. 89, no. 544, 1861, pp. 131–48, *HathiTrust*. Accessed 3 Mar. 2018.
"The Schoolboy of Fiction.'" *The Spectator*, 13 Sep. 1902, pp. 8–9, *The Spectator Archive*. Accessed 8 Feb. 2018.
"School Stories, 1914–1960." *Dictionary of Literary Biography, Vol. 160: British Children's Writers*, edited by Donald R. Hettinga and Gary D. Schmidt, Bruccoli Clark Layman, 1996, pp. 344–50.
Sims, Sue, and Hilary Clare, editors. *The Encyclopaedia of Girls' School Stories*, Ashgate, 2000.
Smith, Karen Manners. "Harry Potter's Schooldays: J. K. Rowling and the British Boarding School Novel." *Reading Harry Potter: Critical Essays*, edited by Giselle Liza Anatol, Praeger, 2003, pp. 69–87.
"Some Changes in School-Girl Fiction." *The Spectator*, vol. 145, no. 5345, 6 Dec. 1930, p. 901. *ProQuest*. Accessed 14 Aug. 2018
Speicher, Allison. *Schooling Readers: Reading Common Schools in Nineteenth-Century American Fiction*. University of Alabama Press, 2016.
Spolton, L. "The Secondary School in Post-War Fiction." *British Journal of Educational Studies* vol. 11, no. 2, 1963, pp. 125–41, *JSTOR*. Accessed 14 Aug. 2018.
Steege, David. "Harry Potter, Tom Brown, and the British School Story: Lost in Transit?" *The Ivory Tower and Harry Potter: Perspectives on a Literary Phenomenon*, edited by Lana A. Whited, University of Missouri Press, 2002, pp. 140–56.
"*A Sweet Girl Graduate* by L. T. Meade (book review)." *The Spectator*, vol. 68, no. 3321, 20 Feb. 1892, pp. 275–76, *ProQuest*. Accessed 13 Aug. 2018.
T., B. E. "Stories for School Girls." *The Spectator*, vol. 139, no. 5188, 3 Dec. 1927, p. 995, *ProQuest*. Accessed 14 Aug. 2018.
"Thomas Hughes." *The Spectator*, 28 Mar. 1896, pp. 11–12, *The Spectator Archive*. Accessed 8 Feb. 2018.
"*Tom Brown's Schooldays* (book review)." *The Edinburgh Review*, vol. 107, no. 217, 1858, pp. 172–93, *HathiTrust*. Accessed 3 Mar. 2018.
Townsend, John Rowe. *Written for Children: An Outline of English Children's Literature*. Garnet Miller, 1965.
Trease, Geoffrey. "Midnight in the Dorm." *Tales Out of School*. William Heinemann, 1948, pp. 125–43.
"The War Schoolgirl." *Nation*, vol. 26, no. 10, 6 Dec. 1919, pp. 364–66, *ProQuest*. Accessed 14 Aug. 2018.
Watson, Benjamin. *English Schoolboy Stories: An Annotated Bibliography of Hardcover Fiction*. Scarecrow Press, 1992.
Waugh, Alec. "The Public School in Fiction [To the editor of the 'Spectator']." *The Spectator*, no. 4672, 12 Jan. 1918, p. 36, *ProQuest*. Accessed 8 Feb. 2018.

Weber, Sandra, and Claudia Mitchell. *That's Funny, You Don't Look Like a Teacher! Interrogating Images and Identity in Popular Culture*. Falmer Press, 1995.

Wells, Bobbie, Maureen Nimon, and Connie Parker. "School Stories." *The Cambridge Guide to Children's Books in English*, edited by Victor Watson, 2001, pp. 630–33.

Westman, Karin E. "Blending Genres and Crossing Audiences: Harry Potter and the Future of Literary Fiction." *The Oxford Handbook of Children's Literature*, edited by Julia L. Mickenberg and Lynne Vallone, Oxford University Press, 2011, pp. 93–112.

Wilby, Peter. "Margaret Thatcher's Education Legacy Is Still with Us—Driven on by Gove." *Guardian*, 15 Apr. 2013, *Guardian News and Media*, theguardian.com/education/2013/apr/15/margaret-thatcher-education-legacy-gove. Accessed 19 May 2018.

Yet Another Schoolmaster. "The Public School in Fiction." *The Spectator*, no. 4665, 24 Nov. 1917, p. 599, *The Spectator Archive*. Accessed 8 Feb. 2018.

Y. Y. "What Katy Did at School." *New Statesman*, vol. 23, no. 586, 1924, pp. 403–5, *ProQuest*. Accessed 14 Aug. 2018.

CHAPTER 2

Giving Education a Bad Name

Bookish Boys in Contemporary American School Stories

While some might think of the school story as a niche topic for studies in children's literature, its arcs of learning, growth, and socialization suggest a significant overlap with the broader category of *Bildungsroman*, variously understood as "novel of development," "novel of education," or as a synthesis of both.[1] As Franco Moretti notes in *The Way of the World* (1987), the emergence of the European *Bildungsroman* at the end of the eighteenth century signaled a field of cultural production giving unprecedented attention to youth: contrasting with the "mature" and "adult" sensibilities that had governed classical epic, youth came to the fore as a cipher for "modernity's essence," which Moretti parses in socioeconomic and psychocultural terms of "mobility and interiority," "dynamism and instability" (3–5). Despite that preoccupation with young life, and despite "the growing influence of education" (5), Moretti detects a "striking ... antipathy between School and the Novel: School condemns novel reading as having bad effects on students—and the novel, for its part, requires its hero to leave his studies early on, and treats school as a useless interlude that can be done without" (247, n. 3). Whether or not we are persuaded by such a sweeping claim, a comparable sense of school experience as something outgrown in the development of the novel informs the earlier and more foundational study of the *Bildungsroman* by Mikhail Bakhtin, whose theories of language and literature continue to influence studies in the novel and in children's literature.[2]

In "The *Bildungsroman* and Its Significance in the History of Realism" (composed 1936–1938, published 1979), Bakhtin gives a promising introduction to what he calls the "didactic-pedagogical" novel, only to sideline it. He proposes a typology of the novel comprising four types of plot classified "according to how the image of the main hero is constructed: the travel novel, the novel of ordeal, the biographical (autobiographical) novel, and"—for Bakhtin, the most important in preparing the way for nineteenth-century realism—the "novel of education" (10). The last category he applies to a range of fictions depicting human growth and learning: from Xenophon's *Cyropaedia* (c. 370 BC), Rabelais's *Gargantua and Pantagruel* (1532–1564), and Rousseau's *Émile* (1762) to Goethe's *Wilhelm Meister's Apprenticeship* (1795–1796), Dickens's *David Copperfield* (1849–1850), and Mann's *The Magic Mountain* (1924). Because the plots in these works vary so much—in some "the organizing basis is the purely pedagogical notion of man's education, while this is not even mentioned in others; some of them are constructed on the strictly chronological plane of the main hero's educational development, and have almost no plot at all" (20)—Bakhtin narrows his terms to describe how "the aspect of man's essential becoming" is depicted, a qualification that allows him to distinguish between, on one side, the travel novel, novel of ordeal, and biographical novel; and, on the other side, the novel of education, or of "human emergence" (also equated with "human development"). Under this new term, he identifies five subcategories, representing increasingly nuanced stages in depicting the relation between hero, world, and time: idyllic (human life is represented from childhood to old age as cyclical, repeating in each life); experiential (development is still cyclical, but each life progresses by way of experience from "youthful idealism" to "mature sobriety"); biographical/autobiographical (each life is unique, passing through unrepeatable stages); didactic-pedagogical (development now hinges on processes of education); and realistic-historical ("man's individual emergence is inseparably linked to historical emergence," meaning that "he emerges along with the world") (21–23). Bakhtin argues that, compared to the realistic-historical stage (represented by *Wilhelm Meister*), the preceding stages including the fourth (represented by *Émile*) are limited in their historical consciousness: "Man's emergence proceeded against the immobile background of the world, ready-made and basically quite stable. If changes did take place in this world, they were peripheral, in no way affecting its foundations. Man emerged, developed, and changed within one epoch. The world, existing and stable in this existence, required that man adapt to it, that he recognize and submit to the existing laws of life. Man emerged, but the world itself did not.... In and of itself the conception of the world as an experience, a school, was very productive in the *Bildungsroman*.... But the world, as an experience and as a school, remained the same, fundamentally immobile and ready-made, given" (23).

For a study of the school story, what is surprising about Bakhtin's typology is that it puts an expiry date on the didactic-pedagogical novel, a form "based on a specific pedagogical ideal, understood more or less broadly, and depict[ing] the pedagogical process of education in the strict sense of the word" (22–23). It is as if we must understand pedagogical fiction not as a discrete accomplishment in a pluralistic typology (as the title of Bakhtin's essay leads us to expect) but as a rudimentary stage in a hierarchical teleology (as his actual account describes). And I question that—both the valorization of world-conscious realism as the touchstone by which we reckon the historical telos of the novel, and the tacit denigration of the pedagogical novel as a subgenre superseded in that telos. We do better, I think, to keep hold of the didactic-pedagogical as an enduring category, one that not only allows us to consider the prolific role of school experience in children's literature (and vice versa) but also affords critical insights into the processes of education shaping our vaster historical reality.

Not all stories set in school, of course, yield a coherent pedagogical imagination; indeed, scholars of children's literature are often at pains to distinguish between works in which the school experience is integral to plot and character development, and those in which the school setting is merely incidental.[3] As it happens, a number of contemporary young adult books by American authors do offer impressive depictions of student development in the realm of formal education: Laurie Halse Anderson's *Speak* (1999), Stephen Chbosky's *The Perks of Being a Wallflower* (1999), and David Lubar's *Sleeping Freshmen Never Lie* (2005), for example, all give compelling accounts of how teens might successfully develop intellectually, emotionally, and socially under the influence of attentive teachers. But also commonplace are books, often for younger readers, purveying more troubling conceptions of what it means to study, learn, and grow. I am thinking of American middle-grade novels such as Andrew Clements's *Frindle* (1996), James Patterson's *Middle School: The Worst Years of My Life* (2011), Tommy Greenwald's *Charlie Joe Jackson's Guide to Not Reading* (2011), and Chris Grabenstein's Mr. Lemoncello series (*Escape from Mr. Lemoncello's Library*, 2013; *Mr. Lemoncello's Library Olympics*, 2016; *Mr. Lemoncello's Great Library Race*, 2017; *Mr. Lemoncello's All-star Breakout Game*, 2019; and *Mr. Lemoncello and the Titanium Ticket*, 2020); and middle-grade/young teen novels such as those in Jennifer Chambliss Bertman's Book Scavenger series (*Book Scavenger*, 2015; *The Unbreakable Code*, 2017; and *The Alcatraz Escape*, 2018). All these works feature young protagonists who succeed in bookish ways as readers, researchers, or writers.[4] But the kinds of success they valorize evince a vexed understanding of education: one that conflates fact-finding with learning, confuses materialistic ambition with studious engagement, and in many cases passes off the habitual failure to meet academic expectations as a kind of resilient individualism. Keeping in mind that learning and literacy are catchwords for educators dedicated to remedying neoliberal inequities, these novels appear to offer figures of hope in young, bookish characters, whose narrative arcs actually celebrate the market consciousness, deregulation, and excessive individualism for which neoliberalism is known. More to the point, to the extent that it has become increasingly difficult to separate school experience from the world system of the neoliberal marketplace, the didactic-pedagogical novel seems to carry a more substantial world consciousness than Bakhtin gave it credit for.

In this chapter, I examine the ways in which such novels pay lip service to the idea of learning and literacy as a democratic good while actually undermining democratic possibilities by teaching young readers to think of academic inquiry as a means to selfish, proprietorial ends. Focusing on *Frindle* and *Charlie Joe Jackson's Guide to Not Reading*, two books that merit special attention for their flamboyant mockery of formal education and teacher authority, I consider how the didactic-pedagogical imagination in American fiction for young people promotes an ideologically problematic conception of student development and life preparedness. The protagonists of both stories could easily take their place in a tradition of American boyhood literature going back to Mark Twain's *The Adventures of Tom Sawyer* (1875), whose title character gave an early glimpse of the schoolboy entrepreneur who seeks success by way of marketplace exchanges rather than learning—as when Tom stands at the church door to waylay local boys on their way to Sabbath school, trades "lickrish" and "fish-hook[s]" for the tickets they earned by memorizing Bible passages, and then redeems the tickets for a "Dore Bible" (a Bible illustrated with woodcuts by Gustave Doré) from the superintendent, an exchange meant to signify his having read two thousand verses of scripture. As Twain explains, "Only the older pupils managed to keep their tickets and stick to their tedious work long enough to get a Bible, and so the delivery of one of these prizes was a rare and noteworthy circumstance; the successful pupil was so great and conspicuous for that day that on the spot every scholar's heart was fired with a fresh ambition that often lasted a couple of weeks. It is possible that Tom's mental stomach had never really hungered for one of those prizes, but unquestionably his entire being had for many a day longed for the glory and the eclat that came with it" (34). It is also possible that middle-grade school fiction is currently making more room for boy characters of this kind than for girls, as if authors have in mind a gendered sphere of young entrepreneurship. Yet, as noted, more generally, the kind of fiction I discuss seems just as ready to accommodate girls as much as boys, with girls taking the lead, as in *Book Scavenger*, or collaborating with boys, as in the *Lemoncello* series. For this reason, this chapter is concerned more with the bookish than the boyish implications, on the understanding that further inquiry is called for to work out whether or not the literature is singling out boys rather than girls as agents of neoliberalism—in ways that might be compared, say, to the classic British boarding-school story of the late nineteenth century, which cultivated narratives of elite schoolboys groomed for serving the British Empire at the height of colonial expansion (see Quigly).

I take *Frindle* and the *Guide to Not Reading* to be structured around a shared binary of education and entrepreneurship, terms introduced as competing with one another in conflicts that seem to be resolved in a mutual compromise but that ultimately end in a hierarchy privileging one term (entrepreneurship) over the other (education). Of all the forms considered by Caroline Levine (*Forms*, 2015)—wholes, rhythms, hierarchies, and networks—she describes hierarchies as the "most troubling." As she explains, "it is not difficult to understand hierarchies, like bounded wholes and rhythms, as forms: hierarchies arrange bodies, things, and ideas according to levels of power or importance. Hierarchies rank—organizing experience into asymmetrical, discriminatory, often deeply unjust arrangements. The most consistent and painful affordance of hierarchical structures is inequality" (82). True to her general theory of forms, however, Levine also offers the qualification that hierarchical forms, which rarely operate in isolation, "exert a far less orderly and systematic kind of domination than we might expect" (85). "Hierarchies," in fact, "interfere with one another's capacity to organize the world" (86); should they collide, "they are capable of generating more disorder than order" (85).

The routines and structures of school, of course, abound with hierarchies. Curriculums are organized according to subject and discipline hierarchies determined by educational policy, which in our current neoliberal age tends to rank mathematics over humanities disciplines (see, for example, Lynch and McGarr). Students, too, have informal but influential opportunities to rank classes and teachers through online review sites such as Rate My Teachers and Rate My Professors. More formally, schools at all levels are structured according to hierarchies of authority, students answering directly to teachers, librarians, and principals, and indirectly to superintendents, school boards, parents' groups, and educational authorities at various scales. At the same time, teachers, substitute teachers, assistant teachers, instructors, lecturers, and professors occupy positions within a highly stratified system affording more or less privilege in terms of teaching loads or opportunities for professional development, research, and governance. Meanwhile, in much the same way that faculty are subjected to evaluation procedures that weigh professional performance and growth, students are tracked according to developmental hierarchies, by which they are often deemed "behind," "on track," or "ahead."[5] Age and grade hierarchies also inform students' social standing when their accomplishments and abilities are ranked "below" or "above" those of their peers. Social hierarchies, indeed, take many forms in school, privileging some students (and teachers) more than others along lines of gender, sexuality, class, race, ethnicity, religion, ability, and experience. And if graduation marks the highest achievement in a child's school career, it simultaneously marks their official entrance into the world of work and social "climbing," yet more fields governed by hierarchical metaphors of physical movement to describe the cultural ideal of ceaselessly improving income and quality of life relative to both one's own circumstances and those of others. While school stories definitively attest to many if not most such hierarchies, it seems reasonable to recognize, with Levine, that such hierarchies do not always align or bolster a single dominant power, an insight especially important if we care about democratic freedoms since it implies room for contesting abuses of power. The underside of that claim, of course, is that democratic structures themselves can be contested or even, to borrow from Wendy Brown, undone (*Undoing the Demos: Neoliberalism's Stealth Revolution*, 2015).

Frindle: Waste Time, Make Trouble, Get Rich

Originally published in 1996, Andrew Clements's debut novel *Frindle* (illustrated by Brian Selznick) remains a representative work of contemporary American school fiction.[6] Like his later novels for young readers including *The School Story* (2001), *The Report Card* (2004), *No Talking* (2007), and *Extra Credit* (2009), *Frindle* is a well-crafted story of young minds and active imaginations in the school realm: on the strength of these and other titles, Clements is appropriately marketed as the "master of the theme-driven, feel-good school story" ("No Talking," *Kirkus*). As a work of school fiction, however, *Frindle* is arguably more distinctive for how it rewards the exploits of bookish characters while simultaneously denigrating the meaning and value of formal education (in the sense, as noted in the introduction to this book, of a shared school experience in an institutional setting governed by trained pedagogues teaching to a standardized curriculum).

Frindle certainly looks like a promising school story with valuable lessons for teachers and students alike in that it imagines breaking down the divide between a strict teacher and her resistant student. The novel takes its title from the schemes of middle school protagonist Nick Allen, who, bent on disrupting the doling out of homework in his fifth-grade classroom, glibly propagates a nonsense word for *pen*: "frindle." Recognizing rightly that Nick is challenging her authority, language arts teacher Mrs. Granger deals out a swift punishment in the form of extra homework: he is to prepare an oral report on the dictionary, knowing full well that she thinks of the dictionaries in her classroom as "the law" (31). Laying bare the traditional hierarchy of the classroom, Mrs. Granger explains: "I have always said that the dictionary is the finest tool ever made for educating young minds, and I still say that. Children need to understand that there are rules about words and language, and that those rules have a history that makes sense" (74). As the story unfolds, however, the dictionary helps Nick find a way to flout Mrs. Granger's authority—in the short term, when he uses his report to waste more class time, and in the long term, when he continues to disseminate his word to the point at which it achieves international circulation as a trademarked name for a commercially marketed ballpoint pen. At which point, the logic of the marketplace trumps all "the rules about words and language, and . . . history" and especially "sense." But even if Clements foregrounds the clash between the authoritative, dictionary-loving Dangerous Grangerous and the homework-hating Nick, what begins as a battle of wills ends in a show of mutual respect when, ten years on, she commends him on the entry of his word into Webster's dictionary, and he establishes a scholarship fund in her name. Wrapped up, the novel asserts both the teacher's enduring influence on her student's future success and the student's fond, eternal indebtedness to that teacher.

But the flouting of curriculum in this novel, which Nick articulates as a democratic challenge to the traditional teacher/student hierarchy of the classroom, is really an act of self-interest displacing rather than deconstructing the power differential. When introduced, Nick is the resident "expert at asking the delaying question . . . guaranteed to sidetrack the teacher long enough to delay or even wipe out the homework assignment" (14). Hence his asking, while reporting on the origins of the dictionary, "why words all mean different things. Like, who says that d-o-g means the thing that goes 'woof' and wags its tail?" (29). Mrs. Granger replies, "You do, Nicholas. You and I and everyone in this class and this school and this town and this state and this country. We all agree. . . . if all of us in this room decided to call that creature something else, and if everyone else did, too, then that's what it would be called, and one day it would be written in the dictionary that way. *We* decide what goes in that book" (29–31). This appeal to consensus is pivotal: while it emerges in what appears to be Mrs. Granger's genuine concern for how language serves the needs of the whole community, it is immediately appropriated to serve the petty desires of the one rather than the needs of the many. Defending himself by parroting, "It's how words really change, isn't it?" (44), Nick compels all his chums in school to call their pens *frindles*: not to enrich the common understanding of pens, but simply to score a point over Mrs. Granger. So, paying lip service to democracy, Nick really acts like a demagogue, proving that even the most meaningless words can have currency. But the real challenge to the traditional hierarchy of the classroom comes when Nick is bolstered not by willful personality but by marketplace privilege.

Put another way, *Frindle* is a fantasy of free enterprise and entrepreneurship in the age of commodity capitalism, updating the schoolboy dream of sudden wealth that, for George Orwell ("Boys' Weeklies," 1940), characterized the corrupt ideology of early twentieth-century popular school fiction. It tells the story of an evolving brand name, tracing the expanding commercial horizons of the nascent trademark from school community, through local and national news media, to international marketplace where it renames—without reconceiving—the common ballpoint pen. Except Nick is not so much brand-building as rebranding, at least if rebranding is "to apply a new brand identity, name, logo, etc., to (a product, service, or company). In extended use: to change radically the presentation of" ("rebrand, v."). Taking a brand to be "a name, term, symbol, design or a combination of them intended to identify goods or services of one seller or a group of sellers and to differentiate them from those of competitors" (from the American Marketing Association, cited in Muzellec and Lambkin 804), then Clements's readers are compelled to recognize not only the sudden and strange entrance into the marketplace of Nick but also the implicit designation of both the classroom as a field of marketplace competition and the teacher as a competitor. In the process, the new word certainly accrues meaning, signifying not only the pen it brands but also Nick's appeal to consensus: as he puts it, "It's not my word anymore. *Frindle* belongs to everybody, and I guess everyone will figure out what happens together" (76). But this appeal to consensus is undermined by the private rewards awaiting Nick, when the word is trademarked to become his legal property: while the press applauds Nick for having "masterminded this plot that cleverly raises issues about free speech and academic rules" (68), "the checks that went into Nick's trust fund got bigger and bigger" (85), so that by his junior year of college, "Nick was rich. Nick was very rich" (95). The singular schoolboy profits from the word in ways that "everybody" else does not; and as a proprietor asserting exclusive rights over the word's commercial possibilities, he forecloses on the possibility of democratic consensus. Put another way, if "democracy" denotes "a method of group decision making characterized by a kind of equality among the participants at an essential stage of the collective decision making," and if, "strategically, democracy has an advantage because it forces decision-makers to take into account the interests, rights and opinions of most people in society" (Christiano), then democracy is an insufficient term to explain the privilege enjoyed by this individual who exploits for private gains a word that publicly "belongs to everybody." Even though the traditional hierarchy of the classroom has been disturbed, hierarchy as such remains intact in the form of a hidden marketplace power advantaging the one over the many.

Invoking consensus only to undercut it, *Frindle*'s protagonist poses a problem for those who care about democratic theories of education, which tend to work toward leveling rather than bolstering hierarchies. Notably, while Nick self-identifies as an avid reader, the story of his success begins with neither reading pleasure nor intellectual curiosity but a dread of homework, girded by a resolve to disrupt the class and distract his teacher, whose words he exploits to serve his own ends—parroting her appeal to consensus, but disregarding the imperative to make sense. But the new word, *frindle*, like Nick himself, is too idiosyncratic to be properly democratic: a word serving the one in ways it does not serve the many, it expands a vocabulary reckoned not by its meaning-making but by its market value. It is possible, of course, that Clements is rightly acknowledging how a certain kind of school experience could ready the child for the communitarian task conventionally given mass education in the USA, by leading him into the realms of industry and economy on which the nation depends. But even if the public-school system in America has historically justified mass education on the strength of its potential to ready young people for the world of work, reducing the curriculum to economics and commerce at the expense of literacy acquisition is precisely the kind of neoliberal hierarchization of the curriculum that empties education of its democratic and moral possibilities.[7]

It is worth noting that the frindle paradigm—the way in which the narrative valorizes a certain idiosyncratic bookishness at the expense of formal education—is no bad thing as far as Clements is concerned. This is confirmed at the end of the novel when Mrs. Granger, writing to Nick in college, recalls her initial anger on "[seeing] the word *pen* pushed aside as if it did not matter" (98), but then confesses to finding consolation in having had "the kind of chance that a teacher hopes for and dreams about—a chance to see bright young students take an idea they have learned in a boring old classroom and put it to a real test in their own world" (99). In prioritizing the lessons of student-directed experience over abstract dictionary exercises, Mrs. Granger reveals an understanding of literacy intervention currently valued in theories of reading resistance and struggle.[8] But at stake is more than just a mode or style of learning. Early in the story, when she explains the etymology of *pen*—a word with roots in the Latin *pinna*, denoting the feathers from which early quills were made—she shows concern for language's meaningful developments. Not all words need classical etymons to be valid, of course, but for Nick to posit *frindle* as an alternative to *pen* is, as his teacher knows, to strip away context that might otherwise help to make sense of how and why particular words denote particular things. Arguably, of course, Nick's intervention could be appreciated from a structuralist or poststructuralist perspective, in that it seems to confirm Ferdinand de Saussure's influential description of "language as a system of arbitrary signs" (73). Still, no matter how arbitrary the original word choice for feather might be, the etymology associating feather, quill, and pen enriches cognition in ways that Nick's random word cannot. As such, with Mrs. Granger's capitulation to Nick's force as a word creator, Clements calls into question everything she stands for as an advocate of literacy and language, even as she assumes what Mark Lewis and Ian Renga identify as the role of "teacher as devoted guide of students with potential" (68). Indeed, this latter role situates the novel in what Jason Whitney terms "the inspirational subgenre" of school fiction—an "idealistic subgenre . . . in which teaching is portrayed as a means to a meaningful and worthwhile life" (40). As Whitney notes in his discussion of teacher movies, such representations can influence real-life teachers, serving to "activate and confirm the idealism that often carrie[s] them into the profession" (40–41). The problem is that Mrs. Granger sends out mixed signals: she is a traditional, curriculum-driven teacher, set in her ways, who also assumes a revisionist role (as described by Parton) by privately signing off on Nick's free enterprise. In effect, in defying the traditional hierarchy of the classroom, Nick compels Mrs. Granger to be complicit in undermining her own old-school rigor, an act that in turn makes for a new curricular hierarchy by replacing literacy acquisition with entrepreneurship as the measure of success.

It is possible, however, that this particular problematic of curricular hierarchy helps Clements's middle-grade story transcend what Bakhtin describes as the limits of the didactic-pedagogical novel. As noted, accounting for the different ways in which the novel of education has represented growth and learning, Bakhtin identifies five subcategories denoting evolving novelistic conceptions of the relation between hero and world: idyllic, experiential, biographical, didactic-pedagogical, and realistic-historical (21–23); and the shortcoming of the fourth stage, along with the first three, is that "man's emergence proceeded against the immobile background of the world"; that is, "if changes did take place in this world, they were peripheral, in no way affecting its foundations": "Man emerged, but the world itself did not" (23). Hence Bakhtin considers the didactic-pedagogical to be a lesser form compared to the realistic-historical. Yet in *Frindle*, a novel conscious of the ways in which pedagogical processes facilitate developmental opportunities, we have a work in which the educational process itself (and especially the derailing of that process) signifies a dramatically changing world. Nick's emergence as a new adult carries with it the emergence of the increasingly totalizing reality of capitalism at a precise moment in late twentieth- and early twenty-first-century history: when the American system of mass education—subordinating the humanist, interdisciplinary concerns of the liberal tradition—seems inclined to conflate learning, growth, and development with readiness for the marketplace. *Frindle* is, as such, an important novelization of education in the age of neoliberalism, a gentle, feel-good study of the classroom when conventional literacy is under duress; when the word is emptied of sense and history, reified and made to serve the commodity marketplace; when the classroom is conceived as a realm of competitive individualism; and when readers are primed to recognize the monetary rather than the intellectual hierarchy of academics.

Charlie Joe Jackson's Guide to Not Reading: Slack, Cheat, Publish

Though a far cry from the decorum of *Frindle*, *Charlie Joe Jackson's Guide to Not Reading* by Tommy Greenwald (illustrated by J. P. Coovert) yields a comparable understanding of academic experience in middle school; and, again, what reads like a story of school success turns out to be a homage to profiteering on a lackluster academic performance. Like *Frindle*, the *Guide to Not Reading* is a debut novel depicting an imaginative American middle school boy bristling under the academic demands of his teachers. But where Clements conjures a boy who confidently challenges the curriculum and beats his teacher at her own game, Greenwald imagines a schoolboy who, in faking the learning process, is compelled to conceal (albeit, not to his readers) his resistance. To its credit, as a didactic-pedagogical novel foregrounding the exploits of a committed resistant reader, the *Guide to Not Reading* raises valuable questions about childhood literacy especially in terms of what it means to encourage struggling learners and the role of original thinking in assessment. The title character, Charlie Joe, dislikes reading so much that, for years, he has not read a single schoolbook all the way through, relying instead on strategically skimming his books and bribing his peers for synopses. From the outset, we are invited to find this schemer, cheat, and liar relatable: "I hate reading," he says, "And if you're reading this book, you hate reading, too" (3). When he draws attention to the social rewards of non-reading, confessing that "I'm proud of my perfect record. All the kids knew about it, and were mighty impressed" (29), the novel conceives middle school as a realm of qualified slacking: provided one appears to perform adequately, it is possible to gain prestige by neglecting core literacy outcomes. In other words, social hierarchy in the *Guide to Not Reading* interferes with the hierarchy of academic outcomes and stage development that conventionally underpins school experience.

Greenwald's narrative does, however, put critical pressure on Charlie Joe's dishonest resistance to reading when it depicts the gradual disclosure of his cheating and underscores the emotional turmoil it brings to friends, teachers, and parents. Notably, this moralistic thread is bound up with Charlie Joe's coming round to identifying as a reader: the boy who early describes the library as "a kind of hell on earth" (61) later discovers that he actually enjoys reading: "So THIS," he says of one reading experience, "was what it was like to identify with a character in a book [....] all of a sudden I was acting like a ... wait for it ... *reader*. I was thinking about the book and [...] my heart sank—I *cared* about what happened" (111–12; bracketed ellipses mine). But still he continues to slack and cheat his way through the novel, stopping only when it comes out in public that his friend Jake did the reading for Charlie Joe's end-of-term position paper. Not insignificantly, Charlie Joe frames his paper, titled "From Friends to Rivals: How the Pressures Facing Kids Today Makes Them Form Cliques, or Teams, to Face Off Against One Another," as a more or less democratic work in the *Frindle* vein. "It is my contention," he explains (with conspicuous eloquence) while presenting his paper, "that because kids in today's society are under so much pressure to excel, and they spend so much time in studies and extracurricular activities, that they don't develop the necessary social skills to interact with all their peers, and therefore only socialize with those with their immediate interests, leading to cliques, clubs, and other forms of separation that are ultimately detrimental to the developmental and maturation process as kids try to become adults" (158). As part of his project, Charlie Joe sets in motion a social experiment in breaking up the social hierarchy of the school that does, in fact, impact positively on the student population, but the motivation is driven purely by self-interest: he sets up two students from different cliques—the unrequited love of his life, Hannah Spivero, and Jake—on the presumption that Jake will be amenable to reading and reporting on the books for Charlie Joe's paper. After the big reveal, with Charlie Joe on the brink of alienating himself from friends, family, and mentors, honesty seems to count for Greenwald, though what matters most are the personal rather than the academic stakes: not the cheat's deficient reading experience, but his potential to "crush" (189) and "shame" (194) those who care about him.

More to the point, whatever moralism Greenwald brings to bear is short lived, as is Charlie Joe's repentance, with the novel in its last pages affirming the rewards rather than the regrets of freewheeling entrepreneurship. As Charlie Joe puts it, "I came to the conclusion that I wasn't a completely horrible person.... I was definitely a careless person. Possibly a lazy person.... And maybe I was a slightly scheming person.... And yeah, I did some dumb things.... I still felt bad, but I was done beating myself up. In fact, if I'm not mistaken, it's exactly that kind of good old-fashioned creativity that's made America the great nation it is today" (196–97). Echoing Ronald Reagan's 1980 presidential campaign slogan, "Let's make America great again" (reworked by Donald Trump for his 2016 presidential campaign), Charlie Joe taps into the rhetoric of a neoliberal leader, policy maker, and ideologue with a remarkable track record for cutting governmental spending on higher education and turning the management of public education over to corporate interests (see Bauman and Read). While he begins in apparent sincerity, he soon leads into ironic ambivalence, a move that—very much in the Mark Twain vein—makes it easy to spot the humor but difficult to pin down the brunt of the joke. Regardless, the ensuing logic of the novel takes "that kind of good old-fashioned creativity" to heart, when the narrative is revealed as a metafiction and Charlie Joe has turned the story of his academic failure into the market commodity the readers have in their hands. Again, entrepreneurship trumps education.

But that valorization of empty-headed entrepreneurship at the expense of standard literacy learning emerges even more explicitly, and more troublingly, in the sanctions taken by the school against Charlie Joe for cheating. "Apart from finding a suitable punishment for your recent infraction," explains school principal Mrs. Sleep, "it is clear that you need to learn how vital reading is to your growth and development, both as a student and as a young person" (205). Pointing out that Charlie Joe lacks "judgment," English teacher Ms. Ferrell joins Mrs. Sleep in reaching out because he is nevertheless "bright," "imaginative," and "creative—which is to say that such qualities, rather than any actual academic achievement, are what counts at this moment. She gives him a choice: "The first option . . . is to read ten books over the course of the summer, and write a five-page book report on each one" (206), an appropriate assignment intended to encourage a habit of reading and being accountable in writing for that reading. "The other option," the one he settles on, "is to *write* a book. A book no less than 150 pages in length, on any topic you choose" (206). This second option certainly offers a valuable opportunity for writing, yet it loses sight of the pedagogical problem that provoked the academic intervention in the first place: it gives him license to continue not reading as he makes up for not reading. When Charlie Joe then tells us that his summer writing project is in fact the book we are reading, the novel compounds its already problematic conception of writing by suggesting that the literary marketplace also rewards uninformed writing motivated by academic dishonesty. Comparable to *Frindle*'s revisionist schoolboy dream of sudden wealth, here is a fiction of sudden marketplace presence, of a professional occupation achieved precisely in the act of flouting the standard literacy preparation on which such occupations conventionally depend.

While it might be possible to find healthy, Freirean principles at play in Charlie Joe's narrative,[9] in that the resistant reader and writer ultimately comes around to playing an active and productive role as a student, the sanction given by his educators—to write his own book without a reading quota—evinces a suspect understanding of literacy, one that is echoed formally in the final turn taken by the novel. Conspicuously, Charlie Joe ends—as he began—by reaffirming resistance and reluctance: reminding us that "I was born a non-reader, and I was going to die a non-reader" (208), he confesses that "I've come to the conclusion that writing a book is far less annoying than reading one" (214). So, he remains motivated by the same resistance that compelled him to avoid reading in the first place, only now he has institutional validation in being allowed to redeem himself academically as a continuing non-reader, not to mention commercially as a writer celebrating in print his non-reading. In the last instance, once again, character development and academic success are measured by the logic of the marketplace, though where Clements's schoolboy thrives by upending the hierarchy of the curriculum, Greenwald's succeeds because the curriculum is leveled when the academic bar is lowered to such a degree that he can satisfy reading outcomes without doing any actual reading. Such "a radical disregard for school," Elisabeth Gruner notes, is not uncommon in the school story genre, a fact that need not prevent the "education" of young protagonists.[10] But whatever education Charlie Joe receives has less to do with the conventional literacy standards expected in the academic curriculum and more to do with an idiosyncratic mix of ignorance, resilience, and productivity in the marketplace. The pedagogical trouble with Charlie Joe's success is that it seems bent on distracting us from (rather than directing us toward) the dismal condition of educational authorities whose only recourse, when challenged, is to compromise the curriculum by undoing the traditional hierarchy of stage objectives, outcomes, and assessment. And it is a compromise with which the novel seems content, so long as it affords opportunities for "bright," "imaginative," and "creative" boys to apply themselves not as students but as entrepreneurs.

Critical Contexts: Praise and Ambivalence

Critics and reviewers applaud both novels. *Frindle* is typically commended for its "thought-provoking insights about the nature of words and their importance to the lives of regular people" (Engelfried 56). Hailed for its "adventures that will be cheered by etymological enthusiasts" (Baskin 2074) and "dictionary lovers" ("Frindle," *Publishers Weekly*), it is summed up as a story in which "the power of words shines through" (Bomboy 201) or in which "the power of language triumphs" (Weisman 125). Characterizing Nick as "a sharp, creative, independent thinker" (Bomboy 201), "a delightful nonconformist" (Baskin 2074), and "one of the most charming troublemakers since Soup" (Watson 732), reviewers give only a cursory nod to the problem he poses for the school realm. Even Elizabeth Watson, who wryly notes how "the merchandising future of this one is too terrible to contemplate; the cutting-edge gift this Christmas has got to be a frindle," imagines how booksellers might capitalize on the novel but not how the novel itself validates this "merchandising future" at the expense of literacy learning (732).

Comparable attitudes inform the critics' responses to the *Guide to Not Reading*. While some reviewers think that "Greenwald pulls off a clever bit of reverse psychology" ("Charlie Joe Jackson's Guide to Not Reading," *Publishers Weekly* 69), in a story that "speaks straight to other book-averse middle-schoolers" (Rochman 81), others argue that "the narrator's faux I'm-one-of-you tone won't fool reluctant readers" (Jaffee 71). Similarly, while some describe a moral tale, noting how Charlie Joe "is brought down by his own finagling and scheming" (Bange 66), others see it more along the lines of an anti-novel, claiming that "slackers everywhere have a new, likeable hero in Charlie Joe Jackson" ("Charlie Joe Jackson's Guide to Not Reading," *Kirkus Reviews* 12). Put another way still, in the words of Elizabeth Bush, "It's difficult to tell whether Greenwald has created a naïve misfire, intended for reluctant readers who won't ever come near it, or a stroke of subversive genius, skewering those well-intentioned authors who vainly believe theirs is that one magical novel that will finally entice the most obtuse holdout" (520). Bush spells out the difficulty of pinning down a novel that flirts with penance while committing to villainy.

Perhaps the most striking account of Greenwald's novel comes from a research article on reading interventions by Andrew Huddleston and Tara Lowe, "'I Skim and Find the Answers': Addressing Search-and-Destroy in Reading" (2014), which aims to encourage teachers and students "to reconsider what it means to read and how one approaches texts" (71). Pegging the *Guide to Not Reading* as "an excellent children's book to engage students in conversations about what it means to read," Huddleston and Lowe claim that Charlie Joe "does much more reading than he claims and is in fact quite a good reader." As they explain, "Charlie Joe offers 25 nonreading tips for reluctant readers, many of which are actually good reading strategies." Citing Tip #21, they remind us of Charlie Joe's advice on "the things you need to make sure you know when telling someone you did read a book, when you actually didn't read the book"; these include "the title, the author, what's on the cover, how long it is, the name of the main character, the name of anyone who dies, the names of any animals, how long it took to read, what happened in a specific chapter, [and] if you like it or not" (my compressed rendering of the cited text). "Clearly," argue Huddleston and Lowe, "by the time a person finds all the information mentioned in the list, he or she has essentially read the book" (77). That selective reading can enforce comprehension makes sense, but to assert that Charlie Joe's reading strategy is tantamount to "reading the book" alas does not, since he relies on other people to supply such details. Better, rather, to acknowledge the deficiency of the reading experience and how the author, his characters, and his critics show no substantive concern for how that deficiency actually prepares the way for marketplace success. As such, I agree that the novel is an excellent choice for classroom discussion, but not in the way supposed by Huddleston and Lowe, who fail to distinguish between strategies for enriching the learning process and those for exploiting or doing away with it.

Implications and Connections: ~~They Say/~~ I Say

Frindle and *Charlie Joe Jackson's Guide to Not Reading* both raise critical questions as to the nature of reading in and beyond the middle school curriculum. As popular stories of school experience in America, they stand to inform how young Americans understand the meaning and value of resistant or dishonest reading, topics that have long occupied practitioners in, and theorists of, education. As the reviews make clear, Clements and Greenwald encourage us to applaud schoolboys who, though worlds apart in thought and diction, are written to "charm" us even as they "trouble" the classroom (Watson). Above all, both narratives subvert a certain principle intrinsic to current dominant theories of literacy and academic development: that writing should be understood as a responsive and responsible form of inquiry, fairly and honestly representing and engaging with the writings of others. This principle, for example, underpins the articles of the Common Core State Standards Initiative (CCSSI), just as it informs the central paradigm in influential textbooks such as Gerald Graff and Cathy Birkenstein's *They Say/I Say*, a work intended in its 2014 high school edition "to help teachers successfully implement the Common Core State Standards" (preface).

The CCSSI—which has been adopted in more than forty US states, though not without controversy—aims to standardize grade-level knowledge outcomes in literacy and mathematics, for grades K–12, to consistently prepare high school graduates for success in "college, career, and life" ("Key Shifts"). To consolidate our sense of the didactic-pedagogical imagination in *Frindle* and the *Guide to Not Reading*, it is worth reviewing two of the initiative's expectations for skills and knowledge. The first calls for "regular practice with complex texts and their academic language," for "progressive development of reading comprehension," and "for students to grow their vocabularies through a mix of conversation, direct instruction, and reading" ("Key Shifts"). The second calls for "reading, writing, and speaking grounded in evidence from texts, both literary and informational," and for a readiness to "answer questions that depend on . . . having read the texts with care" ("Key Shifts"). Augmenting the state standards, textbooks like *They Say/I Say* insist that the best writing comes when engaging with and responding to the words and ideas of others: student writers are encouraged to read and listen to the voices of others, to accurately represent those voices, and to enter into conversation with them. While the conversational model is not the be-all and end-all of writing instruction or language arts learning, it can and does play a critical role in helping students enter and understand both the scholarly community and the wider world of culture and society. Which is to say that, like the Common Core, it lays out certain rudiments in terms of academic methodologies, practices, and etiquette. In much the same way that schools and colleges offer introductory and advanced or lower and upper classes in writing, the presumption is that development occurs according to a hierarchy of stage expectations: students get to grips with basic principles as prerequisites for more demanding work.

Keeping in mind just how far the state standards and supporting textbooks currently reach, it seems appropriate to acknowledge the extent to which Clements's and Greenwald's schoolboys fall short of expectations. Charlie Joe in particular, as a dedicated non-reader, seems set for failure, since the developmental payoff rests wholly on practicing with texts, which he simply does not do (and his exploits continue in *Charlie Joe Jackson's Guide to Extra Credit* and *Charlie Joe Jackson's Guide to Summer Vacation*, both 2012). But even Nick, an avowed word lover and happy reader, seems set for academic difficulty—since the coining of his new word, in its disregard for existing language, demonstrates a poor grasp of working with texts, while his limited interpretation of Mrs. Granger's words reveals a selective (and so dishonest) rendering of her fuller argument. Elements that would mark these boys for academic mediocrity if not outright failure in real life distinguish them, in both novels, for bookish success: the one publishes his own story of decline and renewal in school, while the other invents a word that gains commercial recognition, enters the dictionary, and makes him rich. Thus, while other American school stories do make promising engagements with academics, also common are works like *Frindle* and the *Guide to Not Reading* that conceive education as something that happens in spite of formal schooling—as a process of aspiring, without necessarily growing, reckoned by a measure of entrepreneurial individualism. Superficially, both books lay claim to a working binary of education and entrepreneurship, but the narrative arcs of their protagonists suggest a troubled and uneven pairing; in good neoliberal form, the logics of the marketplace interfere with the hierarchies of literacy acquisition, stage development, and curriculum, emptying the school experience of education as such and redefining the school as a locus of wealth acquisition and a gateway to the marketplace, if not a marketplace in its own right.

My point, finally, is not to bash books like *Frindle* or *Charlie Joe Jackson's Guide to Not Reading*, nor to censor them, but to encourage readers to reflect on the educative assumptions of binary logics that pit education as a poor alternative to entrepreneurship. If the contemporary American school story has the potential to influence understandings of what it means for young people to study, learn, and prepare for life, then the trouble with authors such as Clements and Greenwald is that they champion an art of dropping out without actually dropping out: they ask us to imagine highly individualistic manipulators, cheats, and liars who are capable of marketplace success precisely because they manipulate, cheat, and lie. Hence, while it has long been commonplace for scholars of children's literature to define the school story as a genre speaking to the social rather than the academic life of school, it seems much shrewder to recuperate the language of education and democracy, and to tackle head on the didactic-pedagogical ideals motivating our authors of school fiction.

NOTES

1. An earlier version of this chapter first appeared in *Children's Literature in Education* vol. 49, no. 1 (March 2018), a special issue on education titled "Education Gone Bad," edited by Elizabeth A. Marshall and Lissa Paul. I extend my thanks to the editors for their help in readying that manuscript for publication, and to the journal's publisher, Springer, for its help in sustaining the scholarly community.

2. Recent Bakhtinian readings in children's literature include Lichung Yang's "Following Reading Primers the Wrong Way: Pedagogical Nonsense in Dr. Seuss" in *Children's Literature in Education* (2017), and Lin Knutson's "Monster Studies: Liminality, Home Spaces, and Ina Vampires in Octavia E. Butler's *Fledgling*" in *University of Toronto Quarterly* (2018).

3. As Sheila Ray puts it, "Many books written for children have scenes set in, or references to, school, but the term 'school story' is generally used to describe a story in which most of the action centers on a school" (467). See also M. O. Grenby on "the three basic criteria of the school story: it is set almost entirely in school; it takes the relationships between the scholars and their teachers as the primary focus; and it contains attitudes and adventures which are unique to school life" (90); and Pat Pinsent, who argues that "the most memorable school stories seem to be those in which the school is almost a character in itself" (238).

4. *Book Scavenger* does not explore the routines or significance of school enough to qualify as a school story, but it does speak to dominant conceptions of learning and literacy, hence its inclusion here.

5. See, for example, Parks, "Metaphors of Hierarchy in Mathematics Education Discourse," which explores the hierarchical implications of describing children's learning by way of the metaphor of traveling along a physical path.

6. Most recently, it earned the Children's Literature Association's 2016 Phoenix Award.

7. For insights into the pedagogical difficulties concomitant with the US democratization of education, see Patrick Hartwell's "Grammar, Grammars, and the Teaching of Grammar" (1985), Mike Rose's "The Language of Exclusion" (1985), and David R. Russell's "American Origins of the Writing Across the Curriculum Movement" (1992), all in Susan Miller's *The Norton Book of Composition Studies* (2009), and Sarah Mondale and Sarah B. Patton's *School: The Story of American Public Education* (2001). For commentaries on the competing purposes of disciplinary specialization, job preparation, and liberal education, see William Cronon's "'Only Connect . . .': The Goals of a Liberal Education" (1998), James Schall's "Liberal Education and Social Justice" (2006), and Nel Noddings's "Renewing the Spirit of the Liberal Arts" (2013).

8. See, for example, Dobson (2016), Jacobs (2011), and Graves and Watts-Taffe (2008).

9. I have in mind the imperatives to act and to create that, in *Pedagogy of the Oppressed* (1968), Paulo Freire describes as life-affirming and humanizing elements of the learning process.

10. Gruner is discussing J. K. Rowling's *Harry Potter* series (1997–2007), Terry Pratchett's Tiffany Aching novels (2003–2006), and Philip Pullman's *His Dark Materials* trilogy (1997–2000); a comparable diagnosis is offered by Karin Westman (2011), who also sees Rowling's protagonists learn, grow, and advocate education in spite of a vexed school realm.

WORKS CITED

Bakhtin, Mikhail. "The *Bildungsroman* and Its Significance in the History of Realism (Toward a Historical Typology of the Novel)." *Speech Genres and Other Late Essays*, translated by Vern W. McGee, edited by Caryl Emerson and Michael Holquist, University of Texas Press, 1986, pp. 10–59.

Bange, Stephanie. "Charlie Joe Jackson's Guide to Not Reading." *Library Media Connection*, vol. 30, no. 3, Nov. 2011, pp. 66–67, *EBSCOhost*. Accessed 9 Apr. 2016.

Baskin, Barbara. "Frindle." *Booklist*, vol. 2074, Aug. 1999, *Literature Resource Center*. Accessed 9 Apr. 2016.

Bauman, Dan, and Brock Read. "A Brief History of GOP Attempts to Kill the Education Dept." *Chronicle of Higher Education*, 21 Jun. 2018, *Chronicle of Higher Education*, www.chronicle.com/article/A-Brief-History-of-GOP/243739. Accessed 30 Dec. 2019.

Bertman, Jennifer Chambliss. *Book Scavenger*. Illustrated by Sarah Watts, Henry Holt and Company, 2015.

"binary, adj. and n." *OED Online*, Dec. 2019, *Oxford University Press*, www.oed.com/view dictionaryentry/Entry/19111. Accessed 26 Dec. 2019.

Bomboy, Pamela K. "Frindle." *School Library Journal*, vol. 42, 1996, p. 201, *Literature Resource Center*. Accessed 9 Apr. 2016.

Bush, Elizabeth. "Greenwald, Tommy: Charlie Joe Jackson's Guide to Not Reading." *Bulletin of the Center for Children's Books*, vol. 64, no. 11, 2011, p. 520. *ProjectMUSE*. Accessed 9 Apr. 2016.

"Charlie Joe Jackson's Guide to Not Reading." *Kirkus Reviews*, vol. 79, no. 12, 2011, *MasterFILE Premier*. Accessed 9 Apr. 2016.

"Charlie Joe Jackson's Guide to Not Reading." *Publishers Weekly*, 69, 2011, *PWxyz, LLC*. Accessed Apr. 9, 2016.

Chbosky, Stephen. *The Perks of Being a Wallflower*. Pocket Books, 1999.

Christiano, Tom, "Democracy." *The Stanford Encyclopedia of Philosophy*, fall 2018 edition, edited by Edward N. Zalta, Stanford University, plato.stanford.edu/archives/fall2018/entries/democracy. Accessed 26 Dec. 2019.

Clements, Andrew. *Frindle*. Atheneum, 1996.

Cronon, William. "'Only Connect . . .': The Goals of a Liberal Education." *American Scholar*, vol. 67, no.4, 1998, pp. 73–80, *JSTOR*. Accessed 9 Apr. 2019.

de Saussure, Ferdinand. 1916. *Course in General Linguistics*. Translated by Wade Baskin, edited by Charles Bally and Albert Sechehaye in collaboration with Albert Reidlinger, Philosophical Library, 1959, *Internet Archive*. archive.org/stream/courseingeneralloosaus/courseingeneralloosaus_djvu.txt. Accessed 30 Dec. 2019.

Dobson, Meaghan Hanrahan. "The Importance of Real Reading for Resistant Readers." *Education Week Teacher*, 13 Apr. 2016, *Editorial Projects in Education*, www.edweek.org/tm/articles/2016/04/13/the-importance-of-real-reading-for-resistant.html. Accessed Apr. 9, 2016.

Engelfried, Steven. "Frindle." *School Library Journal*, 56, 2004, *Literature Resource Center*. Accessed 9 Apr. 2016.

Faggella-Luby, Michael N., Sharon M. Ware, and Ashley Capozzoli. "Adolescent Literacy Reports: Key Components and Critical Questions." *Journal of Literacy Research* vol. 41, 2009, pp. 453–75.

Freire, Paulo. 1968. *Pedagogy of the Oppressed*. Continuum Publishing Company, 1997.

"Frindle." *Publishers Weekly*, 1998, *PWxyz, LLC*, www.publishersweekly.com/978-0-689-81876-9. Accessed 9 Apr. 2016.

Grabenstein, Chris. *Escape from Mr. Lemoncello's Library*. Yearling, 2013.

Graff, Gerald, and Cathy Birkenstein. *They Say/I Say: The Moves That Matter in Academic Writing*. 3rd ed., foreword by Jim Burke, W. W. Norton & Company, 2014.

Graves, Michael F., and Susan Watts-Taffe. "For the Love of Words: Fostering Word Consciousness in Young Readers." *The Reading Teacher*, vol. 62, no. 3, 2008, pp. 185–93, *JSTOR*. Accessed 9 Apr. 2016.

Greenwald, Tommy. *Charlie Joe Jackson's Guide to Not Reading*. Illustrated by J. P. Coovert, Square Fish, 2012.

Grenby, M. O. "The School Story." *Children's Literature*. Edinburgh University Press, 2008, pp. 87–116.

Gruner, Elisabeth Rose. "Teach the Children: Education and Knowledge in Recent Children's Fantasy." *Children's Literature* vol. 37, 2009, pp. 216–35, *ProjectMUSE*. Accessed 9 Apr. 2016.

Gurdon, Meghan Cox. "Darkness Too Visible." *Wall Street Journal*, 4 Jun. 2011, *Dow Jones & Company, Inc.*, www.wsj.com/articles/SB10001424052702303657404576357622592697038. Accessed 31 Aug. 2015.

Huddleston, Andrew P., and Tara N. Lowe. "'I Skim and Find the Answers': Addressing Search-and-Destroy in Reading." *The Reading Teacher*, vol. 68, no. 1, 2014, pp. 71–79, *JSTOR*. Accessed 9 Apr. 2016.

Jacobs, Alan. "We Can't Teach Students to Love Reading." *Chronicle of Higher Education*, 31 Jul. 2011, *Chronicle of Higher Education, Inc.*, www.chronicle.com/article/We-Cant-Teach-Students-to/128400. Accessed 9 Apr. 2016.

Jaffee, Cyrisse. "Greenwald, Tommy: Charlie Joe Jackson's Guide to Not Reading." *The Horn Book Guide*, vol. 71, 2012, *Literature Resource Center*. Accessed 9 Apr. 2016.

"Key Shifts in English Language Arts." *Common Core State Standards Initiative*. www.core standards.org/other-resources/key-shifts-in-english-language-arts. Accessed 9 Apr. 2016.

Knutson, Lin. "Monster Studies: Liminality, Home Spaces, and Ina Vampires in Octavia E. Butler's Fledgling." *University of Toronto Quarterly*, vol. 87, no. 1, 2018.

Lewis, Mark A., and Ian Parker Renga. "(Re)Imagining Life in the Classroom: Inciting Dialogue Through an Examination of Teacher-Student Relationships in Film." *Exploring Teachers in Fiction and Film: Saviors, Scapegoats, and Schoolmarms*, edited by Melanie Shoffner, Routledge, 2016, pp. 65–75.

Lubar, David. *Sleeping Freshmen Never Lie*. Dutton Books, 2005.

Lynch, Raymond, and Oliver McGarr. "Negotiating Subject Hierarchies: Neo-Liberal Influences on the Comprehensive Curriculum in Ireland." *Educational Policy*, vol. 30, no. 5, 2016, pp. 721–39. *EBSCOhost*. Accessed 28 Dec. 2019.

McGee, Chris. "The Power of Secrets: Backwards Construction and the Children's Detective Story." *Telling Children's Stories*, edited by Mike Cadden, University of Nebraska Press, 2010, pp. 44–61.

Miller, Susan, editor. *The Norton Book of Composition Studies*. W. W. Norton & Company, 2009.

Mondale, Sarah, and Sarah B. Patton. *School: The Story of American Public Education*. Beacon Press, 2001.

Moretti, Franco. *The Way of the World: The* Bildungsroman *in European Culture*. 1987. New Edition. Translated by Albert Sbragia. Verso, 2000.

Muzellec, Laurent, and Mary Lambkin. "Corporate Rebranding: Destroying, Transferring or Creating Brand Equity?" *European Journal of Marketing*, vol. 40, no. 7/8, 2006, pp. 803–24, *Semantic Scholar*. Accessed 26 Dec. 2019.

Noddings, Nel. "Renewing the Spirit of the Liberal Arts." *Journal of General Education*, vol. 62, nos. 2–3, 2013, pp. 77–83. *JSTOR*. Accessed 9 Apr. 2016.

"No Talking." *Kirkus Reviews*, vol. 75, no. 11, 2007, *Kirkus Media LLC*. Accessed 29 Jul. 2017.

Orwell, George. "Boys' Weeklies." 1940. *Inside the Whale and Other Essays*, Victor Gollancz Ltd., *Orwell.ru*, www.orwell.ru/library/essays/boys/english/e_boys. Accessed 9 Apr. 2016.

Parks, Amy Noelle. "Metaphors of Hierarchy in Mathematics Education Discourse: The Narrow Path." *Journal of Curriculum Studies*, vol. 42, no. 1, 2010, pp. 79–97, *EBSCOhost*. Accessed 26 Dec. 2019.

Parton, Chea. "Revisionist Films: Detaching from Teacher as Hero/Savior." *Exploring Teachers in Fiction and Film: Saviors, Scapegoats, and Schoolmarms*, edited by Melanie Shoffner, Routledge, 2016, pp. 149–59.

Patterson, James. *Middle School: The Worst Years of My Life*. Illustrated by Chris Tebbetts, Little, Brown and Company, 2011.

Pinsent, Pat. "School Story." *The Routledge Companion to Children's Literature*, edited by David Rudd, Routledge, 2010, pp. 238–41.

Quigly, Isabel. *The Heirs of Tom Brown: The English School Story*. Chatto & Windus, 1982.

Ray, Sheila. "School Stories." *International Companion Encyclopedia of Children's Literature*, edited by Peter Hunt, Routledge, 2004, pp. 467–80.

"rebrand, v." *OED Online*, Dec. 2019, Oxford University Press, www.oed.com/view/Entry/247467. Accessed 26 Dec. 2019.

Rochman, Hazel. "Charlie Joe Jackson's Guide to Not Reading." *Booklist*, vol. 81, 2011, *EBSCOhost*. Accessed 9 Apr. 2016.

Schall, James. "Liberal Education and Social Justice." *Liberal Education*, vol. 92, no. 4, 2006, pp. 44–47, *ERIC*. Accessed 9 Apr. 2016.

Scholastic. *Kids and Family Reading Report*. 5th ed., 2015, *Scholastic Inc.*, www.scholastic.com/readingreport. Accessed 1 Sep. 2016.

Twain, Mark. *The Adventures of Tom Sawyer*. 1875. Grosset & Dunlap/Harper & Brothers, 1920.

Watson, Elizabeth S. "Frindle." *The Horn Book Magazine*, vol. 732, 1996, *Literature Resource Center*. Accessed 9 Apr. 2016.

Weisman, Kay. "Frindle." *Booklist*, vol. 125, 1996, *Literature Resource Center*. Accessed 9 Apr. 2016.

Westman, Karin E. "Blending Genres and Crossing Audiences: Harry Potter and the Future of Literary Fiction." *The Oxford Handbook of Children's Literature*, edited by Julia L. Mickenberg and Lynne Vallone, Oxford University Press, 2011, pp. 93–112.

Whitney, Jason. "The Role of the Teacher, Real and Imagined." *Exploring Teachers in Fiction and Film: Saviors, Scapegoats, and Schoolmarms*, edited by Melanie Shoffner, Routledge, 2016, pp. 36–46.

Wilingham, Daniel T. "For the Love of Reading: Engaging Students in a Lifelong Pursuit." *American Educator*, spring 2015, *American Federation of Teachers, AFL-CIO*, www.aft.org/ae/spring2015/willingham. Accessed 9 Apr. 2016.

Yang, Lichung. "Following Reading Primers the Wrong Way: Pedagogical Nonsense in Dr. Seuss." *Children's Literature in Education*, vol. 48, no. 4, 2017, pp. 326–40.

CHAPTER 3

Darkness as Heuristic

Care and Development in Pathological School Fiction

In her now notorious *Slate* article "Darkness Too Visible" (2011), children's book reviewer Meghan Cox Gurdon stirred controversy when she accused publishers of "bulldoz[ing] coarseness or misery into ... children's lives" by way of "dark" teen novels mired in "pathologies" and "profanity." Much like Victorian critics of school fiction who criticized authors for untruthful representations, Gurdon complains that, "if books show us the world, teen fictions can be like a hall of fun-house mirrors, constantly reflecting back hideously distorted portrayals of what life is." Though primarily interested in contemporary novels such as Chris Lynch's *Inexcusable* (2005), Cheryl Rainfield's *Scars* (2010), and Lauren Myracle's *Shine* (2011), stories exploring the effects of date rape, childhood sexual abuse, and sexual discrimination, Gurdon characterizes young adult literature in general—from S. E. Hinton's *The Outsiders* (1967) and the anonymous *Go Ask Alice* (1971) to Andrew A. Smith's *The Marbury Lens* (2010) and Jackie Kessler's *Rage* (2011)—as an archive given to increasingly "dark topics." The problem, she argues, is that "a careless young reader—or one who seeks out depravity—will find himself surrounded by images not of joy or beauty but of damage, brutality and losses of the most horrendous kinds." While she acknowledges the common objection that such novels matter because they affirm the experiences of identities that might otherwise go without representation, she insists that it is more likely "that books focusing on pathologies help normalize them and, in the case of self-harm, may even spread their plausibility and likelihood to young people who might otherwise never have imagined such extreme measures. Self-destructive adolescent behaviors are observably infectious and have periods of vogue. That is not to discount the real suffering that some young people endure; it is an argument for taking care." What Gurdon means by "pathologies" is not spelled out, though it is directly associated with "self-harm" in the context of an essay ranging widely in its allusions to abuse, violence, depravity, vampires, suicide, self-mutilation, kidnapping, pederasty, incest, brutal beatings, profanity, damage, losses, class tensions, family dysfunction, disaffected youth, drugs, abduction, rape, gore, and cruelty.

Gurdon's claims deserve attention here to the extent that the young adult novel in the form of the school story, while it need not be as pathological as the kind of book she questions, sometimes can be. In fact, some of the most acclaimed school fictions of recent years are categorically pathological in structure and content, their narratives crafted to express and explore characters and psyches "exhibiting a quality or trait to a degree considered extreme or psychologically unhealthy" ("pathological, adj."). Think no further than Sapphire's *Push* (1996; film adaptation, as *Precious*, 2009, directed by Lee Daniels), Laurie Halse Anderson's *Speak* (1999; film adaptation 2004, directed by Jessica Sharzer), and Stephen Chbosky's *The Perks of Being a Wallflower* (1999; film adaptation 2012, directed by Chbosky), all award-winning problem novels adapted for the big screen, and all undertaking fraught journeys into the inner lives of physically and mentally abused schoolchildren.[1] I would argue that such works negotiate their pathological materials in ways that invite critical rather than copycat thinking: they compel young readers to contextualize rather than essentialize suffering and damage—that is, to read the suffering politically, so as to recognize that certain identities and experiences are not so much pathological in their own right as pathologized by way of social structures and cultural production.[2] In other words, a genuine interest in pathological fiction for young adults would mean, in the words of Anderson's protagonist, "seeing beyond what is on the surface" (*Speak* 119), especially when considering the ways such texts work not to crush readers' spirits but to hearten with stories of academic promise. More to the point, the pathological school stories told by Sapphire, Anderson, and Chbosky remind us that everyday school experience raises comparable questions about crisis, influence, and care—about the narrative process of self-realization in the school years, and about the extent to which families, peers, educators, and policy makers open up or foreclose on individual life trajectories. So, even though I believe that Gurdon is justified in worrying about what she calls the "careless young reader," I hesitate to dismiss the pathological outright.

Since the school as institution plays a defining role in books such as *Push* and *Speak*, and since their protagonists develop according to distinct intersections of cyclical and longitudinal time, in this chapter I draw on Levine's theory of rhythmic forms to consider how Sapphire and Anderson envision protagonists who descend into what Gurdon styles "darkness too visible"[3] yet successfully develop—intellectually, emotionally, and socially—under the influence of attentive teachers. For Levine, temporal patterns work to organize and impose constraints on social life, especially in terms of "the predictable rhythms of everyday life" governed by the large-scale institutions of work and school (49). Levine takes the institution to be a form in the sense that it "afford[s] certain kinds of constraints and opportunities, bringing bodies, meanings, and objects into a political order," arguing that institutions, while also relying on the bounded wholes of buildings and spaces, are definitively "composed of rhythms—patterns of duration and repetition over time" (56). Citing political scientists James March and Johan Olsen, who characterize institutions as "relatively enduring collection[s] of rules and organized practices, embedded in structures of meaning and resources that are relatively invariant in the face of turnover of individuals and relatively resilient to the idiosyncratic preferences and expectations of individuals and changing external circumstances" (qtd. in Levine 58; brackets Levine's), Levine observes that "institutions endure ... only because participants actively reproduce their rules and practices. Whether acting as administrators or parents, macho men or diligent students, poker players or welfare recipients, we play parts set out for us by institutions, and, as we do so, we reproduce the institution itself" (57–58).

Arguably, rhythmic form is *the* critical form for understanding the rationality shaping secondary and higher education in the West, in that educators, administrators, and policy makers are in the business of plotting student pathways according to strict developmental stages in ways that shape both the short-term progress through school and the long-term life course. And since this Western negotiation of short and long terms is increasingly premised on utilitarian, entrepreneurial, and marketplace conceptions of the meaning and value of the diploma and degree, it seems right to acknowledge that neoliberalism has brought its own distinct rhythmic forms to bear on school experience. Still, even if "forms do organize us," Levine brings us back to her guiding claim that not only are they plural but they also compete with one another for dominance—that "they do not work together, and so in the end are not able to impose a single coherent order on experience" (80–81). Applied more specifically to institutional forms, the point is to take school and work institutions to comprise multiple tempos that not only potentially clash with one another but also collide with other forms inside and outside the institution.

In what follows, I consider how Anderson's and Sapphire's narratives of young trauma are organized around institutional tempos of school as well as less predictable tempos of declining health, rehabilitation, and recovery.

In particular, I make a case for reading the pathological in the contemporary school story as a potentially promising heuristic both *in* and *for* the school realm: a way to lay bare the violent rhythms of institutions in an age of weakened public infrastructures and reduced welfare services; a chance to explore developmental stoppages; and a critical opportunity to consider the private possibilities of student development while looking for evidence of institutional care and commitment to victims of race, class, and sexual violence. My intention is not to valorize the damage done to or felt by schoolchildren but to recognize that stories of such damage often anticipate Gurdon's "argument for taking care" at the levels of private, public, and institutional experience. Provided books like *Push* and *Speak* work through their depictions of suffering so as to call out the unjust social structures in which such suffering thrives, I am inclined to argue that pathological teen fiction has the potential to help rather than hurt its audience.

Speak:

Broaching the "dark" territory reviled by Gurdon, *Speak* tells the story of a teenager coming to terms with her identity as a survivor of sexual assault, a schoolgirl with "a chewed up horror of a mouth,"[4] who at her lowest ebb decides to "open up a paper clip and scratch it across the inside of my left wrist. Pitiful. If a suicide attempt is a cry for help, then what is this? A whimper, a peep? I draw little windowcracks of blood, etching line after line until it stops hurting" (87). Raped by a senior at a summer house party but unable to speak of it—indeed, barely able to speak at all—Melinda Sordino, ninth-grade freshman at Merryweather High School in Syracuse, is in the process of unravelling mentally. Because the cops broke up the party when she made an aborted phone call for help, an intervention that led to arrests (presumably for underage drinking), the student body as a whole, including her former best friends, more or less despises her. As she puts it, "I am Outcast" (4). Overlapping with the spatial and hierarchical forms on which the idea of the outcast depends—marking, as it does, a sense of both territorial and social division—are the rhythmic forms of both the school as institution (operating according to traditional routines of academic year, seasonal terms, and weekly and daily calendars) and of the traumatized adolescent (struggling to regain the routines of everyday life and failing to meet stage expectations for social and academic development). Rhythmic form, in fact, is the first dominant paradigm by which we are invited to understand this freshman story, in that Anderson divides the book into four "marking periods," indicating a school system that tracks its students' progress quarter by quarter through the academic year. Indeed, each of the first three periods ends with a section titled "My Report Card," where Melinda records her performance in classes such as Social Studies, English, Art, Spanish, Algebra, Biology, and Gym, and more wryly in other areas including Social Life, Clothes, Attitude, Plays Nice, and Lunch (46, 92, 137). Reckoned by school time, because Melinda's grades in all subjects except Art are more or less in steady decline, *Speak* might seem to comprise a narrative of adolescent failure. But a more encouraging story seems to emerge in the rhythms afforded by the natural cycle of the seasons, which, loosely aligning with the academic calendar, symbolically signposts Melinda's descent as victim into stoppage and isolation (winter) and reemergence as survivor ready to grow again (spring). That the fourth period ends not with a report card but with Melinda poised to tell her story to her art teacher, Mr. Freeman—an educator in his own way at odds with the institution of the school—confirms Anderson's interest in the conflicted rhythms and tempos of school life.

In the thick of teachers caricatured by Melinda, whether for their aggression (Mr. Neck, social studies) or ineptitude (Hairwoman, English), Mr. Freeman figures as an exceptional teacher who succeeds in reaching a promising but damaged student floundering in the school system—a romantic construction that fits well with the neoliberal valorization of individual effort over institutional responsibility. Early in the term, he brings out a broken globe filled with scraps of paper bearing the names of objects. "You will spend the rest of the year learning how to turn that object into a piece of art," he explains. "But there's a catch—by the end of the year, you must figure out how to make your object say something, express an emotion, speak to every person who looks at it" (12). Melinda gets "tree," a random assignment, but one that lends itself to working through the blight and eventual regrowth of life after her rape, an act that, coincidentally, took place "*under the trees*" at the back of the party house (183, italics in original). In other words, as contemporary scholars know well, her art project has a therapeutic function and, as such, registers her character development in terms of a struggle to articulate her thoughts and feelings—another neoliberal strain that puts the burden of change on the individual rather than the social structure. For the most part, she wrestles with her materials and abilities, unable to make her trees "look real" (78): she draws, paints watercolors, sculpts with found objects, and carves linoleum blocks, only to render trees that are "flat . . . cheap, cruddy" (55), as if "dead" (78) or having "died from some fungal infection" (92)—in a word, "pitiful" (118). At stake in this clutch of descriptors is a preoccupation not with what to represent but how to represent it—and while it reads like a problem of modality (striving for "real" over "flat"), it is more properly a problem of expression. As she makes clear, "I can see it in my head.... But when I try to carve it, it looks like a dead tree, toothpicks, a child's drawing. I can't bring it to life" (78).

While Melinda and Mr. Freeman share a number of meaningful exchanges—whether he is "almost faint[ing] with delight" at her work (63), astutely recognizing that her "imagination is paralyzed" (118), or like a "jerk.... criticizing" her efforts (153)—a turning point comes during one particular scene, when he is giving her a ride downtown on a snowy day, and he says, "I'm seeing a lot of growth in your work" (121). Wholly out of character, Melinda speaks her mind, replying, "'I don't know anything. My trees suck.... you said we had to put emotion into our art. I don't know what that means. I don't know what I'm supposed to feel.' My fingers fly up and cover my mouth. What am I doing?" (122). In this rare act of divulging vocally, of all possible characters in the novel—peers, teachers, principal, guidance counselor, parents—it is Mr. Freeman to whom Melinda begins to open up, a teacher who—in keeping with her sense that she must find a way to voice her troubles—confirms that expression is everything. "When people don't express themselves," he explains in the same scene, "they die one piece at a time. You'd be shocked at how many adults are really dead inside—walking through their days with no idea who they are, just waiting for a heart attack or cancer or a Mack truck to come along and finish the job. It's the saddest thing I know" (122). Moving from general principal to specific point, he tells her, "You're a good kid. I think you have a lot to say. I'd like to hear it" (123). It is this invitation that prompts Melinda to search for the feelings she cannot find, even though "they are chewing me alive like an infestation of thoughts, shame, mistakes" (125).

Bearing in mind that art therapy has gained a reputation in recent years for helping sufferers of trauma and other psychiatric disorders give voice to stories and experiences otherwise difficult to express,[5] it makes sense that art figures prominently in Melinda's recovery, compelling her to sound the depths of her feelings in ways organic to the expressive objectives of Mr. Freeman's class. Yet the expression on which her recovery ultimately depends is far more documentary and consciously interventionist than the existential kind that he models. One day in spring, in the fourth marking period, reading graffiti conversations in the girls' toilets, she decides to "start another subject thread on the wall: *Guys to stay away from.* The first entry is the beast himself: *Andy Evans*" (175). In the coming days, she finds that other students—in "different pens, different handwriting"—have lent their voices to the thread, confirming Evans to be a "creep," "bastard," and "pervert" (185–86). This tacit alliance between Melinda and her peers pays off in a dramatic climax, when Evans—furious that she has called his reputation into question—traps her in a janitor's closet and again tries to rape her. It matters not only that she bests him in the tussle, holding a shard of glass to his neck while declaring, "I said no," but also that the moment is interrupted by ex-best friend Nicole and the lacrosse team (195). In the aftermath, Melinda comes around to the realization that "I have suddenly become popular. Thanks to the big mouths on the lacrosse team, everybody knew what happened" (197). By breaking the cycle of silence, then, Melinda disturbs the social and cultural hierarchies between the rapist and his victims, as well as between the broad school community and the outcast. With the addition of her final account from the art classroom—that "my tree is definitely breathing: little shallow breaths like it just shot up through the ground this morning" (196)—the novel ends by drawing the competing rhythms of Melinda's life together. Thus, with the closing lines, when Mr. Freeman says, "You've been through a lot, haven't you?" and she replies, "Let me tell you about it" (198), the reader is to suppose a satisfying convergence of natural, institutional, and developmental tempos as the seasonal, academic, and therapeutic fields of conflict arrive at a shared moment of closure.

The trouble with that reading is that it depends on a "flat . . . cheap, cruddy" conception of Mr. Freeman, a character who is actually rendered by Anderson in the same imagery of trauma used to characterize Melinda. Beginning in the first marking period, Mr. Freeman is revealed as something of an antihero, an artist-teacher who preaches freedom to his students while he himself declines temperamentally under a mounting sense of institutional constraint. Resonant with the connotations of his name, his new-age teaching style is "freeing," as is the learning environment of his classroom: where he can say, with hands covered in red clay, "Welcome to the only class that will teach you how to survive . . . Welcome to Art," at which point he "grabs a piece of chalk without washing his hands. 'SOUL,' he writes on the board. The clay streaks the word like dried blood. 'This is where you can find your soul, if you dare'" (10). But if his name has any allegorical currency in the novel, it is not because he is "a man who is personally free," or "a man who is politically free; a man enjoying the rights and liberties of a free society, as opposed to a tyrannical regime or totalitarian rule" ("freeman, n."). It is, rather—ironically—because he is unfree: a teacher haunted by a school board that has cut his art budget, diminished his teaching materials, and imposed a grade system that cannot account for the exploratory and therapeutic outcomes of his classroom. Traditionally, a US school board comprises "a body of people, typically elected, responsible for the provision, maintenance, and administration of schools, or for determining educational policy" ("school board, n."). In recent decades, however, neoliberal reforms have undermined the school board's provision of public goods. As Matt Hastings spells out, "The field of education, traditionally a site of local democratic control, is increasingly subject to neoliberal governance, as elected school boards are consolidated under appointed leadership, district schools are replaced by charter schools, and school resources, such as curriculum, testing, and even the training of teachers, are provided by private companies." Admittedly, *Speak* does not arrive at the same explicit conclusion as Hastings—that "neoliberalism frames the purpose of education in terms of investments made in the development of students' human capital"—but Anderson does make a point of pitting the affective, expressive, and therapeutic possibilities of Freeman's art class against the financial exigencies of Merryweather's school board. Keeping in mind that budgets deal not only with moneys but also time, managing incomes and expenditures within the limits of discrete periods, we do well to recognize that Mr. Freeman and the school board have conflicting concerns—indeed, conflicting tempos—in mind: while the one has his eye on the long *durée* of his students' lives, the other forecloses on the short-term affordances on which those lives depend.

The school board as cause for concern is first introduced when Mr. Freeman, frustrated with his freshman students' failure to find traction with their projects, invites them to study "the masters."

> He pulls out an armful [of books]. "Kahlo, Monet, O'Keeffe. Pollock, Picasso, Dali. They did not complain about subject, they mined every subject for the root of its meaning. Of course, they didn't have a school board forcing them to paint with both hands tied behind their backs, they had patrons who understood the need to pay for basic things such as paper and paint"... We groan. He's off on the school-board thing again. The school board has cut his supply budget, telling him to make do with the stuff left over from last year. No new paint, no extra paper. He'll rant for the rest of the period, forty-three minutes. The room is warm, filled with sun and paint fumes. Three kids fall dead asleep, eye twitches, snores, and everything. (31, ellipses in original)

At this point in the first marking period, Melinda shows little sympathy for Mr. Freeman's predicament: he rants; he bores. But in the second marking period, he piques her curiosity when, deciding to practice what he preaches, he begins "working on a huge canvas. It started out bleak—a gutted building along a gray road on a rainy day. He spent a week painting dirty coins on the sidewalk, sweating to get them just right. He painted the faces of school board members peering out the windows of the building, then he put bars on the windows and turned the building into a prison" (62). Read as a diagnostic, the painting of this unfree institutional scene suggests a crisis in rationality governing the education sector. And that the belabored coins are "dirty" suggests not only the hard economic facts of budget cuts but also moral quandary, to say nothing of biological contamination, ideas enforced as Mr. Freeman continues to work on his art. At the end of the second marking period—right around the time when Melinda mutilates herself—he "stops in front of his canvas. He hasn't finished painting. The bottom right corner is empty. The prisoners' faces are menacing . . . Mr. Freeman steps back, as if he has just seen something new in his own picture. He slices the canvas with my chisel, ruining it with a long, ripping sound that makes the entire class gasp" (92). When next encountered, in the third marking period, he "mostly sits on his stool and stares at a new canvas. It is painted one color, so blue it's almost black" (103). Asked what it is, he answers: "It is Venice at night, the color of an accountant's soul, a love rejected. I grew mold on an orange this color when I lived in Boston. It's the blood of imbeciles. Confusion. Tenure. The inside of a lock, the taste of iron. Despair. A city with the streetlights shot out. Smoker's lung. The hair of a small girl who grows up hopeless. The heart of a school board director . . ." (103–4, ellipses in original). Mr. Freeman traces a constellation of professions—the accountant, the teacher (implied by "tenure"), and the school board director—held together by dark suggestions of confinement ("a lock," "a city with the streetlights shot out"), deteriorated emotions (between the "soul" and the "heart," a "love rejected," "despair," "a small girl . . . hopeless"), cognitive dissonance ("imbeciles," "confusion," the implicit obscurity of the city without streetlights), and terminal disease ("smoker's lung"). What ought to be stressed is that Melinda now legitimizes Mr. Freeman's plight, so that when "some teachers rumorwhisper he's having a nervous breakdown," she counters with the notion, "I think he's the sanest person I know" (104). So, as much as the art room serves to validate the traumatized student's painful search for herself, Melinda's narrative serves to validate a comparably painful foray by the teacher into "dark" territory. In other words, Melinda as narrator invites us to compare their plights within the institutional confines of the public school—not to suggest that Mr. Freeman is somehow "raped" by the system,[6] but that his struggle to articulate the disturbing presence of the school board in his professional life is akin to Melinda's difficulty in "naming the monster" (85).

If, at first, both student and teacher share a narrative tempo, heading steadily toward their nadirs around the end of the third marking period when she mutilates her wrist and he his canvas, by the end of the fourth period, the student begins to recover her sense of self in ways that the teacher does not. Mr. Freeman has certainly given expression to his feelings, putting into words and images a profound sense of professional and pedagogical despair. But in much the same frame of mind that led him in the second marking period to "g[i]ve up paperwork when the school board Xed out his supply budget" (91), at the end of the fourth period he "is refusing to hand his grades in on time. They should have been in four days before the end of school, but he didn't see the sense in that" (196). Whether or not we read his defiance as a serious challenge to the school board—or, more generally, appreciate him as an antiestablishment figure—the institution of the school remains a field of profound conflict, the teacher and the board vying for the power to determine the meaning and value of school experience. In other words, Mr. Freeman remains embattled in ways that Melinda does not. And, at the level of institution, not much has changed.

Push: "The Way Free Is Hard"

Like *Speak*, Sapphire's *Push* tells a story of school experience troubled by dominant institutional rhythms, describing a young life out of sync with the conventional grade- and class-conscious tempos of the US public-school system. Set in 1987, the novel opens with illiterate, sixteen-year-old African American Claireece Precious Jones still in ninth grade, having been "left back" twice: first in second grade, because she could not read, and again around seventh grade, at the age of twelve, when she had the first of two babies to her father (3). Sexually molested, physically assaulted, and emotionally abused by both parents since she was three, Precious is exactly the kind of character Gurdon finds troubling. When she recollects how her father would rape her, she remembers that "afterward I go bafroom. I smear shit on my face. Feel good. Don't know why but it do. . . . I bite my fingernails till they look like disease, pull strips of my skin away. Get Daddy's razor out cabinet. Cut cut cut arm wrist"—though, as she makes clear, "not trying to die, trying to plug myself back in" (111–12). On publication, the graphic depictions of abuse and punishing representations of Black and illiterate identities alienated many book reviewers (for example, Jacquie Bishop, 1996; Susann Cokal, 1997; and Elisabeth Hayes and Sondra Cuban, 1998); and while some scholars such as Wendy Rountree (2004) were ready to wrestle with the difficulties of the text, as Marlo David confirms, Sapphire's treatment of the "black maternal subject" in particular led to "critical isolation. For years *PUSH* has received limited and uneven scholarly attention. The difficult characters of Precious and [her mother] Mary and, to a certain degree, Sapphire's experimental narrative aesthetics contribute to this critical oversight. Until recently, there have been few scholarly articles or book chapters on *PUSH*, and even fewer that examine the novel as an example of a progressive or empowering maternal narrative" (174). This state of affairs began to change around 2011, when scholars seemed readier to read the novel not for its pathological character studies but for its interest in what Michelle Jarman describes as "disabling traits" that are already "culturally pathologized . . . illiteracy, poverty, abuse" (165).

Explaining that "can't nuffin' fit [in my mind] when I think 'bout Daddy" (58), Precious describes a developmental stoppage in not only her emotional life at home but also her academic life at school. So, at school, she determines to hide both her homelife and her illiteracy. As a result, even though she introduces herself as a student wanting to learn—appreciating, for example, Mr. Wicher's math class—she is ready to move on: as she puts it, "I just wanna gone get the fuck out of I.S. 146 and go to high school and get my diploma" (6). Yet, in spite of this aggressive impatience to be done with school, her implicit trust in the meaning or power of the diploma suggests that she does not actually question the tempo established by the school: the institutionalized ritual of graduation remains the gateway to the future. As such, *Push* helps to clarify an important distinction between spatial and rhythmic forms of school life, in that the student parses her escaping the physical confines of the school realm as "[getting] the fuck out," even though the institutional tempos of grade levels and graduation continue to determine the course of her life (an idea perhaps suggesting that the spatial forms of the institution need not always be the defining ingredients for the school story genre, provided the rhythmic forms of the institution are shaping forces for the narrative). As the story unfolds, however, that relationship changes: first, when Precious transitions to an "alternative" school for students who have fallen off the educational track—where she signs up for "a basic reading and writing class, a pre-G.E.D.[7] adult literacy class, a class for beginning readers and writers" (42) under the tutelage of Ms. Blue Rain; and second, when Precious, who begins to imagine her school experience as a path toward a creative, intellectual life, learns that her social worker, Ms. Weiss, intends to track her into low-skilled service work. Only for a moment, then, does Precious find accord between the space and tempo of school life in Ms. Rain's classroom, though both Rain and Weiss are equally influential in prompting her to work out her sense of self and purpose.

Push explores the meaning of young, Black, female independence in the contexts of home sphere, school community, and broader economy, all linked by a narrative interest in the meaning and value of the welfare state. Conscious of her status as a welfare recipient, Precious sets out in the belief that others perceive her as a "vampire" sucking the system's blood (31). Outlining the historical conditions informing this imagery, David reminds us that

> Precious comes of age in 1980s Harlem, a period and location highly symbolic of the real and imagined inner city, which has become emblematic of black cultural difference in the post–Civil Rights era. The representation of dysfunctional, urban blackness reached a zenith in the 1980s as the figure of the "welfare queen" rose in the national imagination, instigated by a campaign speech by President

Ronald Reagan and continually fed by politicians, academics, and members of the media who draw on racist cultural theories and neoliberal political ideologies to explain black women's failure to belong to the ideological American family. The idea of the welfare queen kept alive fears about the black matriarch, a mid-century figuration of the black mother as an emasculating and harmful maternal stereotype, and turned her into the embodiment of the fallen promise of an American racial utopia. (175)

While noting that "*PUSH* situates Harlem as a critical site for the post–Civil Rights failure that the figure of the welfare queen enacts," David argues that "the novel intervenes in the neoliberal logic of individualism, which privileges the liberties of dominant white men, and it implicates institutional or systemic functions such as increasing concentrations of state power and media inundation—as the causes of familial discord and estrangement from community. In other words, *PUSH* indicts the systemic causes behind the intensification of fear and violence in the inner city rather than simply pointing to a failure of personal responsibility in its black women characters" (175). David brings rich and detailed context to bear on the novel, making an impressive case for recognizing the ways in which *Push* speaks politically to one of many undemocratic turns in modern US history. The problem is that the novel does not so much deconstruct the figure of the welfare queen as transpose it onto the character of the mother, a leeching brute who bullies Precious into collecting welfare checks and food stamps by fraudulently claiming her first child as a dependent in the household even though he lives with his great-grandmother. Sedentary and stagnant, but still physically threatening, the mother orders Precious to "forget school—get down to welfare" (56), as if to say her daughter's education is at odds with their livelihood. When Precious begins to question her mother's authority, her first thought is that "I could be on the 'fare myself now" (34) and "maybe get my own check" (51), though "not sure I know how to be on my own" (34). But in the story that ensues, it is less a matter of learning to "be on my own" (like an "ideal neoliberal child"[8]) and more about finding her place in a community of fellow survivors guided by Ms. Rain, who happens to take a strong stance against welfare, saying, "See how welfare has helped your mother; you could go further" (73). Keeping in mind that, soon after, Precious reorients her ambitions and decides that she "would like a job, a paycheck" (81) rather than a welfare check, the first half of the novel takes an ambivalent look at the state-citizen relationship: in equal parts conservative and progressive, it demonizes dependence on the state and makes a case for economic independence by way of the job market, all while valorizing a radical grassroots experience in the alternative classroom. This ambivalence, in fact, fits well with John Krinsky's account of the effects of neoliberalism on left-of-center social movements and advocacy groups in New York City between the 1970s and 1990s, which tended to both shore up and challenge the individualist values underpinning emergent neoliberal ideals.[9]

Without spelling out the public or private dimensions of the alternative school,[10] *Push* makes a point of distinguishing between learning environments that, against the odds, encourage growth and freedom (represented by Ms. Rain's classroom) and institutional apparatuses that stifle education (symbolized by Precious's academic record on file). Unambiguously, Precious attributes the crisis in her school experience to racialization: early in the narrative, when she states that "crackers is the cause of everything bad. It why my father ack like he do" (34); and later, when she identifies Ms. Weiss as a "cracker" with a "big beige file cabinet behind her desk" (116), attributes suggesting that the individual and the city apparatus behind her are, so to speak, one and the same hue. Fleeing home after the birth of her second baby, with the help of Ms. Rain Precious moves from a homeless shelter to a halfway house ("Advancement House") where she is obliged to meet in "counsel room" with Ms. Weiss. While these sessions help Precious to understand more of her life as an abused child, they miss the mark for a young woman who wants to focus less on the past and more on the future: they make her feel "paralyzed. . . . like second grade again" (115). With this sense of retardation, Precious steals her file from the cabinet and learns of Weiss's evaluation of her academic, personal, and social development. The file records her "outstanding achievement" in literacy acquisition, engagement in the learning process, low scores on the TABE[11] test, conscientious parenting, and "her desire to get her G.E.D. and go to college" (118–19). But regardless of encouraging remarks, Weiss determines that "the time and resources it would require for this young woman to get a G.E.D. or into college would be considerable. Although she is in school now, it is not a job readiness program. . . . The teacher, Ms Rain, places great emphasis on writing and reading books. Little work is done with computers or the variety of multiple choice pre-G.E.D. and G.E.D. workbooks available at low cost to JPTA[12] programs." The report concludes that "Precious is capable of going to work now. In January of 1990 her son will be two years old. In keeping with the new initiative on welfare reform I feel Precious would benefit from any of the various workfare programs in existence. Despite her obvious intellectual limitations she is quite capable of working as a home attendant" (119). Accommodating "the new initiative on welfare reform" by tracking Precious into "workfare programs"—ways of handling welfare benefits so that recipients, to remain eligible, must prepare for active employment through education, training, or work experience—Ms. Weiss figures as a cipher for the neoliberal forces that throughout the 1980s and 1990s were radically transforming the city of New York socially and economically. In response, Precious writes in her journal, "Ms Weiss. Fuck her. I don't need her if all she see me for is wiping ol white people's ass. I ain been going threw all this learning to read and write so I be no mutherfucking hom attendint" (121). Based on the experiences of peers and fellow survivors of abuse such as Rhonda, who "usta hafta go all the way out to Brighton Beech wher she work for them mutherfuckers" (121), Precious reads the workfare solution as one more iteration of racial oppression, an intimation of material and intellectual impoverishment completely at odds with the sense of ambition and empowerment nurtured by Ms. Rain. That is, she rightly identifies Weiss as an agent of narrative foreclosure, a harbinger of radical stoppage in the rhythm of school life clearing the way for reasserting the spatial and hierarchical forms of an institutionally racist neoliberalism.

Published in 1996 but set in late 1980s New York, *Push* speaks to a profound moment in US history, when a distinctly neoliberal calculus was being brought to bear on the pathways afforded disadvantaged demographics including youth like Precious. "During the 1990s," explains Mark Harvey, "neoliberal theory became the dominant paradigm informing United States government policies towards poor persons and places"—a time when

> state and regionally administered market-based approaches to poverty and the economic development of distressed areas displaced more federally administrated and needs-based ones. The most consequential was the Personal Responsibility and Work Opportunity Reconciliation Act of 1996 (PRWORA). More commonly known as "welfare reform," PRWORA abolished the federal entitlement to cash relief for poor families by replacing the Aid to Families with Dependent Children (AFDC) program with Temporary Assistance for Needy Families (TANF), a "workfare" program designed to "reduce dependence" on government assistance by setting a 5-year lifetime limit on receipt of relief and requiring household heads to perform "work activities" in exchange for it, among other things. Administratively, PRWORA ... gave the states significant discretion in determining their own TANF policies, how TANF funds were used and how workfare services were administered. (641–42)

As it happens, New York City—the setting for *Push*—emerged as one "well-publicized model" for such reforms (Krinsky, "The New Tammany Hall?" 1088). As John Krinsky argues in "The Dialectics of Privatization and Advocacy in New York City's Workfare State" (2006), the city's mid-1970s fiscal crisis was a watershed moment in the history of neoliberalism. It transformed abstract ideas about *laissez-faire* capitalist management into an array of governance practices. For proponents of neoliberalism in the presidential administration of Gerald Ford and among New York City's financial elite, the municipal balance-of-payments crisis was a window of opportunity to impose privatization and austerity. Adapted from the restructuring imposed on Chile following the 1973 coup, these became models for urban policy under Ronald Reagan and for "structural adjustment" policies of the International Monetary Fund and World Bank. (160)

Krinksy explains that "the widely accepted story of the fiscal crisis in financial and government circles was that the city had resorted to borrowing in the 1970s to meet the demands of expanded welfare rolls, and especially rising labor costs due to recent unionization" (162). When Mayor Rudolph Giuliani came to office in 1994, he "brought with him a strong anti-welfare agenda, and quickly set his special adviser, Richard J. Schwartz . . . to the task of reforming the city's welfare program. . . . The centerpiece of the program was a huge expansion of workfare and a crackdown on eligibility and enforcement of work-requirements"—which amounted to forcing workers to work for compensation below the minimum wage, while leaving them without labor protections, union rights, and grievance procedures (1095–96). As such, when Sapphire pits Precious against Ms. Weiss, mouthpiece of the "new initiative on welfare reform" and advocate for workfare, the novel takes on a strictly critical view of neoliberal governance as it affects the education system, charging it with a failure to care for and to meet the needs of people like Precious—as described by Kwame Okoampa-Ahoofe Jr., "politically neglected, emotionally traumatized and maladjusted but otherwise intelligent, ambitious and highly motivated 'other' Americans" (35).

If at first Precious recognizes Higher Education Alternative simply as a way to "get out" of her mother's house (35), in time she is able to say with conviction that "Ms Rain make me feel good . . . gonna be a good school for me" (55). The "goodness" that follows comes from learning to read and write, working out how to tell her own story, and gaining a sense of belonging with a cohort of similarly disadvantaged young women who work with their teacher in a way that Paulo Freire in *Pedagogy of the Oppressed* (1968) describes as "co-intentional": "Teachers and students (leadership and people), co-intent on reality, are both Subjects, not only in the task of unveiling that reality, and thereby coming to know it critically, but in the task of re-creating that knowledge. As they attain this knowledge of reality through common reflection and action, they discover themselves as its permanent re-creators. In this way, the presence of the oppressed in the struggle for their liberation will be what it should be: not pseudo-participation, but committed involvement" (51). In keeping with Freire's criticism of oppressive learning environments in which students are alienated from their own decision-making, a process bound "to change them into objects" (Freire 66), Ms. Rain's classroom facilitates empowerment and emancipation—and, in Precious's case, a consciously Black emancipation. The stories that Ms. Rain asks her to read, which include biographies of Harriet Tubman and Malcolm X, along with Alice Walker's *The Color Purple* and *Selected Poems* by Langston Hughes, resonate with Precious, who takes Ms. Rain's gist to be that "the way free is hard" (101). In the spirit of works such as *The Color Purple* (as well as texts not mentioned in the novel, including *Narrative of the Life of Frederick Douglass*, 1845, and *Soul on Ice* by Eldridge Cleaver, 1968), Sapphire tells a story of African American uplift by way of literacy acquisition: Precious learns her ABCs (52–66), writes in a journal (69–73), takes a family literacy class (65), gains recognition from the city with a mayor's-office literacy award (82), and exponentially improves her TABE test score from 2.0 to 7.8 (139), all while crafting her life story for a class project (94). Though she finds it hard to tell her story, she finds purpose in writing to be read by Ms. Rain, saying, "thas what had made me really like writing in the beginning, knowing my teacher gonna write me back when I talk to her" (94). Scholars including Michelle Jarman and Laurie Stapleton see evidence of Freirean principles in the written and spoken exchanges between Precious and Ms. Rain, summed up by Stapleton in terms of a "joint responsibility for a mutually developed growth process" (217), an interpretation Stapleton supports with Freire's claim that "arguments based on 'authority' are no longer valid; in order to function, authority must be on the side of freedom, not against it" (qtd. in Stapleton 217). Either way, the portions of the novel reproducing the notes, poems, and responses exchanged between the two reveal the sense of how to write evolving hand in hand with an increasing sense of independence and purpose. At the same time, while the content—comprising heartfelt reflections on Precious's life, health, and abilities—makes clear the developmental value in personal expression, the letter of the text, which eventually includes score-throughs and rewrites, demonstrates an increasing sense of needing to revise for clarity and standard correctness (98–105). In terms of classic composition studies, *Push* seems to make a case for a Freirean process pedagogy,[13] framing the literacy narrative as a story of social uplift and racial emancipation. Still, even if scholars such as Stapleton and Jarman make a point of tracing Freirean influences, contemporary scholars are more likely to emphasize the particularities of Black, maternal, and sexual identity in the context of a survivor community (Elisabeth McNeil, 2012; Jarman, 2012; Riché Richardson, 2012; Silvia Pilar Castro Borrego, 2014; David, 2016).

Although the uplift narrative is disturbed when Precious finds out that she has contracted AIDS from her father (93), Sapphire suggests that her protagonist's writing holds developmental promise in and of itself: neither a trite means of coping with the uncertainty of how long she has to live, nor a pat way of answering the question of "How cum I'm so young and feel so old?" (128–29), but a locus of purpose and direction. Hence the final section reproducing the collaborative class project, titled "Life Stories" (141–77), which comprises, in order, two poems by Precious (reflecting on her routines as a mother and student); prose by classmates Rita, Rhonda, and Jermaine (collectively telling of rape, drug addiction, prostitution, prison, homelessness, jobbing, and school); and one last poem by Precious declaring

> it's a prison days
> we live in
> at least me
> i'm not really free
> baby. Mama. HIV
> where i wanna be where i wanna be?
> not where I AM (n.p., lines 17–23)

In a spirit reminiscent of Wordsworth—whose "Lines left upon a Seat in a Yew-Tree" from *Lyrical Ballads* (1798) appears as an epigraph to *Push*[14]— Sapphire suggests that this "prison days" is not necessarily the be-all and end-all of Precious's existence, an idea articulated in the poem's—and the novel's— closing sentiments:

> HOLD FAST TO DREAMS
> Langston say.
> GET UP OFF YOUR KNEES
> Farrakhan say.
> CHANGE
> Alice Walker
> say.
> Rain fall down
> wheels turn round
> DON'T ALWAYS RHYME
> Ms Rain say

walk on
go into the poem
the HEART of it
beating
like
a clock
a virus
tick
tock. (n.p., lines 50–69)

That the novel closes with an emphasis on rhythms seems right, though we do well to ask why it has carried us from the tempos of school life (classroom routines, grade-level stages, and ruminations on graduation) to the rhythms of a poem that conflates not only clock and virus (as if time is of the essence) but clock, virus, and heart (as if doubts about longevity are inextricable from, if not constitutive of, the rhythms of life). Responding precisely to the question of "where i wanna be where i wanna be?" the poem points to itself, as if to say that here Precious can find purpose by going imaginatively, existentially, and artistically into "the poem / the HEART of it." If literary form did not also overlap with social form here, we might be right in taking this to be one more iteration of the unsustainable—pathological—morbidity that characterized Precious at her most vulnerable and hopeless. But in light of the critical disposition implied in the Hughes reference, the racial emancipation denoted in the Farrakhan line, the personal-political imperative attributed to Walker, and the command to break with poetic convention from Ms. Rain, it seems fairer to say that the reader is primed to recognize a sense of profound, Black teenage resistance in an age of neoliberal workfare. Admittedly, *The Kid* (2011), Sapphire's sequel to *Push*, undoes the tacit romantic optimism of the first book's ending—not so much with its account of Precious's death (depicted in the opening scene of the novel), but in its unfolding tale of her second son, Abdul, whose young life into and through his teens is marred by a comparably unnerving series of sexual and psychological abuses as both victim and perpetrator. At the end of *Push*, however, even though the body of Sapphire's protagonist is precariously poised—at the mercy of a life cycle according to which biological stoppage, likely sooner rather than later, is a given—what might be mistaken for a defeatist withdrawal from social life into literary reflection takes on political resonance: in the last analysis, the poor, Black schoolgirl defies the institutional forces of the city to situate herself not in the field of service work but in the realm of artistic and intellectual labor, where she is poised to disclose the "darkness" and inequity of contemporary American urban school experience.

The Politics of Silence

At this current moment of renewed critical interest in *Push*, scholars tend to read the novel for its affirmations of young identity and development: from noting how Precious "acquires the tools needed to [come] to terms with her mistreated and 'diseased' body, and is able to achieve personal freedom" (Dagbovie-Mullins 435), to describing "Sapphire's grotesque-erotic story" as "a literary act of resistance to deformation, a voicing of black women's agency and inherent/natural value" (McNeil 12); from speculating that "*Push* will be analyzed as a text that counteracts the politics of silence, transforming fear and difference into speech and telling, adding to the liberatory discourses of contemporary Black women writers" (Borrego 147), to arguing that "literacy provides opportunities for Precious to escape the social silence and invisibility imposed upon her by her race, class, and gender, exemplifying a tradition in black women's fiction that links literacy, motherhood, and resistance" (David 173). Slightly more cautious is Jarman's take on Ms. Rain's students:

> Although many of these young women rely upon welfare and other social-service programs for survival, they also realize that they must somehow liberate themselves from the oppressive grip of a system designed to exploit them as cheap labor by sacrificing their dreams and human potential. By the end of the novel and the film Precious has not solved this dilemma, but she has identified and confronted her most immediate oppressors; she has built a network of friends, mentors, and distinct communities of support—her friends at Each One Teach One and groups of other young women diagnosed with HIV and incest survivors; and she has tenaciously claimed a complex though not impossible vision of herself obtaining her GED, going on to college or vocational education to prepare for a profession, and mothering the children who were forced upon her in a way that will rewrite the childhood she endured. (183)

Taking these various claims together, the case for appreciating Precious Jones seems to rest on the character's arc of development (she is "able to achieve personal freedom," and "to escape the social silence and invisibility imposed upon her"), and on the character's political resonance for readers (she represents "a literary act of resistance," in "a text that counteracts the politics of silence . . . adding to the liberatory discourses of contemporary Black women writers"), but not on the character's situational capacity to actually grasp or change the social and institutional structures abusing her ("by the end of the novel . . . Precious has not solved [her] dilemma"). I point this out because in current scholarship on Anderson's *Speak*, I detect an inverse tendency to gauge Melinda by that third criterion—to reject the inward orientation of the character regardless of her arc of development or political resonance.

I am thinking primarily of Angela Hubler's recent study of the young adult rape novel,[15] a genre that I would situate within the larger archive of trauma literature for child and teen readers that began to emerge in the last decades of the twentieth century.[16] In "It Is Not Enough to Speak" (2017), Hubler builds on Linda Alcoff and Laura Gray's analysis of "the discourse of those who have survived rape, incest, and sexual assault" (Alcoff and Gray 261), to make a case for what she calls a "coalitional consciousness" in the young adult rape novel. "Survivor speech," says Hubler channeling Alcoff and Gray, "is liable to be 'co-opted' (261) when it employs a confessional mode that focuses on the 'survivor's "inner" self and feelings . . . rather than . . . a discussion of links to the "exterior" and ways to transform it' (280)" (114). Situating *Speak* in a cluster of works including Adèle Geras's *Watching the Roses* (1991), Sharon Draper's *Darkness Before Dawn* (2001), and Alina Klein's *Rape Girl* (2012), Hubler makes the point that even if such works are informed by the "feminist insistence that women tell the truth about their lives by making public tabooed issues like sexual assault," certain formal—especially structural—elements of the novels undermine the feminist imperative to articulate the personal as political (114).[17] As Hubler sees it, "the feminist emphasis on women's speech, which seeks to politicize female experience by moving it out of the private and into the public sphere, situating the individual's experience within a collective one, is weakened by first-person narration which depoliticizes and privatizes rape by emphasizing the trauma experienced by survivors without exposing the social origins of sexual violence. Speech becomes not a way to communicate an alternative perspective on reality, but to mark healing and signal closure, imposing a happy ending on the painful narrative" (116). In effect, the "focus on the individual psychology of the protagonist and her solitary journey to healing deemphasizes the social factors contributing to rape" (117), to such an extent that "it doesn't represent the social origins of rape, or a solution to it other than women behaving more courageously as individuals" (119). Against this "neoliberal individualism" as she describes it (114), Hubler proposes an alternative archive including Sandra Scoppetone's *Happy Endings Are All Alike* (1978), Alice Childress's *Those Other People* (1989), and Erika Tamar's *Fair Game* (1993), all novels whose "multiple first-person narrators offer a more complete perspective on social reality" (115).

In light of Hubler, it is not hard to identify in *Push* the beginnings of a coalitional consciousness in the final section comprising the "Life Stories" by Precious, Rita, Rhonda, and Jermaine, which collectively attest to a world composed of social and institutional structures within which rape and impoverishment flourish alongside domestic violence, addiction, prostitution, homelessness, and imprisonment. Some reviewers have indeed described *Push* as a "communal autobiography" of Harlem and Bronx school experience (Okoampa-Ahoofe 35), although others have also argued that "the portfolio of student writing that appears at the end" seems out of place—that it "belongs in another, longer novel, one that more fully develops the other characters" (Pemberton 1). In Anderson's defense, *Speak*, too, shares something of that inclination to multiply perspectives—in the words graffitied on the toilet stall wall, a small but catalytic plot device that transposes the micro problem of the survivor's "inner self and feelings" into a macro realm of public discourse. But Hubler's point has less to do with discrete plot devices and more to do with the structural principles informing the novel as a whole, and—above all—their capacity to address the political imperatives raised by the rape plot.

Reading *Speak* as a rape novel, as much as I admire Hubler, I hesitate to divide the archive between multiple-character and first-person narratives on the presumption that a single voice cannot speak to the social implications of crisis. When Hubler invokes Bakhtin to contrast the novel he theorizes as a form "particularly effective in representing competing perspectives on social reality" with "the first-person narration utilized by *Speak* and by many other young adult rape novels [which] frequently results in a univocal, individual, and psychological focus" (114), she omits Bakhtin's larger point: that discourse in the novel, regardless of narrator count, is categorically diverse, stratified, and many-voiced (Bakhtin, "Discourse in the Novel"). Bakhtin's theory is further enforced by Jean-Paul Sartre's claim that any act of writing is not only intrinsically social (what is written is realized only when turned over to the "other") but also ethical if not political: "to speak is to act. . . . If you name the behaviour of an individual, you reveal it to him; he sees himself. And since you are at the same time naming it to all others, he knows that he is *seen* at the moment he sees himself. . . . Either he will persist in his behaviour out of obstinacy and with full knowledge of what he is doing, or he will give it up. Thus by speaking, I reveal the situation by my very intention of changing it. I reveal it to myself and to others *in order* to change it" ("What Is Writing?" 36–37). What Sartre and Bakhtin tell us is that in the context of the novel as a form it *is* enough for some characters to speak—on the understanding that what is said both carries into the social and carries the social with it, affording opportunities for others to act further. Indeed, the afterlives of both *Push* and *Speak*—the extent to which they have facilitated discussions among students, teachers, and critics—confirm that readers can engage with and respond to a first-person narrative exploring the inner life of a rape survivor without mistaking that narrative for a sufficient model of action. So, I see no reason why a novel that emphasizes the rhythmic forms of one individual's recovery cannot also critically bear witness to the hierarchical forms that sustain rape culture.

Hubler, of course, goes against the grain of most Anderson scholars, who tend to read *Speak* as a progressive if not radical novel in its figuring of recovery and self-determination. Early reviewers praised it as a work "illuminat[ing] the experiences of adolescent girls," comprising not only a "portrait of hardiness and resistance" but also an "urgent resolution, which focuses on the need to take the struggle away from the individual girl and locate it in the school and community" (S. Smith 586). Educators such as Janet Alsup, informed by the same critical-pedagogical approach motivating *Push* critics, argued that "speaking out can be an action in its own right. Discourse of resistance, such as Melinda's loud 'NNNOOO!!!' as she fights off Andrew Evans at the end of *Speak*, as well as her eventual decision to narrate her story to her art teacher ('Me: Let me tell you about it,' p. 198) has power and can have a positive effect on material reality" (185). Since then, teachers and scholars have advocated for using *Speak* as a teaching text, whether for preventing sexual harassment (Mark Jackett, "Teaching English in the World: Something to Speak About: Addressing Sensitive Issues through Literature," 2007), or encouraging scholarly engagement (David Aitchison, "The Young Archive & First-Year Writing: Using School Stories to Encourage Students' Scholarly Identity," 2018). Reporting on a study ascertaining whether *Speak* might rehabilitate eighth-grade students' acceptance of rape myths,[18] Victor Malo-Juvera found that "it is possible to change students' attitudes toward rape by using a young adult novel in the context of English language arts instruction. Addressing the topic of date rape through the young adult novel *Speak* . . . afforded an opportunity to engage students and educators alike in changing not only the attitudes of individuals, but also the culture of a school" (422).

Children's literature scholars, too, generally discuss *Speak* as a rich and valuable novel of young adult experience, though there is certainly a tendency to complicate any straightforward reading of Melinda's recovery narrative: when Don Latham teases out the queer subtext of Melinda's strategies ("Melinda's Closet: Trauma and the Queer Subtext of Laurie Halse Anderson's *Speak*," 2006); when Barbara Tannert-Smith speculates on the anxious implications of the adult author of young adult trauma fiction ("'Like Falling Up into a Storybook': Trauma and Intertextual Repetition in Laurie Halse Anderson's *Speak*," 2010); and when Amber Moore detects in Melinda's story an unresolved relationship with the outdoors ("Traumatic Geographies: Mapping the Violent Landscapes Driving YA Rape Survivors Indoors in Laurie Halse Anderson's *Speak*, Elizabeth Scott's *Living Dead Girl*, and E. K. Johnston's *Exit, Pursued by a Bear*," 2018). But, as Jessi Snider notes, "Most critics view Melinda's confession, both in her art and in coming to voice, as a positive aspect of the novel" (305). Taking the time to conceptualize the character of Mr. Freeman, Snider describes "an enabler of healing, coaching his students in the cathartic value of art, who also happens [to] be an authority figure. Though Mr. Freeman acts as art therapist, he does not mandate confession. He hopes only for revelation" (304). Leading with the observation that "Mr. Freeman wants Melinda to speak the language of art, which can also be the language of subversion" (304), Snider reflects on the political possibilities of the art teacher's domain. "Mr. Freeman's classroom does not represent or reflect the language of dominant cultural forces," argues Snider;

> Instead, it encourages the voice of those actively in defiance of those forces. Melinda's confession and speech through art, through creating trees, brings healing, not judgment, punishment, or forgiveness. Learning to manipulate her creativity is like learning to speak an entirely new language for Melinda. The outsider art of an adolescent exists independently of capital and exchange and therefore is external to, and suspect in, a culture where almost everything is commoditized and sold. Mr. Freeman's own art depicting members of the school board openly critiques the hierarchies of power to whom, incidentally, he must directly answer. Despite the positive attention his painting receives in the press, Mr. Freeman, in a moment of clarity and spite, decides to slice his canvas to shreds. His art too exists outside of the capitalistic system of exchange and his willingness to both create and destroy in the name of art disconnects him from capitalism's essential function. (304)

Snider makes strong claims on politics, aesthetics, and young identity here, but what really piques my curiosity is the way in which she sees the teacher in that act of mutilation, which is clearly a correlative of Melinda's self-mutilation, but does not identify him as one suffering from a comparable crisis of identity and expression. Which is to say that, where Snider reads a politics, I read a pathology. Rather than charge Snider with an insufficient reading, I am more inclined to suggest that this is how the novel invites readers to handle Mr. Freeman: while we encounter him as a teacher with saving power for his students, and as a teacher pained in his working life, the book brings closure to the narrative of his saving power (through Melinda's development) but not to the narrative of his professional and pedagogical pain. Although I have argued elsewhere that narratives of lost causes can have political force ("Lost Causes, Affective Affinities," 2015), I think that Mr. Freeman—utterly at odds with his teaching—ultimately models quietism, a claim that leads me to rework Hubler's terms: it is enough for Melinda to speak if what she says enters and transforms public discourses and practices in the school realm, but it is not enough for Mr. Freeman to speak if no one responds—or, rather, if the only responses come when "some newspaper guy" who writes an article on his painting "claimed Mr. Freeman is a gifted genius who has devoted his life to education" (77–78) or "some teachers rumorwhisper he's having a nervous breakdown" (104).

Reading *Speak* as a school story, then, raises a different set of questions about the book's therapeutic and political structures, a claim that applies equally to *Push*. For all of these characters—Melinda, Mr. Freeman, Precious—may well be outcasts, but none is truly "outside of the capitalistic system of exchange." The substantive difference between them, arguably, comes down to how ready they are to name the other "beast," neoliberalism: while all agree on its punishing and pathologizing power, only Precious names and indicts it as such, disclosing the extent to which the language, rhythms, and traumas of domestic violence and sexual abuse overlap strategically with the language, rhythms, and traumas of rightwing ideologies and neoliberal economics. Regardless of their differences, both novels offer optimistic visions of student care and development, but the narrative burden placed on exceptional teachers to intervene in their students' lives, along with the heavy criticism leveled against the institutions of the welfare and education systems, suggests a genre adapting in its own way to the neoliberal ethos of individualism, entrepreneurship, and privatization.

Afterword: On Paratexts

Since its debut in 1999, *Speak* has been reissued in multiple editions, which collectively reveal an evolving set of paratexts framing the story proper—from notes, letters, and poems to author Q&As and resource lists, all designed to augment the political and ethic lessons of Melinda's plight as a survivor of sexual assault. Especially notable is the twentieth-anniversary edition (released in 2019 to coincide with the publication of Anderson's poetry memoir *Shout*), whose paratextual scaffolding radically reworks earlier explanations of where Melinda's story came from. In the 2011 edition, at the back of the book in a section titled "Laurie Halse Anderson Speaks About *Speak*," Anderson attributes the story to a "nightmare" she experienced in her adult life, waking from which she found "a crying girl . . . in my head," whose character and "secret" only revealed themselves in the process of writing. In the 2019 revision of that section, however, she confesses that her own life experience was the source, explaining, "I was raped the summer before ninth grade, and I didn't tell anyone about it for twenty-five years," a confession also made in the brief preface to the graphic novel and that underpins the autobiographical narrative told in *Shout*.

To be sure, the ethics and politics of sexual consent have long been integral to how *Speak* has been framed, marketed, and received, with paratexts such as the poem "LISTEN"—composed "from lines and words taken from the thousands of letters and e-mails that Laurie has gotten in the past twelve years" (2011)—consolidating the book's purpose in serving the survivor community. It is hard, of course, to speak with real certainty of the ethics and politics of any novel when the publishing industry, driven by profits, knows exactly how to capitalize on and commercialize stories of hardship and struggle. Even so, I get the sense that, in spite of marketplace imperatives, *Speak* carries out good work publicly and socially. Crystalizing in the paratexts of the twentieth-anniversary edition—released in the wake of the rise to prominence of the #MeToo movement—Anderson's calling to account takes its place in a field of cultural production making new room for us to question the uneven and antidemocratic ways in which power is distributed. I applaud the political consciousness and social imperative of *Speak*'s paratextual framework: in Anderson's poetic identification with the "sisterclan brotherclan / otherclan" of survivors ("make some noise"); in the foreword, in which Ashley Ford identifies as a teenage survivor of sexual assault committed to speaking out for the freedom to tell the truth (Foreword); in the letter by Jason Reynold to his "younger brother," urging him to understand consent (Afterword); in the section parsing consent as a "kind of speaking up" ("Use Your Voice and Use Your Words"); in the author Q&A, where Anderson confirms her own experiences as a survivor; in the list of sexual violence resources; and in the final comment about censorship. The accomplishment of these texts combined is that they implicate the novel in a properly social exchange: by way of inviting and affording conversations about sexual assault, they encourage reflections on growth, development, and responsibility for the one and the many. As such, whether the critics find certain characters within the novel politically sufficient or not, I contend that the book as it is framed helps to challenge certain aggressive, sexist, and patriarchal forms of power through which neoliberalism has been channeled in recent decades.

NOTES

1. Although *Push* is not marketed by its publisher, Vintage, as a book for teen readers, it is commonly identified as such. As of October 2020, Barnes and Noble's online bookstore gives *Push* an audience age range of fourteen to eighteen years; it appears in the American Library Association's list of "Frequently Challenged Young Adult Books" on its Banned and Challenged Books website (see Peters); on Goodreads, users tag it more often as "young adult" than "adult" fiction, with a ratio of 256 to 69 ("Push by Sapphire," Goodreads); and, as blogs and study sites testify, teachers assign it to high school students in both young adult

and general English courses (see, for example, "*Push* by Sapphire" on *Teaching Children's and Adolescent Literature: A Blog About Teaching Literature For Youth By Youth*, 2010; and the lesson plans on sites such as Bookrags.com, which identifies a target readership of seventh through twelfth grade ("Push Lesson Plans for Teachers"), and Study.com, which correlates the novel with Common Core ELA outcomes for grades eleven and twelve ("Push by Sapphire Lesson Plan").

2. In making this distinction, I borrow from Sally Chivers and Nicole Markotić's introduction to *The Problem Body: Projecting Disability on Film*, when they declare an interest in "analyz[ing] the problematic construction of bodies as essentialized, rather than merely contextualized, contradictions within an ideological framework. Thus we evoke a status that is both discursive and material" (9).

3. Gurdon adapts the phrase *darkness visible* from John Milton's *Paradise Lost* (1667; 1674), which describes Satan's first glimpse of Hell on waking after being cast out of Heaven, along with the host of rebel angels, following their failed insurrection against God: "At once as far as angels' ken he views / The dismal situation waste and wild, / A dungeon horrible, on all sides round / As one great furnace flamed, yet from those flames / No light, but rather darkness visible / Served only to discover sights of woe, / Regions of sorrow, doleful shades, where peace / And rest can never dwell, hope never comes / That comes to all" (bk. 1, lines 59–67, p. 4).

4. At this point, Anderson's narrator is actually pondering a face she could draw for art class, but the speculation is prompted when she sees herself in a mirror and is followed by the observation that "I can't stop biting my lips" (16–17).

5. As Stuckey and Nobel explain, "Over the past decade, health psychologists have cautiously begun looking at how the arts might be used in a variety of ways to heal emotional injuries, increase understanding of oneself and others, develop a capacity for self-reflection, reduce symptoms, and alter behaviors and thinking patterns. Given the ubiquity of creative expression, as well as the relative ease of engagement, the extent to which psychological and physiological effects are sustainably health enhancing is an important area for public health investigation" (254). For applications more specific to the school context, Susan Loesl attests to the benefits of art therapy in addressing a range of concerns including students' transition anxieties, disruptive behavior, and mental health problems (54–55).

6. That said, when Melinda asks not only "was I raped?" (164) but also "did he rape my head, too?" (165), the novel does raise the possibility of psychic or emotional rape, though whether Anderson is suggesting that such a phenomenon can be separated from bodily rape is not confirmed.

7. *G.E.D.* refers to the set of four General Educational Development subject tests used in Canada and the USA to demonstrate academic skills and competencies for the high school level.

8. I borrow this phrase from Caren Irr, who describes the "ideal neoliberal child" as "a largely independent, unparented, and entrepreneurial self defined by consumption habits and individual rights"—functionally, a "social orphan" and an "entrepreneur" (222). For a fuller discussion, see my chapter 5.

9. In "The Dialectics of Privatization and Advocacy in New York City's Workfare State," Krinsky builds on the insights of state and policy theorists Bob Jessop and James DeFilippis to tell of New York's fiscal crisis in the 1970s, which led to a "neocorporatist" politics of governance "based, at least for social provision, on partnerships between the state and non-profit social service providers. Many of these service providers had roots in urban

movements in the 1960s and 1970s" (158–59). Problematically, "many of these groups, which devoted their energies to housing rehabilitation and tenant organizing, became co-opted as specialized conduits for housing redevelopment and low-income housing management. As a result, many abandoned their roles as agitators for broader change" (159). More to the point, "their political claims grew ever closer to the foundational, individualist ideas of neoliberal theory, even as they became a critique of theory-in-practice" (159).

10. Describing Precious's junior high school, Sapphire uses the designation "I.S. 146," indicating an "intermediate" or middle school, which she situates in a locale occupied by a real-life NYC public school: "134th Street between Lenox Avenue and Adam Clayton Powell Jr Blvd" (4), where NYC district school P.S. 175 Henry H. Garnet currently stands. But the exact nature of the new school, known as "Higher Education Alternative/Each One Teach One," is not specified. When Precious shows up, she is told that "'the principal at I.S. 146 already sent your discharge papers and stuff over,' and that "we had to have ahh certain information before we could accept you into the program. Our students have to meet certain income, residential, and academic requirements before we can let them in the program'" (27). But whether the program itself is private, state-subsidized, public, or allied in any official way with the public-school system is unstated.

11. TABE, Test of Adult Basic Education, is a comprehensive test used to assess adult learners' skills and knowledge in core content areas including reading, mathematics, and language.

12. JPTA—either a deliberate or accidental misspelling of JTPA, the Job Training Partnership Act of 1982 instituted under the Reagan administration, one aspect of which was to track disadvantaged or underperforming youths into employment.

13. Process pedagogy: referring to the "process movement" in the teaching of composition and rhetoric, that emerged in the late 1960s and early 1970s, according to which students are encouraged to pre-write, draft, and revise their writing, focusing on process rather than product so as to afford room for critical interventions from teachers and peers. Freire is often cited as an influence on the field of composition studies in general (see, for example, Guerra, "Putting Literacy in Its Place"), including both process pedagogy and the "post-process" pedagogies that have emerged more recently to challenge it (see, for example, Breuch, "Post-Process 'Pedagogy'").

14. In this, Sapphire closely follows the sentiment expressed in the opening lines of Wordsworth's *The Prelude* of 1805, in which the speaker meets a "gentle breeze" and declares, "A captive greets thee, coming from a house / Of bondage, from yon city's walls set free, / A prison where he hath been long immured" (lines 1–8)—carrying an "association of city and prison" that, as Nicholas Roe clarifies, "was familiar to Wordsworth from the Old Testament, from Milton, Thomson, Cowper, and from Coleridge's poems" (98).

15. But I also have in mind Jeremy Johnston's recent study of the young adult girl protagonists in Anderson's *Wintergirls* (2009), Meg Haston's *Paperweight* (2014), and Julie Halpern's *Get Well Soon* (2007), who undergo therapy for eating disorders. Johnston argues that "therapeutic treatments within these texts not only are substitutes for genuine social change, but that they also actively participate in the ideological social pressures forcing these characters into disordered eating behaviors in the first place" (312).

16. See, for example, Katharine Capshaw Smith's "Forum: Trauma and Children's Literature" (2005) and Kenneth B. Kidd's "'A' is for Auschwitz: Psychoanalysis, Trauma Theory, and the 'Children's Literature of Atrocity'" (2005), both of which attest to an increasing presence of trauma narratives in books for children, particularly historical fiction dealing with the atrocities of American slavery, the Holocaust, and 9/11.

17. "The personal is political": a slogan responding to the Port Huron Statement of 1962—the Students for a Democratic Society manifesto, which called for a "personally authentic" politics—and summing up the definitive consciousness-raising principles of the Women's Liberation Movement (Lauret 46–50), the point being a process according to which "personal experiences, when shared, are recognized as a result not of an individual's idiosyncratic history and behavior, but of the system of sex-role stereotyping. That is, they are political, not personal, questions" (Koedt, Levine, and Rapone 280–81).

18. "Burt (1980) defined rape myths as 'prejudicial, stereotyped, or false beliefs about rape, rape victims, and rapists' that create environment hostile to rape survivors (p. 217), while Lonsway and Fitzgerald (1994) defined rape myths as 'attitudes and beliefs that are generally false but are widely and persistently held, and that serve to deny and justify male aggression against women'" (Malo-Juvera 134).

WORKS CITED

Aitchison, David. "Lost Causes, Affective Affinities: Radical Chronotope in the Age of Liberal Narrative." *JNT Journal of Narrative Theory*, vol. 45, no. 3, 2015, pp. 395–418.

Aitchison, David. "The Young Archive & First-Year Writing: Using School Stories to Encourage Students' Scholarly Identity." *Pedagogy*, vol. 18, no. 3, 2018, pp. 295–316.

Alcoff, Linda and Laura Gray. "Survivor Discourse: Transgression or Recuperation?" *Signs*, vol. 18, no. 2, 1993, pp. 260–90, *JSTOR*. Accessed 1 Nov. 2019.

Alsup, Janet. "Politicizing Young Adult Literature: Reading Anderson's 'Speak' as a Critical Text." *Journal of Adolescent & Adult Literacy*, vol. 47, no. 2, 2003, pp. 158–66, *JSTOR*. Accessed 1 Nov. 2019.

Anderson, Laurie Halse. *Shout*. Viking, 2019.

Anderson, Laurie Halse. *Speak*. 1999. Square Fish, 2011.

Anderson, Laurie Halse. *Speak*. 1999. Square Fish, 2019.

Anderson, Laurie Halse, and Emily Caroll. *Speak* (graphic novel). Farrar, Straus, Giroux, 2018.

Bakhtin, Mikhail. "Discourse in the Novel." Translated by Caryl Emerson and Michael Holquist, edited by Michael Holquist, University of Texas Press, 1981, pp. 259–422.

Bishop, Jacquie. "Precious Life." *Lambda Book Report*, September 1996, pp. 12–13. *EBSCOhost*. Accessed 1 Sep. 2019.

Borrego, Silvia Pilar Castro. "Re(claiming) Subjectivity and Transforming the Politics of Silence through the Search for Wholeness in 'Push' by Sapphire." *Atlantis*, vol. 36, no. 2, 2014, pp. 147–59. *EBSCOhost*. Accessed 1 Sep. 2019.

Breuch, Lee-Ann M. Kastman. "Post-Process 'Pedagogy': A Philosophical Exercise," *JAC*, vol. 22, no. 1, 2002, pp. 119–50, *ERIC*. Accessed 1 Nov. 2019.

Capshaw Smith, Katharine. "Forum: Trauma and Children's Literature." *Children's Literature*, vol. 33, 2005, pp. 115–19, *ProjectMUSE*. Accessed 1 Dec. 2019.

Chivers, Sally, and Nicole Markotić, editors. *The Problem Body: Projecting Disability on Film*. Ohio State University Press, 2010.

Cokal, Susann. "Book Reviews." *Review of Contemporary Fiction*, vol. 17, no. 1, Spring 1997, p. 186, *EBSCOhost*. Accessed 1 Dec. 2019.

David, Marlo D. "'I Got Self, Pencil, and Notebook': Literacy and Maternal Desire in Sapphire's *PUSH*." *Tulsa Studies in Women's Literature*, vol. 35, no. 1, 2016, pp. 173–99, *ProjectMUSE*. Accessed 1 Dec. 2019.
"freeman, n." *OED Online*, Sep. 2019, *Oxford University Press*, www.oed.com/view/Entry/74415. Accessed 27 Nov. 2019.
Freire, Paulo. *Pedagogy of the Oppressed*. Continuum Publishing Company, 1997.
Guerra, Juan C. "Putting Literacy in Its Place: Nomadic Consciousness and the Practice of Transcultural Repositioning." *The Norton Book of Composition Studies*, edited by Susan Miller, W. W. Norton & Company, 2004, pp. 1643–54.
Gurdon, Meghan Cox. "Darkness Too Visible." *Wall Street Journal*, 4 Jun. 2011, *Dow Jones & Company, Inc.* www.wsj.com/articles/SB10001424052702303657404576357622592697038. Accessed 1 Jun. 2018.
Harvey, Mark H. "Inside the 'Smoke-Filled Room': Neoliberal Devolution and the Politics of Workfare in the Rio Grande Valley of Texas." *International Journal of Urban and Regional Research*, vol. 37, no. 2, 2013, pp. 641–62, *EBSCOhost*. Accessed 1 Sep. 2019.
Hastings, Matt. "Neoliberalism and Education." *Oxford Research Encyclopedia of Education*, May 2019, *Oxford University Press*. Accessed 27 Nov. 2019.
Hayes, Elisabeth, and Sondra Cuban. "Book Review." *Adult Basic Education*, vol. 8, no. 1, 1998, p. 47, *EBSCOhost*. Accessed 1 Sep. 2019.
Hubler, Angela E. "It Is Not Enough to Speak: Toward a Coalitional Consciousness in the Young Adult Rape Novel." *Children's Literature*, vol. 45, 2017, pp. 114–37, *ProjectMUSE*. Accessed 1 Dec. 2019.
Irr, Caren. "Neoliberal Childhoods: The Orphan as Entrepreneur in Contemporary Anglophone Fiction." *Neoliberalism and Contemporary Literature*, edited by Mitchum Huehls and Rachel Greenwald Smith, Johns Hopkins University Press, 2017, pp. 220–36.
Jackett, Mark. "Teaching English in the World: Something to Speak About: Addressing Sensitive Issues through Literature." *The English Journal*, vol. 96, no. 4, 2007, pp. 102–5.
Jarman, Michelle. "Cultural Consumption and Rejection of Precious Jones: Pushing Disability into the Discussion of Sapphire's 'Push' and Lee Daniels's 'Precious.'" *Feminist Formations*, vol. 24, no. 2, 2012, pp. 163–85, JSTOR. Accessed 1 Dec. 2019.
Johnston, Jeremy. "'Maybe I Am Fixed': Disciplinary Practices and the Politics of Therapy in Young Adult Literature." *Children's Literature Association Quarterly*, vol. 44, no. 3, 2019, pp. 310–31, *ProjectMUSE*. Accessed 1 Dec. 2019.
Kidd, Kenneth B. "'A' is for Auschwitz: Psychoanalysis, Trauma Theory, and the 'Children's Literature of Atrocity.'" *Children's Literature*, vol. 33, 2005, pp. 120–49, *ProjectMUSE*. Accessed 1 Dec. 2019.
Koedt, Anne, Ellen Levine, and Anita Rapone. "Consciousness Raising." *Radical Feminism*, edited by Anne Koedt, Ellen Levine, and Anita Rapone, Quadrangle, 1973.
Krinsky, John. "The Dialectics of Privatization and Advocacy in New York City's Workfare State." *Social Justice*, vol. 33, no. 3, 2006, pp. 158–74, JSTOR. Accessed 1 Dec. 2019.
Krinksy, John. "The New Tammany Hall? Welfare, Public Sector Unions, Corruption, and Neoliberal Policy Regimes." *Social Research*, vol. 80, no. 4, 2013, pp. 1087–118, *ProjectMUSE*. Accessed 1 Dec. 2019.
Latham, Don. "Melinda's Closet: Trauma and the Queer Subtext of Laurie Halse Anderson's *Speak*." *Children's Literature Association Quarterly*, vol. 31, no. 4, 2006, pp. 369–82, *ProjectMUSE*. Accessed 1 Dec. 2019.

Lauret, Maria. *Liberating Literature*. Routledge, 1994.

Levine, Caroline. *Forms: Whole, Rhythm, Hierarchy, Network*. Princeton University Press, 2015.

Loesl, Susan. "Introduction to the Special Issue on Art Therapy in the Schools: Art Therapy + Schools + Students = ?" *Art Therapy*, vol. 27, no. 2, 2010, pp. 54–55, *EBSCOhost*. Accessed 1 Dec. 2019.

Malo-Juvera, Victor. "*Speak*: The Effect of Literary Instruction on Adolescents' Rape Myth Acceptance." *Research in the Teaching of English*, vol. 48, no. 4, 2014, pp. 407–27, *EBSCOhost*. Accessed 1 Dec. 2019.

McNeil, Elizabeth. "Un-'Freak'ing Black Female Selfhood: Grotesque-Erotic Agency and Ecofeminist Unity in Sapphire's *Push*." *MELUS: Multi-Ethnic Literature of the U.S.*, vol. 37, no. 4, 2012, pp.11–30, *ProjectMUSE*. Accessed 1 Dec. 2019.

Milton, John. *Paradise Lost*. 1674. Penguin, 2000.

Moore, Amber. "Traumatic Geographies: Mapping the Violent Landscapes Driving YA Rape Survivors Indoors in Laurie Halse Anderson's *Speak*, Elizabeth Scott's *Living Dead Girl*, and E. K. Johnston's *Exit, Pursued by a Bear*." *Jeunesse: Young People, Texts, Cultures*, vol. 10, no. 1, 2018, pp. 58–84, *ProjectMUSE*. Accessed 1 Dec. 2019.

Okoampa-Ahoofe, Kwame, Jr. "Sapphire's 'Push' Is No Pushover." *New York Amsterdam News*, vol. 87, no. 45, 1996, p. 35, *EBSCOhost*. Accessed 1 Aug. 2019.

"pathological, adj." *OED Online*, Sep. 2019, Oxford University Press, www.oed.com/view/Entry/138800. Accessed 1 Sep. 2019.

Pemberton, Gayle. "A Hunger for Language." *Women's Review of Books*, vol. 14, no. 2, 1996, p. 1, *EBSCOhost*. Accessed 1 Aug. 2019.

Peters, Patricia. "Frequently Challenged Young Adult Books." *Banned & Challenged Books*. Aug. 2016. American Library Association. www.ala.org/advocacy/bbooks/frequentlychallengedbooks/YAbooks. Accessed 5 Oct. 2020.

"Push by Sapphire." *Goodreads*. Goodreads, Inc. www.goodreads.com/book/show/71332.Push. Accessed 5 Oct. 2020.

"*Push* by Sapphire." *Teaching Children's and Adolescent Literature: A Blog About Teaching Literature For Youth By Youth*. 11 Apr. 2010. Blogger. www.teachingyalit.blogspot.com/2010/04/push-is-story-of-claireece-precious.html. Accessed 5 Oct. 2020.

"Push by Sapphire Lesson Plan." *Study.com*. www.study.com/academy/lesson/push-by-sapphire-lesson-plan.html. Accessed 5 Oct. 2020.

"Push Lesson Plans for Teachers." *Bookrags*. Bookrags, Inc. www.bookrags.com/lessonplan/push-sapphire/#gsc.tab=0. Accessed 5 Oct. 2020.

Richardson, Riché. "*Push*, *Precious*, and New Narratives of Slavery in Harlem." *Black Camera*, vol. 4, no. 1, 2012, pp. 161–80, *JSTOR*. 1 Dec. 2019.

Roe, Nicholas. "Revising the Revolution: History and Imagination in *The Prelude*, 1799, 1805, 1850." *Romantic Revisions*, edited by Robert Brinkley and Keith Hanley, Cambridge University Press, 1992, pp. 87–102.

Rountree, Wendy A. "Overcoming Violence: Blues Expression in Sapphire's *Push*." *Atenea*, vol. 24, no. 1, 2004, pp. 133–43, *EBSCOhost*. Accessed 1 Aug. 2019.

Sapphire (Lofton, Ramona). *Push*. Vintage Books, 1996.

Sapphire (Lofton, Ramona). *The Kid*. Penguin Press. 2011.

Sartre, Jean-Paul. 1948. "What Is Writing." *"What Is Literature?" And Other Essays*, Harvard University Press, 1988, pp. 25–47.

"school board, n." *OED Online*, Sep. 2019, Oxford University Press, www.oed.com/view/Entry/172529. Accessed 27 Nov. 2019.

Smith, Sally. "*Speak* by Laurie Halse Anderson." *Journal of Adolescent & Adult Literacy*, vol. 43, no. 6, 2000, pp. 585–87, *JSTOR*. Accessed 1. Dec. 2019.

Snider, Jessi. "'Be the Tree': Classical Literature, Art Therapy, and Transcending Trauma in *Speak*." *Children's Literature in Education*, vol. 45, 2014, 298–309, *EBSCOhost*. Accessed 1 Dec. 2019.

Stapleton, Laurie. "Toward a New Learning System: A Freirean Reading of Sapphire's *Push*." *Women's Studies Quarterly*, vol. 32, nos. 1–2, 2004, *EBSCOhost*. Accessed 1 Aug. 2019.

Stuckey, Heather L., and Jeremy Nobel. "The Connection Between Art, Healing, and Public Health: A Review of Current Literature." *American Journal of Public Health*, vol. 100, no. 2, 2010, pp. 254–63, *EBSCOhost*. Accessed 1 Dec. 2019.

Tannert-Smith, Barbara. "'Like Falling Up into a Storybook': Trauma and Intertextual Repetition in Laurie Halse Anderson's *Speak*." *Children's Literature Association Quarterly*, vol. 35, no. 4, 2010, pp. 395–414, *ProjectMUSE*. Accessed 1 Dec. 2019.

Wordsworth, William. *The Prelude, 1799, 1805, 1850*. Edited by Jonathan Wordsworth, M. H. Abrams, and Stephen Gill, W. W. Norton & Company, 1979.

CHAPTER 4

Detention, Dis-ease, and Death

Contemporary School Experience in Popular World Cinema

While the school story is certainly capable of representing the more affirming and promising sides of school experience—as in Gary D. Schmidt's *The Wednesday Wars* (2007) and Gordon Korman's *Ungifted* (2012)—the genre has thrived, at times quite spectacularly, on tropes of sadism, spite, and stupidity. This is especially true in the realm of cinema: even the most romantic school films, from Peter Weir's sentimental classic *Dead Poets Society* (1989, USA) to John Carney's song-driven *Sing Street* (2016, Ireland), default to characterizing school as a realm of fear and failure. In this way, they share much with earlier, grittier fictions such as Robert Cormier's *The Chocolate War* (novel 1974; film adaptation by Keith Gordon 1988, USA) and Stephen King's *Carrie* (novel 1974; film adaptation by Brian De Palma 1976, USA), two school novels prominent in the ranks of banned books because of their violence.[1] Also adapted for the big screen, such works helped to consolidate the tropes of bullying, alienation, and revenge characteristic of more recent school films from around the world including *Batoru Rowaiaru/Battle Royale* (2000, Japan), *Dek Hor/Dorm* (2006, Thailand), *Gosa: Piui Junggangosa/Death Bell* (2008, South Korea), *F/The Expelled* (2010, UK), *The Final* (2010, USA), *Detention* (2011, USA), and *Cooties* (2014, USA)—all of which conceive the school environment as a locus of frightful alienation.

As noted, this is nothing new; even seminal works of moral school fiction from the mid- to late nineteenth century invested imaginatively in an underside of school life driven by brute and anti-intellectual sensibilities; think no further than the archetypal bully from *Tom Brown's Schooldays* (1857), Flashman, a minor character resurrected for modern readers as the antihero of George MacDonald Fraser's *Flashman Papers* series (1969–2005). Victorian schoolboy fiction, in fact, owed a tremendous debt to the penny-dreadful tradition for its lurid and violent sensationalism. "Following the success of *Tom Brown* and *Eric*," explains Robert J. Kirkpatrick,

> the 1850s saw the development of periodicals for boys, initially respectable and heavily didactic, but in the 1860s somewhat overshadowed by the emergence of the "penny dreadful," cheap weekly boys' papers full of farce, gothic horror, exaggeration, brutality and melodrama, the precursors of today's "pulp fiction." Such was the popularity of the first two or three of these more sensational boys' papers that an intense circulation battle broke out amongst a group of London publishers, with a bewildering number of titles being published over the following 40 or so years. Many of these papers contained school stories, some of which were later re-issued as separate weekly serials and then as complete volumes. A few, such as *Jack Harkaway's Schooldays*, became as famous in their time as their more modest precursors. (Kirkpatrick, *Encyclopaedia* 2)

John Springhall confirms that *Harkaway* author Samuel Bracebridge Hemyng, building on the innovations of Edwin Harcourt Burrage (known as "the boys' Charles Dickens"), played a critical role in consolidating the "school story formula . . . in the penny dreadful periodicals of the 1870s, '80s and '90s" (81). Introduced in the *Boys of England* weekly, "'Jack Harkaway' was to remain a household name until at least the end of the century and a long-term money-spinner for Edwin Brett, his first but not only publisher. Parents, clergy and teachers considered the stories both immoral and mischievous. . . . When Brett began to serialize 'Jack Harkaway' in the summer of 1871, the circulation of *Boys of England* soared from 150,000 to 250,000 copies. . . . as a result, Harkaway became probably the best known and most popular schoolboy hero since the creation of Tom Brown himself" (86–87). To give readers a taste of the penny-dreadful strain, Springhall recounts a scene from *Jack Harkaway's Schooldays* (1880), in which the headmaster's wife, accidentally injured by a stone thrown by Jack, orchestrates his whipping: "Let him take off his jacket and waistcoat," she instructs master Mole, "and then tie his hands with that string, and haul it up tight, so that his hands will be over his head, and he will be standing upright and unable to escape you. . . . Cane the little wretch as severely as you can, and go on until I tell you to leave off. It will be some satisfaction to me to see him suffer what he so well deserves"—whereupon Mole proceeds to flog Jack until the cane is bloody and the boy has fainted (Hemyng 87–91). Reveling in such scenes of cruel punishment, the school story in its popular weekly form capitalized on the idea of school as a site of sensational violence.

As Kirkpatrick tells it, the penny-dreadful provided one of three paths along which the boys' school story developed, the other two being "the antithesis of the 'penny dreadful' . . . the evangelical school story" and "the trend that had been popularised, if not established, by *Tom Brown*," whose later authors "posed similar moral problems to those tackled by the evangelical writers but who enlivened them by setting them amongst what became the more familiar motifs of the school story—sport, dormitory feasts, fagging, fights, breaking bounds and so on" (2–3). To be sure, as Isabel Quigly documents, the classic works of boys' boarding-school fiction could just as easily tap the penny-dreadful vein, with a book such as *Stalky & Co.* (1899) reviled by critics for its "vulgarity . . . brutality . . . savagery," its characters indicted as "mucky little sadists," "repulsive and disgusting" (110). But it is also worth remembering that Quigly's last word on the classic school story is that it collapsed in "farce" (276), suggesting a tone not too far removed from "the clean-fun, knock-about type of story" (Orwell 95) or the "jolly rabble" (Lamb 68) that, respectively, marked popular boys' and girls' fiction of the early to mid-twentieth century. Such descriptions, no doubt sweeping, do not prepare us for what M. O. Grenby describes as the "brutal, almost Orwellian, education in conformity" inaugurated in the 1970s by Cormier's *The Chocolate War* (Grenby 112), in which Catholic schoolboy Jerry Renault is caught in the middle of a power struggle between sadistic teachers and a vicious student society converging to manipulate a chocolate sale fundraiser. While aware that earlier children's literature critics such as Peter Hunt held Cormier responsible for "demolishing the school story," Grenby rightly acknowledges that, "despite Cormier's nihilism, the school story still flourishes" (112). More remarkable for the present study is the extent to which *The Chocolate War* seems to signal a radically altered sense of modern school experience, in which the psychosocial threads of young life are made to weave with murderously competitive self-interest as well as totalizing marketplace imperatives. For this reason, I take *The Chocolate War* to be a landmark narrative of young identity in the violent age of neoliberalism, a critical touchstone for understanding more recent, popular representations of school experience.

Admittedly, some might argue that school is by no means a privileged site for sensational fiction, whether for print or screen: that, along with the house, apartment block, shopping mall, hospital, asylum, church, factory, underpass, country road, woodland, island, and rustic shack, it figures as just one of countless spaces that—as a familiar but idiosyncratic enclosure—affords unnerving possibilities. Indeed, as Jessica R. McCort spells out in her study of horror in children's literature and culture, "frightening fictions for children and young adults have been holding center court for the last few decades in American publishing houses, suggesting that the turmoil our society has experienced in recent years—war, school shootings, political backbiting, rampant consumerism, economic collapse, and ever-increasing debt and the mortgage crisis—has trickled down to feed our country's youths' obsessions with horror fantasies" (9). As McCort observed in 2016, recent "best-selling young adult series include the *Harry Potter* books, *The Hunger Games* novels, the *Divergent* trilogy, the *Maze Runner* books ('If you aint scared you aint human'), *The Mortal Instruments* books, and the *Miss Peregrine's Home for Peculiar Children* novels, all of which participate in the horror tradition through their use of stock horror characters, body horror, the monstrous, and a variety of other tropes and themes drawn from the genre" (9). But in much the same way that the abandoned asylum has its own capacity to chill, to the extent that what ought to be a site of care and recuperation emerges as a scene of dissolution and torture, so does the school: a place, ideally, of encouragement and development yet repeatedly given to stories of psychological duress, existential angst, and social contagion. Thus, rather than count the school environment as just one of any number of spaces that might fit the horror bill, I want to consider it as a locus of concern in its own right with its own particular set of affordances.

In this chapter, I turn attention to two school stories for the big screen, the English-subtitled edition of *Battle Royale* (Japanese ninth graders forced by the government to fight to the death) and *Cooties* (American elementary school teachers on the run from zombie students), to consider how the rhetorical conventions of horror, sometimes mixed with comedy, are used to parse the school experience as a sum of alienating and totalizing forces. Though officially restricted to different age groups, rated R15+ and R, respectively, both films potentially draw the same late-teen audience on account of the proliferation of teenage protagonists (*Battle Royale*) and the traditional association of horror-comedy (*Cooties*) with teen viewers.[2] More to the point, they invite comparative analysis for their shared obsessions with old-school discipline and the excessive standardization and competitiveness that, along with growing precarity for teachers, have become hallmarks of public education under neoliberalism. Taking up Levine's theory of contending wholes—the general recognition that formal enclosures serve in various ways to contain, constrain, and determine fields of social, political, and aesthetic activity alike, and the more particular insight that such forms "may be nested inside one another," each being "capable of disturbing the other's organizing power" (16–17)—I explore the spatial imaginary in the neoliberal-era school film to consider the ways in which punishing enclosures in these movies provide opportunities for reinforcing or deconstructing damaging constructions of young identity and development. Informed by Mary Helen Immordino-Yang's research on emotional thought (*Emotions, Learning, and The Brain: Exploring the Educational Implications of Affective Neuroscience*, 2015) and Constance Flanagan's understanding of youthful civic engagement (*Teenage Citizens: The Political Theories of the Young*, 2013), I look at popular cinematic depictions of student and teacher suffering and dis-ease to ask what it means when the developmental, social, and ethical possibilities of formal education come under hyperbolic duress—when prevailing logics suggest the need to escape, rather than graduate, from the bounded whole of the school.

Battle Royale: "Fight for Survival and Find Out If You're Worth It"

Following a class of Japanese ninth graders abducted by the government during a school trip, removed to a remote island, and instructed to fight to the death until only one remains, Kinji Fukasaku's 2000 cult horror *Battle Royale* (screenplay by Kenta Fukasaku; English subtitles unattributed) hardly reads like a school story in the usual sense. If measured by the realist criteria conventionally used to define the genre by scholars such as Kirkpatrick ("The school occupies at least one-third of each novel, although in the vast majority of cases it is either the whole novel or at least half" [*Bullies, Beaks* 4]), or Grenby ("It is set almost entirely in school; it takes the relationships between the scholars and their teachers as its primary focus; and it contains attitudes and adventures which are unique to school life" [90]), it might seem to miss the mark entirely. Yet, much like Koushun Takami's 1999 novel (translated into English by Yuji Oniki) which it adapts, *Battle Royale* stands out as one of the most thought-provoking assays of emotional and moral crisis informing school experience in the age of neoliberalism. While it unabashedly exploits the school demographic for horror-shock value, it deserves attention for the ways in which it questions what has been for many critics a mainstay of school fiction: school spirit. Read against the realist grain, *Battle Royale* emerges as a powerful allegory of students and teachers navigating the social relations and moral development critical to school experience, probing what it means for students to know and trust their peers, their teachers, and the wider human community in an age of exaggerated individualism.[3]

Like the later *Hunger Games* series by Suzanne Collins (novels 2008–10; film adaptations 2012–15), often read by critics and fans alike as a *Battle Royale* redux,[4] Fukasaku's *Battle Royale* provoked cries for censorship because of its graphic depictions of children as perpetrators and victims of deadly violence.[5] In addition to sharing fundamental plot elements, *Battle Royale* and *The*

Hunger Games show comparable interest in exploring the moral relationship between the one and the many, along with the ways in which dominant logics—especially those cultivating individualism at the expense of social empathy—try to overdetermine that relationship. While I have suggested elsewhere that Collins's series gives readers productive opportunities for exploring intersections of young identity, political consciousness, and ethics of care ("*The Hunger Games*, Spartacus, and Other Family Stories: Sentimental Revolution in Contemporary YA Fiction," 2015), I here contend that *Battle Royale* is more persuasive than *The Hunger Games* in justifying for the young audience the crisis of competitiveness. That is, although both authors speculate similarly on the potential of the state to control the masses by inducting their children into a cutthroat realm of competitive individualism, Collins imagines a future in which that individualism is imposed artificially upon the realm of childhood (children do not provoke the punishments meted out by the state), whereas Takami reveals a world in which it arises organically from the realm of childhood itself (children provoke the punishments meted out). While both craft allegories, Takami more than Collins invites us to recognize that our children and their school environments are complicit with the deadly competitive cultural logics associated with neoliberalism.

In the English-language subtitled release, Fukasaku's *Battle Royale* begins with a brief account of (implicitly Japanese) economic and cultural collapse at the turn of the millennium, according to which, "10 million were out of work. 800,000 students boycotted school, and juvenile crime rates soared. Adults had lost all confidence, and now fearing the youth, they eventually passed the Millennium Educational Reform Act, AKA the BR Act." The narrative of adult-youth conflict is soon dramatized in a scene from a school hallway: a teacher emerging from a boycotted classroom is inexplicably knifed by a student, a boy, who drops his knife and runs off; the teacher then limps to a sink, where, washing the blood from his hands, he looks meaningfully at a girl student who witnessed the assault and picked up the knife. This episode, which exemplifies the epidemic of youth crime, prompts the state to pass the BR Act, an authoritarian means to instill fear in the youth and so keep them in their place: under the act, a fixed number of randomly selected ninth-grade classes from across the nation are abducted, each class taken to its own remote location where the students are forced to fight one another to the death. This year, a class from Shiroiwa Junior High, which includes the boy (Kuninobu) and girl (Noriko) from the hallway scene, sets out by bus on what appears to be a study trip, only to be plied with a knockout gas en route and stolen away; when they wake they find themselves, along with two unknown "transfer students," in a strange classroom; all are wearing electronic collars. When the BR instructor (Kitano) enters, along with armed guards, we recognize him as the teacher wounded by Kuninobu. To orient the students, Kitano plays an instructional video, in which an unnervingly chipper young woman explains with visual aids how they are on an island "about 10km in diameter," which has been divided by grid lines into smaller areas; at fixed times in the next three days, designated squares will become "danger areas" from which the students must flee or their collars will explode; as the novel clarifies, the purpose is to shrink the field of conflict and force the students into confrontation (61). Along with a backpack containing random weapons and supplies, each student is given a map and a compass. To justify the program, Kitano tells the class, "you don't respect adults," adding, "life is a game. Fight for survival and find out if you're worth it." In blunter terms: "Today's lesson is you kill each other off till there's only one of you left. Nothing is against the rules." Declaring that if more than one student is alive after three days, the collars will explode and all will die, Kitano himself gets the game underway by killing two students including Kuninobu before releasing the class, one boy and one girl at a time, out onto the island terrain.

In the opening movement from the junior high school to the island, spatial thinking plays a critical role for grasping how power works here: the riotous space of the hallway, in which the students terrorize the teacher, gives way to the deceptively safe space of the bus, which transitions to the uncannily familiar space of the classroom—soon revealed as ground zero for an island terrain strictly managed so as to contain, compromise, and destroy the student body. Following Levine, it is not hard to recognize a method of organizing the students by way of the absolute power of the bounded whole: not only is the unruly student body diverted from the rampant space of their old school into the authoritarian space of the island, that same body is situated in such a way within the enclosure so as to turn against itself. The point of the containment, it seems, is to undo the more affirmative emotional relations connecting the students. As it turns out, the bounded whole of the island enclosure figures as a relatively successful, if nefarious, method of organizing the student experience: of the forty-two students conscripted, not counting the two killed by Kitano, six die by suicide and thirty-two are murdered by peers (though, of the thirteen who kill, two are responsible for more than half of the total deaths), leaving only two to make it off the island safely—Shuya (the primary protagonist-narrator of the novel) and Noriko. Since Shuya kills twice during the program, once accidentally and once intentionally, Noriko is the only one who does not fall into the "trap" as Shuya, in the novel, calls the program (62). Yet the closing scene of the film, when Shuya hands Nobu's knife back to Noriko before they go on the run, suggests that both have internalized the murderous sense of suspicion cultivated in the island enclosure. In other words, even though they escape the bounded whole of the island and seem to defy the rule of individualistic absolutism, their sense of themselves as fugitives is tainted with the emotional residue of that enclosure.

The question is, Why imagine the social life of the school community in this way? With a nod to affective and social neuroscience, why boil the emotional relations of schoolchildren down to not only the most basic but also the most negative forms: fear, disgust, sadness? One possible answer is suggested by a *New York Times* editorial from 1986, in which Fred M. Hechinger reported on the arrest of a fourteen-year-old junior high school student in Tokyo for "striking a classmate in the face 20 to 30 times," an incident that "came shortly after a 13-year-old boy in the same school, Nakano Fujimi High, committed suicide after persistent attacks by his classmates." The article discusses a crisis in bullying, citing a *Japan Times* editorial that attributed mounting student violence to the fact that "these young people lack a sense of future, much less past." For Hechinger, however, the problem was less abstractly existential and more specifically educational. Noting a third incident, he tells of how two fifteen-year-olds "attacked a classmate because they felt he was spending too much time preparing for one of the many competitive examinations. The boy had to be hospitalized." "Competition," Hechinger argues, "is fierce for grades needed for admission to elite schools and universities, which, in turn, hold the key to the best jobs and careers. Young people in Japan know that their futures are determined, often unalterably, by their early performance in school. Bullying becomes part of the competition." Compounding the crisis, as Hechinger sees it, "Japanese parents . . . tend to consider corporal punishment in school as part of a sound education, a feeling still shared by many Americans," even though "there is much evidence that children who have been subjected to the officially sanctioned violence of corporal punishment often seek revenge by turning violently on weaker youngsters." Speculating that "perhaps there is a lesson for Japan and the United States," Hechinger signs off with the warning that "there are serious risks in placing children into social, educational pressure cookers, under threats of dire physical or psychological consequences of failure."[6] Whether or not we are persuaded by Hechinger's portrait of the schoolchild as innately violent and volatile, that very possibility is precisely what motivates *Battle Royale*. And rather than presume an epidemic of bullying in general, better to recognize highly specific forms of bullying that correlate with the competitive pressures burdening the curriculum shaped by neoliberal educational policy.

Perhaps unsurprisingly, the rhetoric of the "pressure cooker" to describe Japan's competitive education system figures prominently in discussions of Fukasaku's *Battle Royale*, early critics in particular reading the film as a timely commentary on a critical juncture in modern Japanese history when crisis in school experience coincided with both economic decline and a disturbing escalation in youth violence. Andrea Arai, for example, reads the film against a fraught background of events ranging from Japan's economic devastation following the Second World War, through the period of recovery and growth known as the "economic miracle," to the eventual bursting of that bubble followed by recession, which "led to a deluge of discourse on the impending 'decline' (*suitai*) and 'collapse' (*hōkai*) of the nation" (370). Under the assumption that the "miracle" owed much to a certain cultural resilience,

> during the first years of the twenty-first century, the focus shifted dramatically in the Japanese media onto what became known as the collapsing classrooms (*gakkyū hōkai*), failing homes (*katei hōkai*) and strange kids (*hen da kodomo*) of the new millennium. These descriptions of decline were filled with the details of the frightening deficiencies of academic ability, physical strength and social skills among the young, on the one hand, and their excesses of desire for commodities and death on the other. As examples in the media of the moral and physical decline of the youth preoccupied national interest, a new credence was lent to government proposals for the need to strengthen and revitalize the population. (370)

As Arai tells it, a matrix of problems including "school refusal," "bullying," "inner-school violence," and "fatherless homes" prompted Japan's Ministry of Education to overhaul the education system; that decision was also informed by a survey of popular attitudes to the Kobe child murders of 1997 (when a fourteen-year-old schoolboy from the city of Kobe killed and decapitated an eleven-year-old boy with a handsaw and a ten-year-old girl with a hammer), which found that a high proportion of secondary school students sympathized and even identified with the killer (371). According to Arai, the reforms heralded a neoliberal turn for Japanese education in that they cleared the way for a form of governance that "transfers the responsibility (though not necessarily the means of power) for more of school and local management to the individual and individual community, thereby reducing the financial burden (and blame for problems in the system) on the federal government" (372). Like Hechinger, Arai connects the broad political-ideological climate with the "'examination wars' (*juken senso*)" in the schools, which began to take on a new tenor: "In the post-bubble economy, despite the rhetoric of the end of competition, in education reform, the new reality of survival is that not all will reach the top, but those who do, like the kids in the film, will have to engage desperately (*hisshi ni*) to become worthy competitors for Japan in the amorphous battlefield of the global economy" (374). As Tony Williams explains in his study of the film, "By ninth grade, students have to compete ferociously in nationwide examinations for placement into the more prestigious secondary schools that guarantee eventual entry into quality higher education," during which time "high-school students face great emotional pressures that often result in suicides" (133). To make his point, Williams draws attention to one scene in particular: "When the anxiety-ridden Motobuchi confronts Shuya and Noriko late in the film, he insanely repeats an algebra formation in a parody of rote learning and announces his intention of surviving the Battle Royale; in order to 'go to a good school,' he will kill as many of his former classmates as possible" (133).

Reading *Battle Royale* as a fiction of the emotional life of the schoolchild in an age of hyperbolic, competitive individualism—a framework also informing *Gosa: Piui Junggangosa/Death Bell* (2008, Korea), which follows an elite class of students preparing for a college entry exam suddenly subjected to a deadly game of survival—it is telling that Takami and Fukasaku do not describe the same web of cause and effect. Whereas the novel figures the schoolchildren as, in the first instance, innocent victims of an experimental military program ("Battle Experiment No. 68 Program") operated by a dictator-led "Republic of Greater East Asia," as noted, the film opens with a vision of the students as inherently feral and responsible for the sense of national collapse. That said, both works—like *The Chocolate War* a quarter century earlier—insist on a nuanced reading of young, psychosocial identity: in the film, for example, some students (Kazuo) are psychotic killers, enjoying the killing for killing's sake; some (Mitsuko) are pathological killers, victims of childhood abuse enjoying an opportunity to lash out; some (Shuya) are anguished killers, killing accidentally or reluctantly in self-defense; some (Shogo) at times refuse to kill when they have the chance; some (Yoji) opt out of killing others by killing themselves; some (Ryuhei) collaborate with others to prevent kills; some (Shogo) sacrifice themselves so that others might live; and some (Shinji) unite with others to sabotage the program.

If Levine is right, that "aesthetic and political forms may be nested inside one another ... and that each is capable of disturbing the other's organizing power" (16–17), it seems appropriate to acknowledge the formalist implications of the range of personalities in *Battle Royale*, each grasping the order of things in its own way, each presupposing its own ideal pattern of human action and interaction. Levine's pluralistic approach compels us to recognize how certain oppressed demographics, though under duress in real ways, might nevertheless wield power. One of her examples, though far removed from the present study, is a case in point: a 1298 decree by Pope Boniface III resulted in the cloistering of nuns in medieval Europe, a situation that "drastically restricted these women's movements and their access to donors and influence, while striving to limit sexual temptations and scandals" (37). Yet, as Levine documents, nuns like these came to occupy a privileged place in the "hierarchy of spaces within the church," where they "could cast themselves as especially holy—indeed as more capable than their male counterparts of gaining access to miraculous experience" (37). As tempting as it is to find a comparably hopeful counterpoint in a school film like *Battle Royale*, any such interpretation would misread the dystopian tenor of the film as a whole. On the one hand, the spirit of resistance and ethics of care represented by Noriko (who never kills), Shuya (who protects Noriko), and Shogo (who helps Noriko and Shuya to escape) emerge as powerful alternatives to the individualistic logic of the program. Indeed, especially if viewers are familiar with romantic and horror conventions, it is not hard to read *Battle Royale* as a film with a satisfying conclusion, since it ends with the program hacked, the soldiers withdrawn, Kitano killed, and Shuya and Noriko escaping: literally, against the odds, two young, tender comrades escape a plague of violence and beat the system; symbolically, the bounded whole of the island enclosure is breached, teaching us that absolutism can fail and that resistance is useful. On the other hand, since forty out of forty-two students perish along the way and the last two survivors have internalized the logic of the BR Act, with that romantic reading we fall into the same trap that Shuya cautions against, imagining that the survival of the one (or the few) somehow justifies the punishment or degradation of the many. As in George Orwell's *Nineteen Eighty-Four* (1949), the consummate fiction of state-citizen dystopia, there is an apocalypticism to *Battle Royale*, one that in the last analysis offers no viable alternative form of power. Structurally, nothing has changed. That such apocalypticism has been brought to bear on a school story for the twenty-first century ought to give us pause.

Rather than get snagged on the objection that the actual institution of the school plays only a small part in *Battle Royale*, better to acknowledge that its relative absence exaggerates the sense that school experience has come unhinged from its traditional, formal purpose and democratic promise. When it does appear—as the feral space of the junior high, as the militaristic space of the island classroom, or as the nostalgic space of the junior high gym where the students once played basketball together—it tells of a cohort derailed from the growth and development conventionally favored by democratic educators. "Schools," Mary Helen Immordino-Yang reminds us, "are social contexts. Each school is a community that functions inside a broader culture, and the social and emotional experiences that children have as members of a school's culture will shape their cognitive learning" (72–73). In the political terms of Constance Flanagan's work on teenage citizenship, schools function as "mediating institutions" or "mini-polities," so-called "to emphasize the fact that it is through their experiences in these local, proximal, contexts that teens formulate ideas about their membership rights, and obligations as citizens in the broader polity. In other words, adolescents' concepts of themselves as citizens, as members of the body politic, are built up via their memberships in groups and institutions—peer groups, schools, community-based institutions—spaces where they enact what it means to be part of a group, that is, exercise the prerogatives and assume the responsibilities of membership in the group or institution" (18). In Fukasaku's *Battle Royale*, the constant presence of the school uniforms, along with the remembrances of the school itself, strongly suggests that school experience remains the touchstone for understanding the emotional crisis at the heart of this story. Specifically, in spite of the authoritarian mechanism overdetermining young identity here, it is a peer crisis, a cohort crisis, which is to say that the real interest lies not in the trap as such, but in the trap as a litmus test, a means of forcing to the surface innate psychosocial qualities. In the novel, for instance, Shuya sets out making distinctions between the "insanity" of the program and "the bonds of love" the program "consume[s]" (65); but when a peer, Yoshio, makes an attempt on Shuya's life, the problem is reconfigured along new lines: as Noriko puts it, "I mean, you have no idea who might turn against you" (82). As such, like *The Chocolate War*, *Battle Royale* might be said to comprise not so much a school story but an anti-school story: not dispensing with school experience, nor simply negating it, but making a case for recognizing the detachment of school in its ideal form as locus of development from the emotional life of the child. If, as the columnists suggest, there are strict correlations between competitiveness and violence in school, an accelerated gravitation toward individualism at the expense of solidarity, then it seems reasonable to read Takami and Fukasaku as making critical contributions to understanding that crisis—a crisis in turn correlating with a broader spread of neoliberal principles favoring competitive individualism, aggressive market thinking, and entrepreneurialism over educated, democratic citizenship.

To good effect, again like *The Chocolate War*, *Battle Royale* unsettles its audience, which I would argue has less to do with penny-dreadful sensationalism and more to do with Orwellian moral quandary. For if Shuya is read in the same tradition as Jerry Renault, and both Shuya and Jerry in the same tradition as Winston Smith, then the school story in the age of neoliberalism seems to be reshaping the meaning and value of violence in profoundly political ways. Yet Shuya and Jerry diverge when we acknowledge that the school, which figures as the quintessential (if fiercely contested) mini-polity in *The Chocolate War*, becomes residual in *Battle Royale*, a place remembered and, in that remembrance, deconstructed. That is, in light of how the program turns out, the final flashback to the basketball game makes it difficult for viewers to take the students' former innocence or camaraderie for granted. So, the audience, too, becomes complicit with the culture of suspicion, encouraged to look beyond the positive expressions for hints of unrest or hate. It is as if, regardless of state interventions, the problem was always within the cohort—though whether that speaks to an Orwellian understanding of the totalizing state-citizen relationship, or an anarchic mistrust of the institutional community, remains ambiguous. Put another way, quite at odds with the radical spirit of the novel, expressed in the last chapter when Shuya declares, "Some day I'm going to tear this country down" (614), Fukasaku takes an ambivalent stance on the layering of economic, educational, and cultural crises: he perhaps makes a case for rehabilitating a school system compromised by competitiveness and cramming, but he could just as easily be suggesting a need to disestablish school experience all together.

"It's Not the End of the World. It's Just High School."

At its best, horror cinema has a knack for giving voice to the underside of the social imaginary, fixating on unsettling encounters in ways that speak to fraught real-life conflicts between individuals, types, or groups. Read affirmatively, the disturbance on which horror rests is valuable to the extent it compels audiences to find the fearful watching experience meaningful—to appreciate that fear, of all possible affects, might afford a productive lens through which to reflect on, say, the nature of school experience. A comparable claim is made by Jay McRoy in his introduction to *Japanese Horror Cinema* (2005), in which he reads dominant trends in contemporary Japanese cinema—from the "avenging spirit" film to the "giant monster" film—as "engag[ing] a myriad of complex political, social and ecological anxieties" (1); these range from "recent transformations in the national economy begetting an influx of women in the workforce" to the "dread of mass destruction, mutation and the environmental impact of pollution resulting from rapid industrialisation" (4). Not long after *Time* magazine's Lev Grossman described the zombie as "the official monster of the recession" (qtd. in Vint 172), Torie Bosch made a similar case in her *Slate* article "First, Eat All the Lawyers" (2011), a landmark essay on the contemporary mania for zombie stories in print and on screen. Exploring the ways in which popular shows such as *The Walking Dead* (2010–ongoing) distinguish between socioeconomic classes in their relative capacities for practical survival, Bosch argues that "the zombie apocalypse is a white-collar nightmare: a world with no need for the skills we have developed. Lawyers, journalists, investment bankers—they are liabilities, not leaders, in the zombie-infested world. (The exception to this rule, of course, is doctors.)" For Bosch and McRoy, horror is a deadly serious business, speaking of and to a troubled sense of life in the twenty-first century.

At its worst, horror cinema is not so much gratuitous (that is, emptied of meaning) as hatefully gratifying, both reveling in and rationalizing fantasies of doing physical, psychological, or ecological damage. Whether or not, as T. S. Kord argues, "horror films, particularly those showing evil children, are more concerned with guilt than fear," that "they are also, and perhaps more importantly, guilt trips" (5), horror cinema at its worst dramatizes and aestheticizes a realm of strange feeling. Read negatively, the disturbance on which horror rests becomes unfettered from the social contract; the point is not to sting us, gadfly-like, into thinking expansively or responsibly about the meaning and value of the human community but to persuade us in the bluntest terms that there is no such community. Violently at odds with its deadly serious sister, seriously deadly horror gives license to the most misanthropic and antisocial acts imaginable. Still, while some horror films explicitly gravitate toward one or the other of these extremes, it seems fair to acknowledge that some—like *Battle Royale*—encompass both, thriving on the disclosure as much as the deconstruction of the imagined world of punishment.

The additional trouble with horror cinema, for the present study, is the extent to which it routinely exploits the young demographic, figured variously as innocent victim or sinister conspirator. According to Kord, "If uncanny or killer kids raise their ugly heads in other films as well, they are practically ubiquitous where we would most likely look for them: in horror" (4). More specifically, as Catherine Lester relates, "The presence of evil or mysterious children is a common feature of horror films for adults, so much so that [film theorist Robin] Wood categorizes children as one of the groups of 'others' in horror who signify that which society fears or represses. As such, uncanny children in adult horror films tend to be treated with ambiguity and suspicion" (31). From Regan MacNeil in *The Exorcist* (1973), Damien Thorn in *The Omen* (1976), and the Grady Twins in *The Shining* (1980) to Isaac Chroner in *Children of the Corn* (1984), Sadako in *Ring* (1998), and Toshio in *The Grudge* (2002), horror cinema's child characters either play on social expectations that children need to be saved from worldly corruption or exploit social fears that the child itself is an embodiment of evil. Either way, the distressed, disturbed, or monstrous child has become a mainstay of mainstream horror, a fact that also holds for the subgenre of school horror, and especially the American school horror. Following the innovations of Wes Craven's *Scream* (1996)—a film that broke new ground by meta-theatrically making the clichés of horror cinema integral to developments in plot, character, and theme—recent school horror movies figure schools and colleges as consummate breeding grounds for the sociopathic vengeance with which horror in general is so often infatuated: Joey Stewart's *The Final* (2010), for example, tells of bullies tortured, mutilated, and murdered by their former victims, while Joseph Kahn's *Detention* (2011) tells of a student so disgruntled as to become a serial killer with an apocalyptic appetite for destruction. Compared to Johannes Roberts's British-made *F/The Expelled* (2010), in which anonymous youth in hoodies terrorize and murder a handful of teachers and staff in a near-empty school, *Detention* appears familiar to the point of clichéd in its mix of schlock horror and acerbic comedy. At the same time, even though *F/The Expelled* is just as dependent on clichés—its hooded youth characterized as archetypal bogeymen—its noir treatment offers an unusually despondent glimpse of school experience, shedding an eerily critical light on teacher dispositions and pedagogical practices (not to be confused with the "torture porn" treatment of *The Final*, which is differently dark). Put another way still, there is a distinct lack of humor in *F/The Expelled*, an observation that takes on more meaning when we acknowledge the extent to which popular school horrors like *Scream* and *Detention* rely so much on humor. To be sure, even *Battle Royale* has its comic touches, most obviously in the casting of Takeshi Kitano—a stand-up comedian well known to Japanese audiences—in the role of sadomasochist Kitano. But whatever comedy informs *Battle Royale*, that film's heavy appeals to gravitas and pathos set it apart from the camp, kitsch, and droll horror films with which American audiences are more familiar.

Cooties: "A Line Has Been Crossed; You Can't Eat the Teachers, Man!"

Drawing in part on the sass and satire of conventional coming-of-age, high school movies, and in part on the tongue-in-cheek, camp theatrics of schlock horror, recent zombie films such as Gregg Bishop's *Dance of the Dead* (2008), Alex Craig Mann's *Detention of the Dead* (2012), and especially Jonathan Milott and Cary Murnion's *Cooties* (2014) raise timely questions about school communities and solidarity in the twenty-first century. Though *Dance* and *Cooties* received restricted (R) classifications under the Motion Picture Association of America (MPAA) ranking system, and *Detention* is labeled for 18+ on popular digital download platforms, all three adapt horror-comedy traditions associated with younger audiences. As Chris Yogerst notes, "The mainstream success of films like [Mel Brooks's 1974] *Young Frankenstein* and [Stan Dragoti's 1979] *Love at First Bite*, and the near-cult status accorded to [George A. Romero's 1978] *Dawn of the Dead* by horror fans, opened the way for undead horror filmmakers to incorporate broad comedy and satire, knowing that their target audience would not only 'get,' but quickly find, comfort and enjoyment in the result" (170). Citing Andrew Tudor's work on postmodern horror, Yogerst reminds us that

> the horror-comedy films (and horror films with comic elements) that proliferated in the 1970s and 1980s were . . . aimed squarely at the youth market. Teenagers' reputation as enthusiastic, indiscriminate consumers of horror films—established in the 1950s, when low-budget horror films became staple programming at drive-in theaters—made them the ideal target audience. Having already seen the same genre conventions play out in dozens of formulaic, low-budget horror films, they were well-prepared both to get the joke and to appreciate the mockery. (171–72)

To borrow from Cynthia J. Miller and A. Bowdoin Van Riper's characterization of John Landis's *An American Werewolf in London* (1981), a horror-comedy influencing the tradition of films peaking with *Scream*, the contemporary zombie comedy distinguishes itself by "weaving caustic dialogue and black humor so thoroughly into the horror that the two bec[o]me inseparable" (xviii).

If the emergence of the American school story as a zombie comedy can be understood as a development in the history of Western horror cinema, the recasting of the zombie-comedy as a school story can just as easily be read as a telling development in the history of school fiction, a crossing of genres affording new expressions of school experience qualified by unprecedented—and ridiculous—degrees of fear, disgust, and duress. Parsing the intersection of school experience and zombie outbreak, *Dance of the Dead* is perhaps the weaker cousin to *Detention of the Dead* and *Cooties*, telling a story of cemetery corpses reanimated by toxic waste from a local power plant that rise from their graves to converge on a high school prom; while the horror scenario affords opportunities to explore school demographics, especially in the dynamic between popular and unpopular cliques, pedagogically the outbreak is a matter of happenstance. Commenting more deliberately on school experience, *Detention of the Dead* throws a group of well-worn stereotypes—geek, goth, jock, cheerleader, stoner—together in detention right when a zombie outbreak hits their school, forcing them to forget their differences in their struggle to stay alive. The satire is strong when, needing to hole up "somewhere no one goes to," they set their sights on the library, and again when they find they are trapped and one student realizes, "So we're completely cut off from the rest of the world," to which another replies, "Wow, if this isn't a commentary on the current state of public education, I don't know what is." Horror tropes serve the school story well here, an observation confirmed when one character notes that the student body already comprised "a bunch of mindless zombies before any of this happened." Yet, as in *Dance of the Dead*, the outbreak itself ultimately figures as an interlude in campus life: it appears from nowhere, accelerates enough to wreak havoc and compel action, and dies back under military intervention. What sets *Cooties* apart is how the contagion, though originating outside the school, opens up a critical perspective on teacher-student interactions organic to the school experience.

Scripted by Ian Brennan, writer of popular comedy-drama television series *Glee* (2009–2015), and Leigh Whannell, writer of torture-porn film *Saw* (2004), *Cooties* takes a jaded look at a school community marked by neurodevelopmental, professional, and social deficits. The opening sequence introduces a grisly theme of contamination: a diseased chicken is graphically strangled, plucked, dismembered, pureed, and made into chicken nuggets, which are then shipped out to Fort Chicken Elementary, Illinois, to be served for lunch.[7] After eating a gangrenous-looking nugget, one girl, Shelly, falls ill: her skin shows signs of ulceration, her breathing is labored, and she appears stupefied until class bully Patriot (the villain of the film, played by Cooper Roth) yanks her hair so as to tear a chunk of rotting scalp away, at which point she turns feral and bites him. Between Shelly, Patriot, and his friend Dink, the virus spreads voraciously through the school following two strict biological imperatives. First, for those yet to reach puberty (all but two of the students), their brains begin decomposing so that—according to teacher Doug (played by Whannell), who performs an autopsy on one deceased zombie child—"They can run, jump, eat, but they're not human anymore, not really"; meanwhile, for those who have passed through puberty (primarily teachers and custodians), infection brings on nothing more than flu-like symptoms. Second, whereas contaminated students are satisfied with infecting, rather than killing, their peers, they make a point of dismembering and eating the teachers. Arguably, this segregation of younger and older demographics signals a shift in the contemporary horror-comedy tradition represented by *Scream* and more recent films such as Ruben Fleischer's *Zombieland* (2009). As Yogerst points out, a film like *Zombieland* is able to dispense with expository content that acquaints the audience "with why the film's world is the way it is. It takes for granted that the audience—like the characters—knows that getting bitten by a zombie means becoming one; that zombies, despite their shambling and slow-witted appearance, are a mortal threat, particularly in large groups; and that carefully constructed, scrupulously observed rules are the key to survival" (175). Unlike *Zombieland*, *Cooties* does in fact need to explain the way the world is—by way of Doug's autopsy, or his examination of an injured teacher's feces—because the conventional rules do not apply: getting bitten by a zombie here does not necessarily mean becoming one.

As in *Battle Royale*, the outbreak of violence in *Cooties* seems less like the sudden intrusion of extrinsic forces and more like the exacerbation of intrinsic decline, the virus exaggerating an inner logic within the school system that figures schoolchildren as hostiles. Hence, the dismal scene glimpsed by substitute teacher Clint (played by Elijah Wood) before the outbreak: when he enters his classroom and finds his students taking prescription pills (for attention deficit hyperactivity disorder, ADHD); when one student, Patriot, introduced as an older child "held back," misreads Clint's name on the chalkboard as "cunt"; when Patriot discloses that he is surfing pornography on his smartphone and, refusing to hand over his phone, threatens to accuse Clint of molestation; and when Patriot and Dink set about goading and bullying Shelly, an interaction peaking with her feral reanimation. As one reviewer notes, "Real teachers may find [*Cooties*] an apt allegory for the zombielike charges in their classrooms" (Genzlinger). More to the point, although student disengagement and student malaise are by no means new phenomena, *Cooties* gives them a distinctly neoliberal twist by reading them as inextricable from the rise of teacher precarity.

While rhythmic forms underpin the developmental subtext of *Cooties*—in that the effects of the virus are contingent on natural cycles of human maturation—the zombie narrative dispenses with the fluid, temporal form of the developing human, replacing it with a bifurcation of physiological forms fixed on either side of the pubescent line: here, a naturally grown adult; there, a monstrously mutated child. Complementing this interest in bounded forms, as in *Battle Royale*, the conflict also crystalizes as a problem in and for the spatial imaginary: in part because the filmmakers question the safe, nurturing, and playful spaces of childhood represented by the canteen, classroom, playground, nursery, and (off-campus) entertainment center, revealing them as sites of distress for adults; and in part because the contagion narrative figures the school enclosures variously as sites of refuge, terror, and entrapment. One memorable sequence comprises a montage following the outbreak in the playground when all the children outside have been infected and the vice principal (played by Brennan) and at least two teachers have been attacked, ripped apart, and eaten. At this point, what has been a dialogue- and character-driven narrative peaking in gross-out zombie action transitions into a parodic art-house sequence of slow, quiet shots in the playground with the children awfully at play: we see spring riders with bloody handprints; feet splashing through puddles of blood; gory children climbing frames and pushing swings; on a merry-go-round, a blood-soaked basketball at rest beside human organs; a bike on the blacktop, wheel-spokes sporting a severed finger noisemaker; a child studying a dismembered forearm; on a playframe platform, eyeballs rolled like marbles; a child skipping with a rope of intestines; and a severed head on a swing-ball rope—all interspersed with extreme close-ups of a child's face (presumably Patriot's) staring, smiling, breathing. Since school playgrounds normally serve to facilitate and augment students' intellectual, physiological, and emotional development,[8] it is worth recognizing that this zombie playground remains a place of free, spontaneous play. For Miller and Van Riper, this retention of normalcy is not necessarily normal in films "combining well-crafted horror and well-crafted comedy," where "the cumulative effect is to dissolve normalcy into chaos, overturn the rhythms of the characters' everyday lives, and undermine their (and the audience's) expectations about the bonds that join causes and effects, creating—at least until the resolution of the plot—a world in which (seemingly) anything, no matter how outlandish, can happen at any moment" (xv). The *Cooties* montage makes the opposite case: the zombified children retain their core characteristic of childishness, the horror effect resting on their continuing disposition to play according to the rhythms and characteristics of their young lives—a sentiment confirmed when Wade exclaims to his fellow survivors in the school, "We're on a total lockdown, we have been breached, and there are little cootie kids right out there in the hallway who're willing to rip your fucking face off with their little teeth, with their little baby teeth." Such scenes and sequences prepare the audience to sympathize with the teachers not only as they become physically endangered in the present moment but also as they reflect more broadly on their professional precarity.

Played against the infected space of the playground, the school building—initially represented by the teachers' lounge, where most of the surviving adults witness the carnage outside, but soon encompassing a gamut of hallways, classrooms, library, music room, maintenance rooms, and air ducts—figures as a disaffected space where the teachers, forced to hole up, reflect bitterly on their working lives. Lying low in the library with fellow teacher Lucy (played by Alison Pill), Clint—who until now has claimed he is a novelist returned to his hometown to write—outs himself as a failed teacher regressively returning to both his hometown and his own former elementary school. "I thought I would have free time to write on my free time," he confides, "but as it turns out there is no free time. Teaching's the hardest job in the world. And I would look out at the kids in my class and I found myself getting jealous of them. They have the whole world ahead of them, their whole lives ahead of them, and they have all these opportunities that have already passed me by," to which Lucy replies, "I would tell you you were wrong, but you sort of have a point." Played straight and with pathos, the scene sympathetically characterizes the teacher as resentful of young identity and youthful possibility, lamenting the extent to which the profession, because all-consuming, has stunted his growth and robbed him of promise. Meanwhile, elsewhere in a basement space, Wade exclaims to the rest of the survivors, "You know what I want? I want to know why my brother-in-law makes ten times what I do. You know what he does for a living? He makes giant foam fingers for football games. Like, you tell people you're a teacher, and they look at you like, 'oh, you must have wanted to do something else and couldn't get anything else.' It's like, 'fuck you, man, I'm raising your kids. I love my job. Teachers deserve respect.'" Unlike Clint, Wade indicts not the profession as such but its status in the marketplace and in the popular imaginary, describing a field devalued in spite of its service to the nation. Whether we are genuinely invited to think that parents might be to blame for the cultural slighting of teachers, and whether we read Wade's declamations of love and respect as sincere or ironic, at such moments the zombie narrative literalizes a profound sense of professional disappointment—not by suddenly transforming the school into a site of unprecedented conflict, but by revealing it as the site of conflict it always already was. Simultaneously true to and strangely at odds with Levine's theory of forms, the zombie narrative in *Cooties* clashes spectacularly with everyday reality precisely by holding a mirror up to that reality. In other words, though dispensing with the dream of intellectual growth symbolized by the library (where Clint and Lucy discover student backpacks filled with prescription drugs), and done with the commitment to sustaining the school symbolized by the janitor's basement (where Wade et al. appropriate school equipment to "suit up" for the zombie encounter), the school in the form of beleaguered fortress affords a productive space for these teachers to search their souls, resolve to escape, and prepare to vent their frustrations on the singular demographic of the prepubescent student body. This is not to say that it is characteristic of neoliberalism to pit teachers against students, although neoliberalism does increasingly divide the school community between students primed to think ambitiously about entering the marketplace of work, commodities, and ideas, and teachers disillusioned if not burned out by the actual tenor and practices of that same marketplace.

Stressing the divergence of prepubescent and postpubescent bodies, *Cooties* reconfigures the single developmental form of the human organism as two distinct, contending wholes. As such, it comes close to contemporary accounts of recent films in which, as Sherryl Vint observes, "zombies emerge more clearly as our possible selves, as abjected and expelled parts of the body politic" (173). At the same time, however, it resists the idea that, as Jen Webb and Samuel Byrnand put it, "there is always something 'nearly me' about the monster" (112). The all-important detail for Webb and Byrnand is "how easily we are infected with 'zombieness': a mere bite from one of them, or a drop of their bodily fluid into my eye, and I too become zombie. The transmission of the 'virus' between us and them indicates our closeness: viruses (mostly) travel between like species, and the job of the average zombie seems to be to (1) eat as many people as possible and (2) infect as many people as possible" (112). As applicable as these characterizations are to the "average" zombie, *Cooties* disrupts any such identification—by casting the prepubescent child as a biological other, focalizing the zombie narrative primarily through adult protagonists, and making the point that "I"—whether represented by Wade, Lucy, or especially Clint, who is bitten—do not become zombie.

Like *Battle Royale*, *Cooties* tells the story of a youth crisis that, manifesting in the specific realm of school experience, signals the collapse of the nation—suggested when radio and television broadcasts reveal the spread of the contagion across the country and when the broadcasts themselves are sinisterly cut off in mid-flow. Unlike *Battle Royale*, *Cooties* does not make a nuanced exploration of childhood dispositions. Rather, in fact, the film summarily writes off childhood as a whole, an idea broached when Wade beats Dink to death; confirmed when Clint, in a pickup truck, runs Patriot down and impales him on the cock hood ornament; underscored when, fleeing downtown, Wade traps infected children in an entertainment center (another play space), douses them in gasoline, and sets them on fire, saying, "naptime, motherfuckers"; and reiterated when the gang rides off in the pickup with Clint asking, "Where we going?" to which Wade replies, "Somewhere kids don't want to go." Bearing in mind that film scholars have long read the big-screen zombie as a figure of troubled consumption in the capitalist era, of all possible demographics, *Cooties* singles out and demonizes the schoolchild as *the* hyperbolic consumer. "Capitalism," argue Webb and Byrnand, "works as an analogue of zombiedom because it too is predicated on insatiable appetite and the drive to consume. But it is not necessarily the mindless consumption of the zombie" (116). Furthermore, as Steven Shaviro notes, building on the scholarship responding to George Romero's shopping mall–centered *Dawn of the Dead* (1978), the "life-in-death of the zombie is a nearly perfect allegory for the inner logic of capitalism, whether this be taken in the sense of the exploitation of living labor by dead labor, the deathlike regimentation of factories and other social spaces, or the artificial, externally driven stimulation of consumers" (7–8). True to these accounts, *Cooties* is certainly concerned with both the plight of the child as a consumer (hungry for pills, porn, and petty violence) and its monstrous appetite (hungry for human flesh). But the empathetic core of the film has less to do with the schoolchild as such and more to do with its effect on the teaching profession. Above all, the zombification of the student body forces the teachers to acknowledge their own precarious positions in not only the short-term struggle for bare life, but also—and more importantly at the level of social commentary—in the long-term struggle for existential certainty, economic security, and cultural prestige. Sadly, tragically, all such concerns increasingly inflect the experiences of real-life teachers at all levels under neoliberal administrations that dismantle unions, phase out tenure, and turn teachers into contingent and itinerant workers without prestige, security, benefits, or any lasting sense of institutional belonging.

Embodying in the physically immature child the sense that there is something intrinsically and dangerously uneven in the teacher-student relationship, *Cooties* restates a problem in and for the social as a problem in and for the state of nature: teachers are in conflict with feral children rather than, say, administrators, policy makers, or cultural gatekeepers. What's more, in much the same way that free-market apologists describe the marketplace as a natural order of things best left to its own mechanisms of supply and demand (as stipulated in the work of Milton Friedman), *Cooties* makes no case for intervention beyond addressing the exigencies of bare life. Indeed, in lieu of a state power that is able to contain the youth epidemic, *Cooties* celebrates the ragtag heroics of idiosyncratic individuals poised to make blows that, while symbolic, have no social efficacy whatsoever. Casting the realm of school experience as one of self-survival in the face of indiscriminate, irrational violence, *Cooties* takes its place in what Shaviro calls the "usually reactionary" genre of "survivalist" horror (10). And distinctly at odds with recent trends in horror-comedy films for young audiences ranging from *Beetlejuice* (1988) to *Hotel Transylvania* (2012) and *ParaNorman* (2012), in which "distrust of difference softens into acceptance, and the 'threat' posed by the arrival of the undead comes to be seen (by the newly enlightened living) as an opportunity for growth and new friendships" (Miller and Van Riper xxiii), *Cooties* argues that innate drives and social emotions play out unevenly across immature and mature bodies, making a case, finally, for the purging of young students from the working lives of teachers. To grasp the implications here, consider Immordino-Yang's description of "children's bodies, brains, and minds" as "meaningful partners in learning. Each child builds on his or her biological predispositions, his or her 'nature,' grappling with his or her own biological and psychological 'self' as a platform on which to understand the thoughts and actions of other people, both peers and teachers" (73). If this description is accurate—which I believe it to be—then *Cooties* affords a worrying vision of the immature body as stunted in its capacity for self and social growth.

Conclusion

Half lament for a beleaguered profession and half revenge fantasy, *Cooties* shares much with *Battle Royale* in its conception of students as latent monsters and of teachers as latent authoritarians. In obvious ways, both films speak to anxieties over the violence raised by the late 1990s Kobe child murders in

Japan and the Columbine High School massacre in the USA, incidents that inaugurated an era of youth violence not only still underway[9] but also bound up with neoliberal worldviews—evidenced in the calls for action following the 2018 mass shooting at Marjory Stoneman Douglas High School in Parkland, Florida, where a nineteen-year-old expelled former student armed with a semiautomatic rifle killed seventeen students, teachers, and staff workers and injured seventeen others (see Laughland et al.). As teen survivors agitated for gun reform, rightwing legislators called for arming the teachers, a textbook neoliberal move putting the burden of responsibility on the individual—in this case, the teacher—rather than the institution or the state, while dispensing with any real ethics of social care (see Strauss). We do well to acknowledge that films such as *Cooties* and *Battle Royale*, while entertaining audiences with images of students as bearers and victims of death and disease, tacitly suggest the impossibility of social trust and democratic belonging in a time of alienating and devastating school experiences.

Though diverging in their affiliations, *Battle Royale* for the students and *Cooties* for the teachers, both films give up on the ideal of school as a healthy learning environment, suggesting anxieties about "the unravelling of the social contract" and "the belief that people generally are fair and trustworthy rather than out for their own gain" (Flanagan, 161–62). As Flanagan notes, social trust is a variable, contingent on values informed by personal experience and historical events. Arguing that "trusting others is an important foundation for democratic governance" (162), Flanagan makes the point that "democratic dispositions—to be open-minded, to trust others, to be committed to finding common ground that transcends differences—do not happen by default. People are not born with democratic dispositions. Rather, formative institutions and experiences are critical" (163). By this account, social trust "is a basic for cooperation. When people have faith in fellow human beings, they need not spend time and energy maintaining their own competitive advantage. Instead, they can turn attention and devote time to working together for the benefit of the whole community" (163). Hence Flanagan's interest in young life, in the ways in which young people learn the difference between trust and vigilance, and in the critical role played by school environments in nurturing the dispositions that make the social contract of a democratic society viable. "Feelings of trust in other people," argues Flanagan, "should be learned by specific kinds of interactions with fellow human beings: (a) interactions through which youth gain a sense of group (collective) identity, a feeling of being part of a mutually caring community; and (b) interactions that broaden the circle of humanity with whom youth have contact and allow them to extend their beliefs about how trustworthy people in general are to groups of people with whom they rarely have contact" (171). By way of contrast, both *Battle Royale* and *Cooties* make a point of disavowing social trust, a fact that should prompt us to ask what it is that audiences enjoy so much about these and similar films—although, if the five-hundred-plus reviews of *Cooties* currently on Amazon's US platform are representative, audience members seem to relate to the vision of a divided school community while appreciating the teacher-on-student violence for its authoritarianism (students deserve to be punished) and its entertainment (killing zombie children is funny).

While *Cooties* is a zombie film by genre, both *Cooties* and *Battle Royale* are zombie films by their politics—a zombie politics being one that, in the words of Henry Giroux, "views competition as a form of social combat, celebrates war as an extension of politics and legitimates a ruthless Social Darwinism in which particular individuals and groups are considered simply redundant, disposable" (2)—though, admittedly, *Battle Royale* is more resigned to, rather than reveling in, any "disposal." But while it is tempting to read the monstrous child in these films as a cipher for troubling or troubled students, better to acknowledge how it speaks to a broader sense of academic precarity in the neoliberal era. In keeping with recent scholarship on the zombie as a metaphor for grasping not only the "living death" of higher education, but also a need for "reanimating—or at least 'undeadening'—current debates about the future of the sector" (Whelan, Walker, and Moore 3), *Cooties* and *Battle Royale* imagine teachers to be just as unsettled as their students in terms of self-realization, vocational purpose, and social worth. Which is to say that the same concerns with young identity and development motivating scholars such as Flanagan and Immordino-Yang apply equally to the ostensibly mature bodies, brains, and lifeways of the adult teachers represented by Kitano, Clint, and Wade. In other words, Flanagan's assay of "the developmental imperatives of late adolescence" maps just as easily onto the plights of adult characters forced to doubt their professional choices, to confront "the competitive nature of life," and discard trust in general for extreme vigilance (174)—characteristics fitting the profile implied in real-world calls to arm our teachers. The difference is that the filmmakers more honestly recognize the impossibility of school under such conditions, hence the narrative imperatives to escape, if not deliberately break up, the realm of school experience. If anything is learned it is that a school system that divides its community between the separate spheres of neoliberalism, between the domain of the ideal (students primed to believe that by merit they will succeed in a viciously competitive marketplace) and that of the real (teachers reduced to drudges) is simply unsustainable.

In giving up on the school community, school stories steeped in zombie politics play at taboo-breaking, not only sensationally in their images of murderous teachers and monstrous children, but more subtly by dispensing with the belief in education on which the democratic social contract depends. "The more people develop and educate themselves," claim Immordino-yang and Antonio R. Damasio,

> the more they refine their behavioral and cognitive options. In fact, one could argue that the chief purpose of education is to cultivate children's building repertoires of cognitive and behavioral strategies and options, helping them to recognize the complexity of situations and to respond in increasingly flexible, sophisticated, and creative ways. In our view, out of these processes of recognizing and responding, the very processes that form the interface between cognition and emotion, emerge the origins of creativity—the artistic, scientific, and technological innovations that are unique to our species. Further, out of these same kinds of processing emerges a specific kind of human innovation: the social creativity that we call morality and ethical thought.... Human ethics and morality are direct evidence that we are able to move beyond the opportunistic ambivalence of nature; indeed, the hallmark of ethical action is the inhibition of immediately advantageous or profitable solutions in the favor of what is good or right within our cultural frame of reference. In this way, ethical decision making represents a pinnacle cognitive and emotional achievement of humans. At its best, ethical decision making weaves together emotion, high reasoning, creativity, and social functioning, all in a cultural context. (35–36)

Like Flanagan, Immordino-Yang and Damasio remind us of the politics and ethics bound up in emotional and cognitive development, and of the central role given to the school environment in shaping democratic dispositions and moral action. Laying aside the question of actual influence, of the extent to which school horror movies promote or encourage certain kinds of behavior in the real world, films like *Cooties* and *Battle Royale* make it easy for audiences to imagine school as a locus not of promise and growth but of crisis and regret, a space void of academic learning, emotional development, social trust, and moral growth. And in doing so, they seem to make it easy to rationalize the wholesale abandonment of education. Which is to say that, wittingly or not, the school horror film in the age of neoliberalism does the devil's work of disinvesting in the idea of school as a public and democratic good.

NOTES

1. According to the American Library Association, *Carrie* was still one of the one hundred "most frequently challenged books" of 1990 to 1999 ("100 Most Frequently Challenged Books: 1990–1999") while *The Chocolate War* was still one of the top ten "most challenged books" as recently as 2009 ("Top Ten Most Challenged Books").

2. In its original Japanese theatrical release, *Batoru Rowaiaru* was classified R15+ (see Herskovitz, "The 'Battle' Rattle"), which officially restricted the young audience to older teens. In the USA, in its mainstream DVD distribution and on streaming platforms such as Amazon Prime, *Battle Royale* is labeled "unrated," a designation variously used to avoid censorship from ranking bodies, or as a marketing tool to rouse curiosity in implicitly questionable content. As I discuss later in this chapter, while *Cooties* was rated R by the Motion Picture Association of America (MPAA), it takes its place in a genre of horror-comedy films long marketed to and associated with teenage audiences (See Yogerst, "Rules for Surviving a Horror Comedy" 171–72).

3. Reading *Battle Royale* this way, I follow *Sight & Sound* reviewer Kim Newman, who argues that, "as in *Lord of the Flies*, an obvious precedent, we are in the territory of allegory rather than a study of real world child violence. The teenagers of Class B do not represent the likes of the Littleton, Colorado trenchcoat mafia, the killers of Jamie Bulger or genocidal teenage Khmer Rouge soldiers" (37); but I resist Newman's conclusion that "instead they are ordinary kids, representing people we are or might be, and their actions in extraordinary circumstances are supposed to expose the range of human behaviour on the edge of societal madness," arguing instead that the film tackles not a general but a particular crisis specific to the realm of school experience.

4. As Susan Dominus acknowledges, "The parallels are striking enough that Collins's work has been savaged on the blogosphere as a baldfaced ripoff"; or, phrased more generously in the words of Marc Walkow, *Battle Royale* is "considered by many to be an unacknowledged inspiration for *The Hunger Games*" (54). As of December 2019, of the four-hundred-plus customer reviews on Amazon's US platform, the single most common claim is that *The Hunger Games* is an inferior remake lacking the subtlety and consistency of the original.

5. According to Tim Larimer, "Education Minister Nobutaka Machimura had urged the filmmakers to tone down the brutality, while members of parliament sought to ban the film. The bluster led to long lines outside theaters two days before its premiere. As Japan has seen a rash of violent youth crimes recently, the film hits close to home: the day *Royale* opened, a 17-year-old boy wielding a baseball bat injured eight" (12).

6. Bullying in Japanese schools continues to rise. For academic year 2016, while high school incidents were comparatively low, junior high incidents peaked at around 70,000 and elementary incidents at around 325,000; compared with the previous year (and discounting verbal forms of bullying such as "ridicule and slander"), "the number of violent acts at elementary, junior high and senior high schools rose 2,651 to 59,457 cases" ("Reports of School Bullying in Japan Rise to Record High"; see also "An Education in Violence").

7. It is worth acknowledging that the school cafeteria often figures more generally in school stories as a site of anxiety in its own right (for example, in a range of works including the *Captain Underpants* series, *Frindle*, *Charlie Joe Jackson's Guide to Not Reading*, *The Perks of Being a Wallflower*, and *Speak*), where unpalatable foodstuffs, obnoxious peers, or both

offend the sensibilities of sensitive protagonists. Summed up by *Speak*'s Melinda Sordino: "Nothing good ever happens at lunch. The cafeteria is a giant sound stage where they film daily segments of Teenage Humiliation Rituals. And it smells gross" (104).

8. See, for example, Hyndman et al., "Exploring the Influences on Children's School Playground Activities," in which the authors discuss efforts to integrate "active play" in the school curriculum for young students.

9. In 2018, for example, in the USA alone, school shootings accounted for 387 killings and 1,274 injuries, numbers making it clear that the incidents given the most sensational media coverage—recently, at Marjory Stoneman Douglas High School in Parkland, Florida (2018), and STEM School Highlands Ranch in Colorado (2019)—only skim the surface of the intersection of school experience and deadly violence in the neoliberal era.

WORKS CITED

Aitchison, David. "*The Hunger Games*, *Spartacus*, and Other Family Stories: Sentimental Revolution in Contemporary YA Fiction." *The Lion and the Unicorn*, vol. 39, no. 3, 2015, pp. 254–74.
Anderson, Laurie Halse. *Speak*. Square Fish, 1999.
Arai, Andrea G. "Killing Kids: Recession and Survival in Twenty-First-Century Japan." *Postcolonial Studies*, vol. 6, no. 3, 2003, pp. 367–79. *EBSCOhost*. Accessed 1 Jul. 2019.
Batoru Rowaiaru (Battle Royale). Directed by Kinji Fukasaku, performances by Tatsuya Fujiwara, Aki Maeda, and Takeshi Kitano, Toei Company, 2000.
Bosch, Torie. "First, Eat All the Lawyers." *Slate*, 25 Oct. 2011, The Slate Group, www.slate.com/culture/2011/10/zombies-the-zombie-boom-is-inspired-by-the-economy.html. Accessed 3 Jul. 2019.
Cooties. Directed by Cary Murnion and Jonathan Milott, performances by Elijah Wood, Alison Pill, Rainn Wilson, and Cooper Roth, Lionsgate Premiere, 2014.
Cormier, Robert. *The Chocolate War*. Ember, 2002.
Dominus, Susan. "Suzanne Collins's War Stories for Kids." *New York Times Magazine*, 8 Apr. 2011, The New York Times Company, www.nytimes.com/2011/04/10/magazine/mag-10collins-t.html. Accessed 21 Jun. 2019.
"An Education in Violence." *Japan Times*, 13 Dec. 2009, The Japan Times Ltd., www.japantimes.co.jp/opinion/2009/12/13/editorials/an-education-in-violence/#.XQkA4B7QjOR. Accessed 18 Jun. 2019.
Flanagan, Constance A. *Teenage Citizens: The Political Theories of the Young*. Harvard University Press, 2013.
Genzlinger, Neil. "Cooties: Back to School with Zombies and Gore." *New York Times*, 17 Sep. 2015, The New York Times Company, www.nytimes.com/2015/09/18/movies/review-cooties-back-to-school-with-zombies-and-gore.html. Accessed 21 Jun. 2019.
Giroux, Henry. *Zombie Politics and Culture in the Age of Casino Capitalism*. Peter Lang, 2011.
Grenby, M. O. "The School Story." *Children's Literature*, Edinburgh University Press, 2008, pp. 87–116.
Hechinger, Fred M. "School Violence: The Japanese Version." *New York Times*, 11 Mar. 1986, The New York Times Company, www.nytimes.com/1986/03/11/science/about-education-school-violence-the-japanese-version.html. Accessed 18 Jun. 2019.

Herskovitz, Jon. "The 'Battle' Rattle." *Variety*. 19 Dec. 2000. *Variety Media, LLC*. www.variety.com/2000/film/news/the-battle-rattle-1117790773. Accessed 3 Oct. 2020.

Hyndman, Brendon, et al. "Exploring the Influences on Children's School Playground Activities." *American Journal of Play*, vol. 8, no. 3, 2016, pp. 325–44, *EBSCOhost*. Accessed 20 Jun. 2019.

Immordino-Yang, Mary Helen. "Implications of Affective and Social Neuroscience for Educational Theory." *Emotions, Learning, and the Brain: Exploring the Educational Implications of Affective Neuroscience*, W. W. Norton & Company, 2016, pp. 69–75.

Immordino-Yang, Mary Helen, and Antonio R. Damasio. "We Feel, Therefore We Learn: The Relevance of Affective and Social Neuroscience to Education." *Learning, and the Brain: Exploring the Educational Implications of Affective Neuroscience*, W. W. Norton & Company, 2016, pp. 27–42.

Kirkpatrick, Robert J., editor. *The Encyclopaedia of Boys' School Stories*, Ashgate, 2000.

Kirkpatrick, Robert J. *Bullies, Beaks and Flannelled Fools: An Annotated Bibliography of Boys' School Fiction, 1742–1990*. Robert J. Kirkpatrick, 1990.

Kord, T. S. *Little Horrors: How Cinema's Evil Children Play on Our Guilt*. McFarland, 2016.

Larimer, Tim. "Tokyo Teens Flock to Flick—Art Imitates Life?" *TIME Magazine*, vol. 157, no. 1, Jan. 2001, p. 12, *TIME USA, LLC*, content.time.com/time/magazine/article/0,9171,998928,00.html. Accessed 20 Jun. 2019.

Laughland, Oliver, Richard Luscombe, and Alan Yuhas. "Florida School Shooting: At Least 17 People Dead on 'Horrific, Horrific Day.'" *Guardian*, 15 Feb. 2018, *Guardian News and Media Ltd.*, www.theguardian.com/us-news/2018/feb/14/florida-shooting-school-latest-news-stoneman-douglas. Accessed 23 Jul. 2019.

Lauro, Sarah Juliet, editor. *Zombie Theory: A Reader*. University of Minnesota Press, 2017.

Lester, Catherine. "The Children's Horror Film." *Velvet Light Trap: A Critical Journal of Film & Television*, no. 78, 2016, pp. 22–37, *EBSCOhost*. Accessed 20 Jun. 2019.

Levine, Caroline. *Forms: Whole, Rhythm, Hierarchy, Network*. Princeton University Press, 2015.

McRoy, Jay, editor. *Japanese Horror Cinema*. University of Hawai'i Press, 2005.

Miller, Cynthia J., and A. Bowdoin Van Riper, editors. *The Laughing Dead: The Horror-Comedy Film from* Bride of Frankenstein *to* Zombieland. Rowman & Littlefield, 2016.

Newman, Kim. "Reviews." *Sight & Sound*, vol. 11, no. 9, Sept. 2001, pp. 37–38, *EBSCOhost*. Accessed 20 Jun. 2019.

"100 Most Frequently Challenged Books: 1990–1999." *Banned and Challenged Books: A Website for the ALA Office of Intellectual Freedom, American Library Association*, http://www.ala.org/advocacy/bbooks/frequentlychallengedbooks/decade1999. Accessed 1 Jun. 2019.

Orwell, George. "Boys' Weeklies." *Inside the Whale and Other Essays*, Victor Gollancz, 1940, pp. 89–128.

Orwell, George. *Nineteen Eighty-four*. Penguin Classics, 2019.

Quigly, Isabel. *The Heirs of Tom Brown: The English School Story*. Chatto & Windus, 1982.

"Reports of School Bullying in Japan Rise to Record High, Education Ministry Survey Shows." *Japan Times*, 26 Oct. 2017, *The Japan Times Ltd.*, www.japantimes.co.jp/news/2017/10/26/national/social-issues/reports-school-bullying-japan-rise-record-high-education-ministry-survey-shows/#.XQkErR7QjOR. Accessed 18 Jun. 2019.

Shaviro, Steven. "Contagious Allegories: George Romero." *Zombie Theory: A Reader*, edited by Sarah Juliet Lauro, University of Minnesota Press, 2017, pp. 7–19.

Springhall, John. "'Boys of Bircham School': The Penny Dreadful Origins of the Popular English School Story, 1867–1900." *History of Education*, vol. 20, no. 2, 1991, pp. 77–94, *Taylor & Francis*. Accessed 1 Jun. 2019.

Strauss, Valerie. "Florida Legislators Take Steps to Arm Teachers—Despite Opposition from School Shooting Survivors." *Washington Post*, 28 Feb. 2018, www.washingtonpost.com/news/answer-sheet/wp/2018/02/28/florida-legislators-take-steps-to-arm-teachers-despite-opposition-from-school-shooting-survivors. Accessed 16 Aug. 2019.

Takami, Koushun. *Battle Royale*. Translated by Yuji Oniki, VIZ, 2003.

"The Top Ten Most Challenged Books." *Banned and Challenged Books: A Website for the ALA Office of Intellectual Freedom*, American Library Association, www.ala.org/advocacy/bbooks/frequentlychallengedbooks/top10. Accessed 1 Jun. 2019.

Vint, Sherryl. "Abject Posthumanism: Neoliberalism, Biopolitics, and Zombies." *Zombie Theory: A Reader*, edited by Sarah Juliet Lauro, University of Minnesota Press, 2017, pp. 171–81.

Walkow, Marc. "The History of Postwar Japan as Told by a Radical Anarchist." *Film Comment*, vol. 52, no. 1, Jan. 2016, pp. 52–59, *EBSCOhost*. Accessed 1 Jun. 2019.

Webb, Jen, and Samuel Byrnand. "Some Kind of Virus: The Zombie as Body and as Trope." *Zombie Theory: A Reader*, edited by Sarah Juliet Lauro, University of Minnesota Press, 2017, pp. 111–23.

Whelan, Andrew, Ruth Walker, and Christopher Moore, editors. *Zombies in the Academy: Living Death in Higher Education*. Intellect, 2013.

Williams, Tony. "Case Study: *Battle Royale*'s Apocalyptic Millennial Warning." *Japanese Horror Cinema*, edited by Jay McRoy, University of Hawai'i Press, 2005, pp. 130–43.

Yogerst, Chris. "Rules for Surviving a Horror Comedy: Satiric Genre Transformation from *Scream* to *Zombieland*." *The Laughing Dead: The Horror-Comedy Film from* Bride of Frankenstein *to* Zombieland, edited by Cynthia J. Miller and A. Bowdoin Van Riper, Rowman & Littlefield, 2016, pp. 169–84.

CHAPTER 5

Teenage Authors, Marketplace Consciousness, and the Deregulation of Childhood in the Age of Neoliberalism

As scholars of literature give increasing attention to the complex of economic, political, sociocultural, and ontological conditions informing neoliberalism, some have begun to explore how childhood in the age of neoliberalism is lived, represented, and understood. Of especial note is Caren Irr's "Neoliberal Childhoods" (2017), a study of fictions about children written for adult readers foregrounding what she calls the "ideal neoliberal child": "a largely independent, unparented, and entrepreneurial self defined by consumption habits and individual rights"—functionally, a "social orphan" and an "entrepreneur" (222). For Irr, novels about children matter because they afford readers a chance to "sort through a matrix of competing ideologies of the child," allowing them to glimpse the "social subject in formation" and thereby examine the effects of neoliberalism on social life (220–21). Among the books Irr discusses is Vikas Swarup's *Q & A* (2005), perhaps better known in its big-screen adaptation, *Slumdog Millionaire* (2008). Drawing attention to the novel's protagonist, Ram, a teen from a Mumbai slum who competes in a cash-prize television quiz show to get revenge on the host (a sadist who has tortured two women in Ram's life), Irr argues that such characters take on a distinctly neoliberal narrative function: they "tour, expose, and reject" social institutions, and when they experience injustice, they find that "no social institution is capable of redressing [that] injustice"; instead, "the marketplace is the only sphere in which a self strong enough to meet this need [for justice] is able to flourish" (231). Confirming the ontological conditions of neoliberalism, Irr's reading of authors like Swarup suggests a totalizing experience for children in fiction, according to which resisting the rationality of the marketplace becomes tantamount to resisting satisfaction or success.

But even if the drives and actions of children in fiction might be complicit with neoliberal structures, scholars recognize that children in real life have a capacity to question and resist neoliberalism. This is Caitlyn Howlett's stance in "Neoliberalism, Critical Pedagogy, and the Child" (2017), in which she wrestles with the critical pedagogy of Paulo Freire, bell hooks, and Henry Giroux. For Howlett, while these theorists might be cognizant of the sociopolitical positioning of children, they do not sufficiently recognize children themselves as knowledgeable or political: there is not enough evidence that hooks or Giroux take children to be questioning the neoliberal reality of their existence. In response, Howlett encourages us to grasp children as critically conscious of neoliberalism. To do otherwise, she says, is to relegate children precisely to the "position required for neoliberalism to succeed: as passive, moldable, not-fully-human subjects" (72). To clarify, she appeals to Daniel Thomas Cook's *The Commodification of Childhood* (2004), explaining that, "in America, our very conception of the child as person has always been understood in capitalist and neoliberal terms, and that neoliberalism has always seen the child as central to its growth and power" (Howlett 70, paraphrasing Cook). Perceiving a broad structure of exploitation, Howlett urges us "to treat children as always already both political and knowledgeable," on the understanding that "the political actions and knowledge of children pose [threats] to neoliberalism ... in which we ought to revel" (72).

Between Irr and Howlett, childhood in the age of neoliberalism bifurcates, finding purpose here, in a story of personal success informed by marketplace consciousness (cognition defaults to entrepreneurial and economic frameworks of exchange and action), and there, in political possibility informed by marketplace skepticism. In this chapter, I consider both, but I follow Howlett's lead in giving attention to narratives by young readers (though, admittedly, she has in mind a younger demographic than I do). Singling out stories concerned with the democratic possibilities of education, a topic currently motivating some of the most pressing debates over neoliberalism, I discuss two young adult works by teenage authors: Faiza Guène's *Kiffe Kiffe Tomorrow* (2004), a novel about a girl in the Moroccan-Parisian projects bristling under welfare-state interventions at home and at school; and Malala Yousafzai's *I Am Malala: How One Girl Stood up for Education and Changed the World* (2014, young readers edition), a memoir recounting the author's activism in Pakistan for girls' schools and her subsequent persecution by Islamist fundamentalists. Neither is a school story in any strict or conventional sense: errant and exiled, the schoolchildren in both books mostly move far beyond the topos of the school. But rather than take this at face value and reach, instead, for more obvious stories negotiating the flux of students, teachers, and classrooms, it seems enriching to spend time with stories such as these on (or over) the edge of the genre. After all, even if these protagonists are rarely on school grounds, they are consistently weighed down if not haunted by the idea of school life. What's more, both stories clearly attribute their protagonists' crises with education to neoliberal pressures, whether in the form of individualist creeds working through realms of discourse, or of occupying armies fighting in the thick of a creeping free market. As such, the school story in the age of neoliberalism—that is, in an age of increasing hostility to public education—might just have begun to register the absence as much as the presence of school. So, without meaning to undermine the working terms of the genre, in this chapter I make some room for stories of errant and exiled schoolchildren, whose narratives hinge on questions of learning, education, and vocation, but whose everyday school routines are all but gone under neoliberal duress.

Both Guène and Yousafzai compel us to think of schoolchildren situated at distinctly neoliberal intersections in their lives: moments when finding purpose and making life choices entail reading the world through the lens of the commercial marketplace, entering into contractual associations, and having to think like an entrepreneur. I want to suggest that such books, in their various acts of negotiating the relation between the individual's sense of self and understanding of the wider world, show children wrestling with the narrative and social concerns raised by contemporary theorists such as William Randall (*The Stories We Are: An Essay on Self-Creation*, 2014; *The Narrative Complexity of Ordinary Life: Tales from the Coffee Shop*, 2015), Bruno Latour (*Reassembling the Social: An Introduction to Actor-Network Theory*, 2005), and Caroline Levine (*Forms: Whole, Rhythm, Hierarchy, Network*, 2015): they understand identity as a narrative matter, recognize the social as a site of flux and controversy, and confirm the idea that radical social change is a formalist concern. Together, Guène and Yousafzai make a strong case for recognizing young people as knowledgeable and political, though not necessarily in compatible ways.

Specifically, Guène and Yousafzai function as theorists of social relations, thinking and writing about the one and the many in ways that resonate with the concerns motivating Levine and Latour. In her study of network forms, Levine draws particular attention to the social insights gleaned when literary narratives are structured around not characters *per se* but character networks. With a nod to Franco Moretti's work on literary plot analysis informed by network theory ("Network Theory, Plot Analysis," 2011), Levine reads Charles Dickens's *Bleak House* (1854) as a novel that "uses networks to reconceptualize character. . . . By organizing the narrative around networks rather than persons, *Bleak House* does for character something like what Marx did for commodities: casting narrative persons less as powerful or symbolic agents in their own right than as moments in which complex and invisible social forces cross. Network form therefore prompts a rethinking of novelistic character" (126). Comparing Dickens to Marx, Levine attributes a critical, political, and perhaps even revolutionary potential to the novel as a form; and in showing us how to read characters less for their individual and more for their social roles, she implies a form of political novel resisting the individualist creed on which neoliberalism depends.[1] In my readings of *Kiffe Kiffe Tomorrow* and *I Am Malala*, while I do not offer a formalist map of character networks, I consider the extent to which the young, first-person narrators are conscious of such networks. I read both books as prose narratives that—without drawing on the technical terms of "vertices" or "edges" (Moretti) or "nodes" or "hubs" (Levine)—comprise network-conscious studies of relations between the self and the social. Such a reading suggests a need to broaden our understanding of the narrative paradigms that govern discussions of children's and young adult stories, which sometimes focus on dramatic (externalized) events at the expense of cognitive (internalized) ones—for example, when the journeys of young protagonists are described as circular and restorative in their physical movements away from and back toward home, even if those journeys have harrowed or altered them.[2] As common as such journeys might be, as definitive reference points they privilege lives actualized in realms of action and mobility, a nexus making little room to appreciate the more peripheral lives of onlookers and nonparticipants—a distinction critical for grasping the uneven ways that children, whether in fiction or in real life, are poised to understand the world, navigate it, and succeed in it under neoliberal conditions.

A Note on Editions

My two primary texts in this chapter have been published in multiple editions featuring either coauthors or translators, which obviously alters the kinds of claims that might be made about young authorship and identity.

Malala's story has appeared in three major variants: *I Am Malala: The Girl Who Stood Up for Education and Was Shot By the Taliban*, written with war correspondent Christina Lamb (2013); *I Am Malala: How One Girl Stood Up for Education and Changed the World* (young readers edition), written with journalist and young adult novelist Patricia McCormick (2014); and, in chapter book form, *Malala: My Story of Standing Up for Girls' Rights*, abridged and adapted from the McCormick by Sarah J. Robbins with illustrations by Joanie Stone (2018). The third book, apart from the illustrations, is recognizably a variant of the second, with shared content and structure, albeit cut and condensed. The same cannot be said for the Lamb and the McCormick, which certainly share an overall narrative movement but constitute different texts in terms of what is said and how. While the peritexts in the books avoid spelling out the exact nature of the collaborations, statements from the coauthors published elsewhere describe a journalistic working relationship for each book, according to which the coauthor carried out substantive in-person interviews with Malala and then went on to write on their own (see, for example, Lamb's "My Year With Malala" and McCormick's "I Am Malala FAQ"). The difference between the first and second books—which McCormick explains as a shift toward "a much more personal, less political story"—understandably has left some readers guessing where, if at all, Malala's voice figures in the works. As scholar-blogger Kasey Butcher sees it, "Malala's experiences are woven into Lamb's research in a way that distances the narrative voice from Malala whereas the young readers edition is more directly Malala's story and therefore either reflects more narrative agency on her part or at least reads as though it does." I, too, favor the young readers edition for the present study, on account of its incidence of teen elements: teenage author (Malala), author for teens (McCormick), and teenage audience (young readers). I also appreciate Butcher's closing comment, with which she reminds us that these books are in the business of constructing, rather than merely representing, Malala's identity. Regardless of voice, all three books with their cover shots, titles, and first-person accounts situate the reader so as to imagine Malala as the principle author, suggesting to me that the story, rather than the letter of the text, is Malala's. Much like the blogs that she wrote for BBC Urdu in Pakistan in the years prior to her attempted assassination, *I Am Malala* belongs to a tradition of war correspondence that, because of conflicts and aftermaths, sometimes compels authors to turn over their stories to others, a fact that should open up, rather than foreclose on, what we mean by authorship.

Guène's novel, meanwhile, was originally published in French as *Kiffe Kiffe Demain* (2004) and subsequently translated into English by Sarah Adams under the titles *Just Like Tomorrow* (2006) and *Kiffe Kiffe Tomorrow* (2006). Much like coauthors, translators seem to risk unsettling critical analytics, especially when lauded for their own literary merit—as was Adams, when *Just Like Tomorrow* won the 2007 Scott Moncrief Prize for French to English translation. As with Malala's story, Guène's comes to the Anglophone world channeled by another author, which might seem to undercut this chapter's interest in correlating teenage authors and their works—although that particular problem could be easily overcome by any French speaker capable of appealing to the original language edition. As it happens, I am interested less in pinning down who these young authors are biographically and more in working through how they are constructed in the experience of reading their books, along with the popular press reviews and opinion pieces surrounding them. As such, I take the translated text to be just as deserving of attention as the original—as a novel marketed and read as the work of a young best-selling author.

Neoliberal Childhoods in Fiction: "Faceless and Fucked Over"

Faiza Guène's *Kiffe Kiffe Tomorrow* tells the story of Doria, a fifteen-year-old daughter of Moroccan immigrants living in a housing project in Paris. The title fuses the Arabic expression *kif-kif* ("same old, same old; it's all the same") with the French *kiffer* ("to be really crazy about something"), hinting at a story about anticipating or hoping for change (epigraph). Though few scenes actually take place in school, *Kiffe Kiffe Tomorrow* merits attention for its depiction of the errant schoolgirl who cannot shake the underwhelming presence of school, which is mostly recalled as a locus of guidance counselling rather than academic activity. Doria retreats to the projects, where she watches the people around her negotiate various forms of material and spiritual impoverishment. Especially conscious of trapped individuals who ultimately find ways to escape, she registers character developments that, while not always satisfying to her, confirm the possibilities of social mobility: in the story of her mother, an illiterate, isolated, and exploited hotel worker who, by way of job training, gains literacy, finds friends, and embarks on a new career as a canteen lady; of Hamoudi, the poetry-loving, neighborhood drug dealer who, feeling his age at odds with his activities, gives up dealing to marry and settle down; of the girl in the projects held prisoner by her father for fear her blossoming sexuality will bring shame, who runs away to join the state circus; and of Doria herself, downward spiraling and "no good at school" (14), who eventually—in the closing pages of the book—makes a fresh start as a hairdressing student.

Opening six months after her alcoholic father has abandoned them for a new family back in Morocco, the narrative follows Doria and her mother as they live a hand-to-mouth, low-wage existence characterized by welfare subsidies, loans from moneylenders, and handouts from neighbors. From first to last, Guène's protagonist exhibits a bitter sense of dependence and lack of autonomy, traits that seem to place her in the ranks of Irr's ideal neoliberal children. Indeed, at odds with the school therapists assigned in the wake of her father's departure and the social workers who pour through her home, Doria's character functions in a comparable way to "tour, expose, and [largely] reject" social institutions. The difference is that she scathes internally without taking action, living her critique cognitively rather than dramatically. In other words, without actually entering the marketplace to redress the injustices of her young life, she identifies that marketplace all the same, as Irr puts it, as "the only sphere in which a self strong enough to meet this need is able to flourish" (231). Guène thus invites us to expand Irr's paradigm to distinguish between the ideal and the potential, nascent, or even skeptical neoliberal child, the one an externalizing agent who actively finds power within a realm of marketplace action, the other an internalizing dreamer on the periphery of that realm.

Comparable ambivalence toward marketplace mechanisms informs Doria's relationship with school therapist Madame Burlaud, who figures in the novel as Doria's only substantive attachment to formal school life. "For all I know," Doria thinks, "Mme Burlaud isn't really a shrink. Maybe she works in TV and all the bullshit I tell her feeds into her sitcom. Burlaud, I bet that's a pseudonym, and . . . she's part of the scriptwriting team . . . That's got to be it . . . Maybe the concept is already being made into a series, it will be a smash hit and get broadcast all over the world . . . And me? I don't hold any rights. I'll just be one of the millions of fans, faceless and fucked over, like all the rest" (63). What starts off as a tacit yearning for authenticity morphs into a critique of unequal relations: the problem is not that the school therapist might be a phony but that she is positioned to gain cultural capital at Doria's expense. This sense of nonreciprocal exchange crystalizes when Doria probes the nature of their sessions together: "What's so tired about psychologists, psychiatrists, psychoanalysts, and all things that start with *psy* . . . They want you to tell them your life story, but them, they don't tell you one thing about themselves. Mme Burlaud knows stuff about me I don't know about myself. After you realize all that, you don't want to talk to them anymore. It's a rip-off" (32). Why resort to an economic metaphor to make sense of mental health and academic well-being in a school setting? Why imagine this flow of personal information—which, in a state-subsidized therapy session is conventionally one-sided—as, of all things, a "rip-off"—a theft, fraud, or swindle ("rip-off, n.")? On the one hand, Guène's protagonist reads like an ideal neoliberal child in the making: construing her personal information to have market value, raising the cry for rights seems less a critique of the market and more an expression of chagrin at being excluded from it. On the other hand, speaking for the "faceless and fucked over," she makes a point of disclosing the abusive potential of uneven market relations.

So, a first distinction between those who practice marketplace power in the school realm and those who covet it clashes with a second distinction between those who abuse that power and those who suffer from it, a collision also evident in Doria's observations of a divisively gendered Muslim community beyond the world of school. Three brief examples show Doria knowingly invoking the language of the marketplace to disclose the dehumanizing effects of uneven gender relations. First, accounting for her father's disappointment in her being a girl and not a boy, she says, "You could say I didn't exactly meet customer specifications" (2). Second, recalling Tahar Ben Jelloun's *The Sand Child* (1985), a novel in which a girl is raised as a boy because her father wants a son, we learn, "Back when the book is set, there wasn't any ultrasound or contraception. It was no refunds, no exchanges" (9). Third, closer to home, she perceives the men from the Parisian Muslim community who marry girls from Morocco to be operating in the "importexport" business (101). At such moments, the language of the marketplace serves to characterize domestic situations in which girls and women are treated as objects: bought, sold, shipped, returned. While the point is to draw attention to failures in the human community, it is telling that Guène's young protagonist resorts to marketplace paradigms to make sense of those failures. The problem is not simply that patriarchs and misogynists abuse familial and social relations; it is, rather, that husbands and fathers grasp familial and social relations as commodity associations. At home, as at school, Doria's rhetorical choices draw attention to how the intimate connections between individuals become overdetermined by the possessive and proprietorial interests of the marketplace, confirming it as a realm of not merely unequal but categorically dehumanizing exchanges.

Unsettled Childhoods: "Precocious ... Political"

On the publication of Sarah Adams's 2006 English translation, *Kiffe Kiffe Tomorrow* garnered praise for its political consciousness from high-profile US periodicals. In a *Salon* article titled "The Other Paris" (2006), Marisa Meltzer drew attention to Guène's timely commentaries on the race, class, and gender tensions then plaguing multicultural Paris. "A year before the riots," Meltzer begins, "this remarkable debut novel about growing up female and poor in Paris's Muslim housing projects was a sensation in France." Admittedly, Meltzer seems disappointed when she notes that "Guène was sought out as a voice of the suburban teen during the riots, but refused to comment." Even so, Meltzer lets the following gambit stand: that "it's tempting to see *Kiffe Kiffe Tomorrow* as prescient, to try to find a few answers to France's recent social unrest, from the riots to last spring's student protests over new labor laws unfavorable to young employees."

In the same period, writing for the *New York Times*, Lucinda Rosenfeld similarly introduced *Kiffe Kiffe Tomorrow* favorably as a "political tract"—or, more correctly,

> not just a political tract. What makes it appealing is its sharply drawn profile of a precocious adolescent. In Sarah Adams's highly colloquial translation, the narrator's scorn extends to areas unrelated to the sociocultural circumstances of her family. A state-appointed shrink smells like "anti-lice shampoo." A classmate enlisted to help Doria with her homework is a "fat loser." A social worker has a "scary voice, the kind of voice you can imagine saying: 'I am Death! Follow me, it's your time!'" In this way and others—her propensity to daydream about Hollywood stars, her obsession with acne and breast size, her aversion to all traces of phoniness or unctuousness in others—Doria is a typical teenager.

Conspicuously, Rosenfeld separates out the political from the precocious, as if "typical teenager" and political consciousness are mutually exclusive. And as rich in social criticism as *Kiffe Kiffe Tomorrow* is, calling it a "tract" seems like a category mistake, mostly because it has not made up its mind on everything it questions: as noted, it appeals to the marketplace as a locus of rights even while lamenting it as a realm of unfreedom, in much the same way it moves back and forth between denouncing and salvaging the school experience. There are, however, two exceptional moments when the first-person narrator propagandizes for democratic participation. In the first, Doria ponders her home turf in the projects: "I wonder if this is why these housing developments are left to decay, because so few people around here vote. You have no political usefulness if you don't vote. Me, when I'm eighteen, I'll go vote. Here, a person never gets a chance to be heard. So when we get the chance, we have to take it" (89). As is common in literature immersed in experiences of minority identities, articulated here is a desire for recognition and representation. This same desire is revisited in a second moment, from the closing passage of the novel. Acknowledging that "lots of things need changing around here," Doria says, "Hey, that gives me an idea. Why don't I go into politics? . . . I'll lead the uprising in the Paradise Estate . . . It will be an intelligent revolution, with no violence, where every person stands up to be heard." And to clarify the sensibility here, in the very last words of the novel, she terms it an expression of "serious democratic fever" (179).

Leading up to the explicit—and distinctly optimistic—politics of the conclusion, Guène anchors Doria socially, emotionally, and vocationally: first, when she reveals Doria's newfound purpose in "going for a hairdressing certificate," which prompts the reflection that "the one thing that comforts me is that I'm coping all right with school this year. Note: If I'd been useless in a hairdressing class, then I really would be worried" (166); and second, when Doria shares the news that "Mme Burlaud told me my therapy was finished" (167), which prompts her not only to acknowledge that "that means I'm doing well" (167), but also to make the point that "I know it's thanks to all this I'm doing better. I don't deny she helped me big time" (168). Despite the tidiness of these narrative threads, she clarifies, "I still don't know what I really want to do in life. Because hairdressing, let's say it's something you do while you're waiting for something else to come along" (169). Uncertainty aside, the resumption of normality in the realm of school experience, in both finding purpose in her studies and dispensing with the therapy, seems to prepare the way for the more active and activist outlook that follows. The mundanity of school life matters here, a detail that seems to get lost when magazines like *Salon* speculate on the radical potential of *Kiffe Kiffe Tomorrow*. For those familiar with the recent critiques of neoliberalism by David Harvey, Henry Giroux, Wendy Brown, and Naomi Klein, in which democracy figures as both avowed enemy and inevitable victim of neoliberalism, it would not be hard to extrapolate from the novel a radical commentary on the possibilities of young life specific to the age of neoliberalism: participatory democracy is proposed as an antidote to a marketplace rationality that, definitively, makes for unequal exchanges. At the same time, and lending credence to the claim that Guène shied away from justifying student riots, the novel suggests that the critical work in preparing for any such participation comes from learning to settle down, at school and at home, before daring to stand up.

The trouble with that reading, which certainly does justice to the political consciousness that wraps up *Kiffe Kiffe Tomorrow*, is that it is not always enough for Guène's reviewers, some of whom in making sense of the novel look less to the uplift registered in its narrative closure (when the expression of political optimism coincides with Doria finding new purpose in pursuing her hairdressing certificate) and more to its commercial status in the literary marketplace. This is Meltzer's point after all when she highlights how Guène's biography both intersects with and departs from the story of Doria's life:

> Like Doria, 20-year-old Guène is the daughter of Algerian immigrants and she grew up—and still lives—with both parents and two siblings in public housing in the volatile northeastern suburbs. By the age of 13, Guène was the editor of her junior high literary magazine and also involved in a publicly funded neighborhood cultural center where teens worked on scripts for short films for television. She showed the first 40 pages of what would become *Kiffe Kiffe Tomorrow* to the director of the center. He then sent them to his sister, an editor at the French publisher Hachette, who bought the book for a reported $1,800 advance.

Bearing in mind that the novel meditates obsessively on the possibility of finding ways out of the diminished existence of the projects and ends on a note of democratic promise, Meltzer traces a dramatically different network of associations when she invites us to recognize something more concrete in the portrait of the schoolgirl as entrepreneur, turning the narrative of young, impoverished life into a marketable commodity. For Meltzer, what counts is not the substantive construction of a character who is doubtful about the marketplace, nor the mapping of lives marred by uneven development, but the more straightforward—and commercially more palatable—financialization of the story. In effect, the complex of the social depicted within the novel is reduced to a character study of the author as entrepreneur. Inviting readers to imagine a book like *Kiffe Kiffe Tomorrow* as somehow embodying that individualist creed, critics such as Meltzer begin to look less like critics and more like social engineers, carrying out the persuasive work of neoliberal ideology.

The Work of the Child Author

If the teenage author is remarkable because of her age as much as her abilities, then it might seem reasonable for critics to take the writing and the writer hand in hand—a move all the more understandable when reading not a novel but a memoir such as Malala Yousafzai's *I Am Malala*. As noted, the presence of coauthors Christina Lamb and Patricia McCormick makes it difficult to speak of Yousafzai as an author with indisputable autonomy: she models, rather, what Marah Gubar, in her study of nineteenth-century child actors, calls "a form of nonautonomous agency in which being scripted by adults did not necessarily preclude them from functioning as intelligent, creative individuals" (159). Without knowing whether or not, or the extent to which, Yousafzai was actually "scripted by adults," we can recognize her as a collaborator in the writing process, a teenage memoirist with agency and presence in the mainstream literary marketplace. For contemporary scholars, the memoir as a form occupies an embattled position: for some, it figures as either "the generic queen of neoliberal literature" (Michaels 27), or symptom of a period in which "neoliberalism no longer needs innovative or speculative forms to anticipate its implementation" (Huehls and Smith 13, paraphrasing Mathias Nilge); for others, it nonetheless has a more critical potential to "estrange us from ourselves and make visible the structures that produce our subjectivities, the rules that bind us to a way of life that is in constant crisis yet also shows no sign of ebbing" (Worden 176). Either way, collapsing distinctions between author and narrator, teenage books like *I Am Malala* explicitly invite us to read the thing made for what it tells us of the maker—and perhaps vice versa, too. Not only suggesting a truer-to-life glimpse of the social subject in formation, they make it easier for critics to judge the literary work less by what it says at the level of narrative and more by how it appears to function, instrumentally, in the commercial life of the young writer. Such books emerge as hubs of concentrated marketplace activity—in part because their stories consciously comment on events inextricably bound up with economics and commerce, in part because their commercial success draws media attention, and in part because of the broader implications of what it means, legally and contractually, to be a teenage author.

Admittedly, in the realm of children's and young adult literature, authors of school age are nothing new, especially when it comes to writing about school experience: Alex Waugh was seventeen when he published *The Loom of Youth* (1917); S. E. Hinton wrote *The Outsiders* (1967) between the ages of fifteen and sixteen and published it at eighteen; and Gordon Korman published his first three school novels at the ages of fourteen (*This Can't Be Happening at Macdonald Hall*, 1978), fifteen (*Go Jump in the Pool*, 1979), and sixteen (*Beware the Fish*, 1980). But more recently, since the turn of the millennium, we have seen a flurry of prominent, published teenage authors around the world: to name but a few, Benjamin Lebert (*Crazy*, 1999), Ned Vizzini (*Teen Angst? Naaah . . .*, 2000), Risa Wataya (*Keritai Senaka/I Want to Kick You in the Back*, 2003), Irina Denezhkina (*Дай Мне!/Give Me (Songs for Lovers)*, 2002), Kody Keplinger (*The Duff*, 2010), Jake Marcionette (*Just Jake*, 2014), Maya Van Wagenen (*Popular*, 2015), and Amy Zhang (*Falling into Place*, 2015), all telling tales of students in or around school or college. Bearing in mind that the nostalgic sensibilities of adult authors have until now dominated almost all fiction about young lives—one of the circumstances that compelled Jacqueline Rose in *The Case of Peter Pan, or, The Impossibility of Children's Fiction* (1984) to question the very possibility of children's fiction—the rise of the teenage author signals a critical moment.

First, it suggests a substantive shift in a literary marketplace making (almost) unprecedented room for the voices and visions of the young.[3] Not insignificantly, around three decades ago, when literary juvenilia studies were beginning to gain traction, Gillian Adams could speculate that the "kind of children [who] are most likely to produce juvenilia that survives" probably enjoyed the support of a "tightly-knit, well-educated, financially secure family" (2, paraphrasing A. O. J. Cockshutt). But if the autobiographical details in contemporary teen narratives are to be trusted, the literary marketplace is now making it possible for young authors from a far more diverse range of milieus to share their work with mass audiences. Second, it unsettles the common understanding that, as Mike Cadden puts it, "it is the reader alone for whom the genre [of children's literature] is defined—a reader almost certainly not present either in children's literature classes or in the ranks of those authors on the syllabus and certainly not among the scholars" (xiv). As it happens, the rise of the teenage author makes it possible to demarcate a new archive under the auspices of a literature not only read but also written by children, whether autonomously or collaboratively. Third, it promises new narrative attitudes to young life potentially unlike those of adult authors whose childhood experiences are behind them—attitudes informed by conceptions of growth, development, and closure possibly unique to the age of neoliberalism.

It is also worth keeping in mind that, under common law, children enter the marketplace on exceptional terms. In the first instance, as Douglas E. Abrams and Sarah H. Ramsey note in discussing American practices, the "operative policy [of the law] is to protect children from overreaching by adult parties," with the "general age of contractual capacity [set] to eighteen" in "virtually all" US states (853). Minors who wish to void a contract may disaffirm (that is, repudiate or void) it "during minority or within a reasonable time after reaching majority" (853). In cases of disaffirmance, if minors have received anything of value under contract, they might be required to return it, though legal precedents suggest that intangible gains—provided, for example, by services rather than goods—typically are not repaid; and for contracts cosigned by parents or "other competent adults . . . the adult co-obligor has responsibility for the obligation" (853).

I do not mean to cast aspersions on actual authors who publish as minors; in fact, authors such as Hinton and Korman, who were generous enough to share with me their recollections of publishing as minors, speak incredibly fondly of their entry, helped by family, into the publishing world.[4] My point, rather, is to acknowledge that the recent influx of teenage authors into the marketplace suggests an increase in the very activity that the legal system purposefully discourages: contracts for labor undertaken by minors. To be sure, the reason for that discouragement is that the law deems the minor's position to be precarious. Yet, as certain legal cases show, minors voiding contracts sometimes make considerable gains at the expense of adult contractors (e.g., *Mitchell v. Mizerski, Court of Appeals of Nebraska*, 1995; see Abrams and Ramsey 849–59). In effect, children contracting to sell their work in the conventionally adult realm of labor relations enjoy protections under contract law that allow them to opt out of agreements that for adults are binding, and potentially to their benefit. With this flexibility in mind, I ask if we are witnessing a "deregulation" of childhood, a term from economics to describe the stripping away of rules and restrictions in the name of individual freedoms, used here to draw attention to at least two things: the renegotiation of childhood that takes place when child authors enter the labor force in numbers and contract (whether or not through third parties) to sell their labor; and the part that the presence of child authors plays in encouraging a maverick neoliberal economy (*if* they are afforded unprecedented freedoms in the marketplace without wholly giving up traditional protections, thereby affording a lopsided model of nonbinding contracts).

Between the stories they tell and the stories told about them, authors such as Guène and Yousafzai—with varying degrees of autonomy—suggest a radical loosening of child/adult boundaries, along with a lifting of traditional restraints on childhood. At the same time, as fresh as this rise of teen authors feels, it could easily be said to belong in the same tradition of children's literature and culture described by Gubar in *Artful Dodgers*, according to which Golden Age children's authors[5] cast children less as "artless" children of nature and more as "artful" collaborators negotiating with and alongside adults (vi). Gubar argues that authors such as Robert Louis Stevenson, E. Nesbit, Lewis Carroll, and J. M. Barrie, who were "self-conscious about the fact that adult-produced stories shape children ... represented children as capable of reshaping stories, conceiving of them as artful collaborators in the hope that—while a complete escape from adult influence is impossible—young people might dodge the fate of functioning as passive parrots" (6). As Gubar persuasively puts it, "Far from being oblivious to the ways fantasies about childhood impinge on children, Golden Age children's authors grappled with this very problem, constructing narratives that raise the question of whether and to what extent young people can rewrite the scripts handed to them by adults, taking a hand in the production of stories and their own self-fashioning" (7). While remaining mindful of the considerable gap between Gubar's "child narrators" (constructed by adult writers) and my "teenage authors" (ranging from autonomous to collaborative), the same critical terms of narrative production and self-fashioning apply to the contemporary field of young authorship. That said, it is imperative that we recognize how these same terms, beyond their personal affordances as expressions of agency and identity, have just as much potential to serve a marketplace with more insidious investments in deregulating childhood.

Neoliberal Imaginaries in Nonfiction: "Living under Wraps"

In many ways, *Kiffe Kiffe Tomorrow* and *I Am Malala* are worlds apart in the stories they tell of young life: the one, in Paris, France, broods edgily on the misfit, dreamer, dropout, and antihero; the other, in Mingora, Pakistan, much more reverently portrays the valedictorian, would-be prophet, agent of change, and unequivocal hero. Alternatively, while the one makes a case for a working-class escape from gendered Muslim traditions, the other takes a more middle-class stance within those traditions in the hope of reforming them. But the real difference, I argue, comes down to their contrasting understandings of individual and social agency: while the one narrator identifies with the peripherally "faceless and fucked over," stifled by a market rationality endangering the human community, the other much more confidently rises to the ranks of the global elite to offer a critique of Islamic fundamentalism that, as commentators have noted, seems to conceal the role of market forces in the rise to prominence of both the fundamentalists and the author.

As an autobiographical narrative, *I Am Malala* turns on the moment when fifteen-year-old Malala—riding the Khushal school bus through Mingora City in northwestern Pakistan's Swat region—is waylaid by two Talibs and shot in the head. Opening on the morning of her attempted assassination, the prologue leads up to the moment when one of the young men boards the bus to ask, "Who is Malala?" only to stop short of describing the actual shooting, which is deferred until the final third of the book, which traces her near-fatal injury, her rescue by British doctors, and her hospitalization and recovery in Birmingham, England. Connecting those opening and closing sections is a backstory suggesting that to know who Malala is necessitates knowing why she was marked for death by Islamist terrorists. On the one hand, the backstory tries to persuade us that Malala is "a girl like any other" (11), in the thick of everyday goings-on with family, friends, and classmates that Western readers will likely find familiar. On the other hand, it distinguishes Malala as a girl quite unlike any other: chaffing at her Pashtun culture's separation of male and female spheres and agitating for school reform after Islamist fundamentalists occupy Mingora City and—in the course of imposing Sharia law—attempt to abolish formal education for girls. She is singled out and shot not only because she persists in going to school but also because she goes out of her way publicly—in newspapers, on radio, and on television—to challenge their prohibition (though real-life Taliban spokesman Adnan Rasheed puts it in stronger terms, accusing her of an anti-Islam smear campaign; see DeHart, "Why Did the Taliban Shoot Malala?").

As a political narrative, *I Am Malala* turns on that same moment to work through competing theories of social relations: on the one side, the schoolgirl's vision of human connections that are open and fluid enough to allow for democratic reform (affording girls and women increasing opportunities for self-empowerment, professional work, and public recognition); and on the other side, the fundamentalists' efforts to craft a limiting order of things (foreclosing on the social as a site of multicultural flux to render in its place a contained society in which all social ties become religiopolitical). In formalist terms, what sets Malala apart from the handful of other girls who, like her, continue to attend her father's school in spite of threats, is her persistence in breaching a fiercely policed bounded whole. The function of her character—and of the book as a whole—is to network with listeners and readers beyond the scripted territories, disclose the assault on democratic promise, and encourage intervention. Taking her at face value, in fact, it is not far-fetched to argue that Yousafzai understands social conflict in the same way that Latour in *Reassembling the Social* understands sociology: both caution against positing society as something fixed and scripted according to a master discourse, just as both make an alternative case for grasping the social as a site of movement and controversy.

From the outset, then, Yousafzai is conscious of the politics of connectivity. Before the arrival of the Taliban, her cognitive map of her homeland is marked primarily by kin, friend, and school relations in Mingora City and in the neighboring mountain village of Shangla, though her social ties extend further. She describes herself as "a member of a proud tribe of people spread across Afghanistan and Pakistan" (12). She identifies with a range of cultural heroes including "the great young Pashtun heroine Malalai, who inspired her countrymen with her courage" (12), "Mahatma Gandhi, the great pacifist, and Mohammad Ali Jinnah, the founder of Pakistan" (15). And, speaking frankly of and to God, she styles herself as a prophet agitating against women's repression. At first, that repression figures as residue of outdated cultural traditions—primarily "the code of *purdah*," or "living under wraps" wearing *niqabs* and *burqas*—that Malala decides are not for her: "From an early age, I told my parents that no matter what other girls did, *I* would never cover my face like that" (17). But once the Taliban move from Afghanistan—where they had "taken over the country," where "schools for girls had been burned to the ground, and all women were forced to wear a severe form of *burqa*" (24)—into Pakistan, that repression is renewed as a living tenet of Islam. Hence the *mufti*, or Islamic scholar, telling Malala's father, who runs three schools, "I am representing good Muslims . . . And we all think your girls' high school is a blasphemy. You should close it. Teenage girls should not be going to school. They should be in *purdah*" (32). Here, and throughout her story, Yousafzai casts fundamentalism as a narrowing of the kin, friend, and school relations on which, as she sees it, liberal-democratic opportunities for growth and change depend.

Notably, a sense of crisis in and for education defines both the narrative situation unfolding (fundamentalists become increasingly aggressive in their attacks on Pakistani girls' schools) and in the characterization of the fundamentalists and their followers. Tracing the rise of the Taliban in Mingora, Yousafzai draws attention to two ideologues: Sufi Mohammad, leader of the TNSM (Tehrik-e-Nifaz-e-Sharia-e-Mohammadi/Movement for Enforcement of Islamic Law), who preaches that an earthquake "was a warning from God" (31); and his son-in-law, Maulana Fazlullah, who takes to the airwaves as a "radio *mullah*" preaching that Western culture is corrupt and that girls' schools are *haram*, forbidden by Islamic law (43). Fazlullah in particular figures as a powerful propaganda hub, winning over the radio audience and joining with Taliban militants to consolidate his religious influence. At the same time, he is described by Malala's father as "a high school drop-out," who "doesn't even have religious credentials," a "so-called *mullah* [who] is spreading ignorance" (41). Fazlullah's followers are similarly described when Malala observes the women who "gathered around the radio" to listen to him "sobbing" and "cry[ing]": "*Stop listening to music*, he begged. *Stop going to movies. Stop dancing. Stop*, he begged, *or God will send another earthquake to punish us all*" (39). Concerned that the women have "romanticized" Fazlullah, Malala says, "I knew what this radio *mullah* was saying wasn't true. An earthquake is a geological event that can be explained by science, I wanted to tell them. But these women, many of whom had no education and who were brought up to follow the dictates of their religious leaders, were frightened. As the mullah wept, so did they" (40). Such disclosures work to disparage what the memoir as a whole indicts as a closed-circuit worldview—a strict encoding of Islamic law intended to restrict the movements of not only schoolgirls but also a broad range of individuals, artifacts, and discourses—all given, in the ensuing "reign of terror" (49), a totalizing application: live by the code or die.

Unsettled Childhoods: "Stooge," "Machine"

The democratic sensibility in *I Am Malala* no doubt explains the book's popularity with Western readers, written as it was to contrast with the same terroristic-fundamentalist others long figured as the antagonists of Anglo-American democracy. Yet that resonance itself has become cause for concern with critics who question Yousafzai's ethnic, religious, and national affiliations and consider her to be an ideologue for the neoliberal West. Put another way, even though Yousafzai's first-person narrator seems entirely at odds with Irr's ideal neoliberal child—to the extent she confirms the bonds of family and kinship, reaches out to the free press rather than the free market, and agitates in the name of democratic good—in certain critics' eyes she comes into focus as a child parsing international conflicts in ways that justify US interventions driven by neoliberal imperatives.

The book's popular-press reception, in fact, calls into question not only the memoir's politics, and not only its facts, but also its composition. Following publication of the young readers edition, Ajachi Chakrabarti, writing for Indian news magazine *Tehelka*, refuted the book's political value ("The Sanctification of Malala Yousafzai," 2013). Claiming "it is as much [Malala's] story as it is of her father, Ziauddin, a Swati activist who was one of the most prominent voices in the Valley against the Taliban," Chakrabarti suggests that the valency of the storied situation has less to do with the daughter's near-assassination or narration and more to do with the father's former achievements as an activist. Troubled that "Western television anchors use Malala's story to demonstrate the backwardness of the Taliban, and by extension Islam," while "they completely ignore the role the West has played in maintaining that volatility," Chakrabarti asserts that "Malala herself hasn't rocked the boat—she has seldom spoken out against the consequences of the US War on Terror, even though the influx of the Taliban into Swat was a direct result." For Chakrabarti, Yousafzai's attempted assassination is summed up as a "brutal, senseless act [that] changed a precocious child with political ambitions into a cause célèbre"; and "in the reams that have been written about Malala ever since that act, not one concrete suggestion has emerged that will carry tangible benefits for girls, or boys, who are denied an education. Like with all icons, the medium has become more important than the message." Unlike Rosenfeld in her review of *Kiffe Kiffe Tomorrow*, Chakrabarti does not segregate the precocious from the political; all the same, his article as a whole works to disavow the child's political power, displacing agency onto the activist father and the Western journalists with whom he networked.

That construction of Yousafzai as an "icon" carries into discussions of the backlash against her in Pakistan. If Filipa Ioannou is correct, the idea that Malala had "become a symbol of malignant Western influence among some factions in Pakistani society" ("Group of Pakistan Schools Disses Nobel Peace Prize Winner With 'I Am Not Malala Day,' 2014) peaked in 2014 after she and Kailash Satyarthi jointly won the Nobel Peace Prize "for their struggle against the suppression of children and young people and for the right of all children to education." Along with Ioannou, Adam Withnall ("Pakistan Schools Denounce Nobel Peace Prize Winner Malala Yousafzai with 'I Am Not Malala' Day, 2014), and Salman Masood ("Malala Yousafzai, Nobel Laureate, Is Assailed by Schools Group in Pakistan," 2014) confirm that many Pakistanis read the book as an "anti-Pakistan and anti-Islam" text, taking Yousafzai to be "a tool in the hands of the Western powers" (Mirza Kashif Ali, qtd. in Ioannou). Citing Mirza Kashif Ali, president of the All Pakistan Private Schools Federation, who in protest inaugurated "I Am Not Malala Day" in the school network, Masood documents a widespread belief that "the West has created this persona who is against the Constitution and Islamic ideology of Pakistan" (Kashif, qtd. in Masood), while "others portray her as a Western stooge who has maligned both country and religion" (Masood).

Whether "icon," "symbol," "tool," "persona," or "stooge," Yousafzai figures in the accounts of her critics as an individual emptied of identity: she is an instrument, a conduit, channeling the values and ideas of other more responsible or efficacious entities. Even sympathetic accounts tend to disavow her agency. Consider *Al Jazeera* contributor Bina Shah's argument that "it's not Malala the person, but Malala the symbol whom Pakistanis have wrongly identified as a Western provocation against the entire nation." In an effort to humanize Malala the person and distinguish her from Malala the media construct, Shah asks, if Malala is a "Western puppet," then "Who's controlling the narrative?" By way of answer, Shah first points the finger at coauthor of the first edition Christina Lamb for making "anti-military insertions" in the memoir that seem "to promote an anti-Pakistan agenda." Shah then reminds readers that Malala began her writing career with her secret diary for the BBC, telling how "the Malala narrative was wrested away and fashioned by anti-Pakistani groups to suit a 'Western' agenda and malign the country." Comparing the daughter-father relationship to that of "Anne and Otto Frank: the brilliant daughter facing death with courage, the protective but proud father doing all he can to spread her message to the world," Shah leaves us with an image of Malala as a modern martyr, a "naïve" victim of a "powerful global media juggernaut."

But where Shah sees naivety, many commentators see conspiracy. In fact, as Withnall notes, "Some in Pakistan continue to say that the attack didn't really happen," a topic taken up by Michael Kugelman in his *Foreign Policy* article "Why Pakistan Hates Malala" (2017). Though acknowledging that "many Pakistanis admire and embrace Malala," Kugelman focuses on the popular perception of Malala as "shameful and traitorous" and of her shooting as "preplanned and staged by a variety of players—and with official Pakistani government connivance." "Conspiratorial thinking about Malala," argues Kugelman, "is strengthened by Pakistanis' deep mistrust of the West, where she is now based. Many suspect it of harboring designs on their country"—a perception he claims is "at least somewhat valid" for a number of reasons: the "extensive role" enjoyed by the CIA in Pakistan; the West's "strong embrace of Malala and the allegedly unlimited access it grants her to prominent platforms and top power corridors"; the "disclosure in 2013 that Malala's family had retained Edelman, a top American public relations firm, to assist with her media management"; and her work in writing for and interviewing with the *New York Times* and the BBC. Ultimately, Kugelman puts the backlash down to lower-class chagrin at Malala's near-impossible rise "from schoolteacher's daughter to embodiment of the global elite," suggesting a "rags-to-riches" narrative of self-made individualism. Yet the connection with Edelman complicates any such narrative.

In the same spirit that prompted Mark Mackinnon to claim that "Ms. Yousafzai's story is certainly worthy of telling. But she's had an unprecedented amount of help getting her message out," and returning to the same questions of agency raised by Chakrabarti and Shah, journalists take issue with the business dealings undergirding the "mighty machine" that is Malala Yousafzai. For some, economic disparity is the sticking point—for example, when Palash Ghosh, writing for the *International Business Times*, appeals to the Pakistan Bureau of Statistics to note that "the per capita income in the country for the 2011–2012 [year] amounted to a paltry $1,257," which "means that it would take almost 24,000 years for the average Pakistan [sic] to earn what Malala will receive from her memoirs." For others, the issue is not so much earning power as business acumen. As Pakistan's English-language daily *Dawn* reported, "Pakistani schoolgirl Malala Yousafzai has become a formidable force for rights in the year since the Taliban shot her, but an equally formidable public relations operation has helped her spread her message. One of the world's biggest public relations firms, Edelman, has a team working on her behalf while politicians, journalists and book publishers are making her into something of a global brand" ("Malala Inc"). Interestingly, whereas most journalists usually disavow Yousafzai's political agency, in describing a business-savvy operation, *Dawn* cites sources who claim that "although she is only 16 it is very much driven by her personality." According to *Dawn*, "The Malala machine really grew in November 2012 when the PR agency Edelman, whose clients include Starbucks and Microsoft, started working for her family. . . . Edelman said its role 'primarily involves providing a press office function for Malala' and 'helping to advise the family on how to engage with the huge media and public interest in Malala's campaign.'" Despite emphasis on presumably nonprofit "campaign" work, it is public knowledge that Yousafzai and her family have thrived under the auspices of Salarzai Ltd., a private company established by Yousafzai and her parents to protect the rights to the book. Writing for British daily *The Times*, Fariha Karim spelled out the company's early business transactions and profits: a UK book deal with Weidenfeld & Nicholson worth "about 2 million" GBP; initial paperback and hardback sales earning 2.2 million including "a pre-tax profit of 1.1 million"; and the fact that, "according to research by the US-based Institute for Policy Studies, she is one of the higher-earning Nobel laureates, bringing in 114,000 per speech, compared with 64,000 for Desmond Tutu." All in, much like Guène's, Yousafzai's critics and commentators lead us to think not of the substance of the story told in the memoir but of its afterlife as a commodity in the hands of a teenage entrepreneur contracting for profit in the marketplace. In the process, Yousafzai emerges as something more than Irr's ideal neoliberal child: no mere character in a narrative, she is a flesh-and-blood youngster who, in ways worth comparing to Swarup's Ram, purposefully resorts to the literary marketplace for justice.

The Work of the Teenage Narrative

With *I Am Malala*'s reception in mind, at least three things matter here. First, that championing democracy in print can have a literal and not insubstantial payoff in terms of private gains. Second, that broader publics are competing over the meaning and value of that payoff: here vindicating it as a natural expression of free-market individualism, and there lambasting it as the ill-gotten gains of deception, treason, sacrilege. And third, that the work of the critics figures the economy as a critical tool, a heuristic, for parsing and evaluating literature in the age of neoliberalism. At which point we seem to enter into a well-trodden debate on the relative impossibility of literature, no matter how democratically minded, to escape the capitalist conditions of production on which it depends for publication (a debate crystalized between the call of Jean-Paul Sartre's *What Is Literature?*, 1948, and the response of Theodor Adorno's "Commitment: The Politics of Autonomous Art," 1962). Yet the nature of that debate seems to alter when attention turns to child authors; and this seems especially true if we are familiar with the line of argument inaugurated by Jacqueline Rose when she called into question the very possibility of children's fiction, arguing that "children's fiction"—as a field not only determined by adults but wholly conditioned by adult desires—"sets up the child as an outsider to its own process, and then aims, unashamedly, to take the child *in*" (2).

With books like *I Am Malala* and *Kiffe Kiffe Tomorrow*, it turns out that teenagers, at least, need not be outsiders to that process—that the market can readily make room for teens, as much as adults, to "constru[e] the child" (Rose 2). The question, then, is whether or not anything of substance actually changes: whether young writers and young readers genuinely obtain new freedoms, or whether they simply enter into a new "fantasy of childhood," as Rose calls it—in this case, a neoliberal fantasy of the entrepreneurial entrance of the child author into the conventionally adult realm of contractual labor relations. Either way, the conventional understanding of children's literature is unsettled to the extent that the young author relinquishes something of childhood, at least as construed in the modern era of child protections, children's rights, child labor laws, and compulsory education, a nexus that functions to segregate the world of growing up from the world of work. To be sure, scholars in cultural and childhood development studies have long recognized the marketplace as an issue of concern both in and for childhood, arguing that the commercial and technological saturation of children's culture, along with the commodification of childhood itself, puts children in jeopardy—cognitively, psychologically, and physiologically (see, for example, Neil Postman's *The Disappearance of Childhood*, 1982; Barry Sanders's *A Is for Ox: Violence, Electronic Media, and the Silencing of the Written Word*, 1994; Shirley Steinberg and Joe Kincheloe's *Kinderculture: The Corporate Construction of Childhood*, 1997; and Richard Louv's *Last Child in the Woods: Saving our Children from Nature-Deficit Disorder*, 2005).

But perhaps more relevant for the present study are those scholars currently thinking of children as producers rather than consumers of culture. Some, represented in the collections edited by Christine Alexander and Juliet McMaster (*The Child Writer from Austen to Woolf*, 2009) and David Owen and Lesley Peterson (*Home and Away: The Place of the Child Writer*, 2016), identify as scholars of literary juvenilia, mostly (though not entirely) exploring the unpublished writings of "scribbling children who achieved greatness as adults" (Alexander and McMaster 2), the task being "to catch these precocious experimenting children in the act of growing into the great authors we have come to admire" (4). To be sure, as Alexander and McMaster spell out, "alongside these child incarnations of adult authors [from Jane Austen and the Brontë children to George Eliot and Louisa May Alcott] are some whose writing is also full of percipience and zest, but who did not become adult writers" (2). Either way, most juvenilia scholars seem to have their sights set firmly on past times and traditions. Others, meanwhile, like Evelyn Arizpe and Morag Styles with Abigail Rokison (2010), draw attention to young writers in the twenty-first century publishing through blogs, social media, and fan-fiction websites, suggesting a whole new world of possibility afforded by the rise to dominance of digital technologies and online networks.

What sets the present study apart is my interest in young authors from around the world who in growing numbers have broken into the mainstream literary marketplace *as* young authors, a fact significant for children's literature in general but also for stories of education and school experience in particular. I say this, in part, because—as explained in chapter one—critics in the past made concerted efforts to define the school story genre according to age-based aptitudes and engagements: they denied young writers attention on the grounds that they lacked worldly experience, emotional maturity, and stylistic or technical expertise. But it is possible that authors of school age speculate on the ends of educational experience in ways that adult authors do not: for example, when in the final chapters of *Kiffe Kiffe Tomorrow* Doria confesses, "I still don't know what I really want to do in life" (169), and Yousafzai in her last chapter (before the epilogue) reflects, "I wonder sometimes if I will be the same Malala in the future" (187), they comprise sentiments expressed while still in the process of learning and growing. Rather than deem this a handicap, I wish to consider it more properly an affordance: a condition not of ignorance but of expectation and anticipation, one that compels distinct narrative solutions to the question of how to imagine the future in terms of growth, development, and learning.

Accepting that the teenage sense of the future is put under a particular kind of duress in the age of neoliberalism—when students, for instance, are increasingly expected to commit prematurely to majors and career tracks at a time of life arguably better suited (from a developmental standpoint) to experimenting across disciplines—I say that such narratives matter precisely because of how they grasp, engage with, and respond to modern ways of living within and around the market structures of global capitalism in the twenty-first century.

Questions of time are rightly foregrounded in narrative studies, as in the landmark contributions of Gérard Genette (*Narrative Discourse*, 1980) and Paul Ricoeur (*Time and Narrative*, 1983). As I have argued elsewhere, our sense of ethical action and political possibility are inextricably caught up in narrative attitudes to time, best expressed in the competing alternatives posed by the conservative appeal to traditional values (looking to a past) and the progressive anticipation of reform or revolution (looking to a future) (see Aitchison, "Lost Causes, Affective Affinities"). And if scholars of gerontology such as William J. Randall are right, we do well to recognize the extent to which our very identities, along with our life possibilities, live and die by the narratives we are able to tell about ourselves, the world, and the relation between. This is not just to reiterate Fredric Jameson's gambit in *The Political Unconscious: Narrative as a Socially Symbolic Act* (1981) that "the process of narrative . . . is the central function or *instance* of the human mind" (13, italics in original) but more specifically to take to heart Randall's insights into the role of narrative in aging and development. Though primarily interested in adult subjects, Randall gives thought to students of traditional college age to consider the ways in which educational institutions and curriculums afford opportunities for young people to build what he calls "good, strong stories" ("Composing a Good Strong Story: The Advantages of a Liberal Arts Environment for Experiencing and Exploring the Narrative Complexity of Human Life," 2012). Conceiving identity formation as a narrative process, he makes the point that the stories young people craft about their lives play an instrumental role in either opening up or foreclosing on actual life choices. Making a case for recognizing the traditional, multidisciplinary liberal arts campus as the consummate locus of experimentation for young, developing identities, he compels us to take seriously the identity work undertaken in stories by and about young people.

To some extent, Randall confirms Alexander's claims regarding the role of writing in making the transition into adulthood—when, discussing the juvenilia of Victorian novelist and spiritualist Rosa Praed, she argues that "the early practice of writing provided intellectual, emotional, and spiritual continuity for this young woman from colonial Queensland as she entered an adult life fraught with hardship and dislocation" ("Nineteenth-Century

Juvenilia" 25). But I would be wary of suggesting a writing experience that fully transcends time and place—as if to say that the nature or role of writing in identity development remains constant in spite of the world-changing shifts in industry, economy, education, and government that has taken place between the nineteenth century and the twenty-first. More with Randall's contemporary scene in mind, the stories told by Guène and Yousafzai—along with others by Lebert, Vizzini, Wataya, Denezhkina, Keplinger, and Zhang—raise a number of remarkable concerns: about the extent to which the young sense of self rests on the promise of democracy; the extent to which formal education, along with its meaning and value, appears to be under duress; the extent to which the marketplace seems to perpetuate nineteenth-century social-realists' vision of fortune as a wheel raising some to meteoric heights while lowering others to abysmal depths; and the extent to which stories of young life are political, not only parsing but also intending to shape social relations—at the very least, giving voice to certain factions agitating for change, but possibly also serving as agents of change in their own right. Understandably, the politics and aesthetics in these and other teenage narratives are by no means settled: they are here preciously wrapped up in the life of the one, and there more conscientiously reaching out to the many. Some might read that as an impasse; others still might even read it as hypocrisy; but if we are at all curious about the narrative dimensions of identity, I would recommend reading it as a glimpse of politics and ethics in the ongoing process of formation.

Conclusion: The Deregulation of Childhood

In a real sense, debate over regulation and deregulation has been the mainstay of the modern education tradition inaugurated by John Locke and Jean-Jacques Rousseau in earlier centuries: the point of seminal works such as *Some Thoughts Concerning Education* (1693) and *Émile, or On Education* (1762), after all, was to champion a form of regulation (guardians purposefully scaffold early learning experiences so as to reduce children's risk of social contamination) in the guise of deregulation (children are given unrivaled freedoms to explore and learn). That is, even the most experimental, liberatory pedagogies tend to regulate childhood's freedoms—as in Rousseau's providing a pedagogically overdetermined space for Émile to find things out for himself in a "natural" way. What Rousseau models, in a work sometimes said to have inaugurated the school story as a genre (Spolton 1963), is a set piece made possible by a sleight of hand: it suggests an upbringing defined by young autonomy and self-actualization, while simultaneously giving license to an environment that is strategically constructed by adult others. Not insignificantly, Rousseau's appeal to "natural consequences" rather than social influences is an appeal echoed in neoliberal defenses of a self-regulating market undergirded by the early theories of Frank Knight, Milton Friedman, and Friedrich Hayek (see Klein 56–65).

It is worth noting that, of the two terms, "regulation" has a broader, more general currency beyond the realm of economic debates, to the extent that it is a fundamental of socialization: from cradle to grave, the human community is drawn into rule-governed realms—of language, manners, customs, traditions, edicts, laws, vocational practices, fields of study—in which more or less correct ways of doing things are enforced. "Deregulation," meanwhile, tends to circulate in a more select discourse community concerned primarily with tariffs, prices, and, more and more, environmental impacts. As a negative term, "deregulation" figures as a catchword for the collective forces of neoliberalism: denoting, broadly, the disestablishment of governmental control of the capitalist market; but also connoting, more narrowly, the purposeful dismantling of policies and attitudes that inhibit the one-sided movement of capital from public to private goods. With Rousseau's childhood enclave in mind, we do well to recognize that the so-called "deregulated" market operates by a comparable sleight of hand: as David Harvey's work in *A Brief History of Neoliberalism* (2005) and "Contradictions of Neo-Liberalism" (2018) makes clear, what is announced as a realm of fair and free competition is in actuality an overdetermined structure. As documented by Naomi Klein in *The Shock Doctrine: The Rise of Disaster Capitalism* (2007), it comprises a mechanism that, from the 1973 coup in Chile to the ongoing wars in the Middle East, demands ceaseless intervention in facilitating and sustaining a global market for the benefit of the few rather than the many. Which is to say that deregulation in the age of neoliberalism indexes neither the avowal of the market in its capacity to self-regulate, nor the disavowal of market interventions as such. As Wendy Brown confirms, "Neoliberalism is not about the state leaving the economy alone. Rather, neoliberalism activates the state on behalf of the economy, *not* to undertake economic functions or to intervene in economic effects, but rather to facilitate economic competition and growth and to economize the social, or, as Foucault puts it, to 'regulate society by the market'" (62). It is in this sense that deregulation is synonymous with the undoing of democracy.

To borrow the language of deregulation to think about childhood and young adulthood, then, is not wholly explained by revisiting Rousseau, since Rousseau's didactic-pedagogical project, as individualistic as it appears, is far more moral than the dominant strain of conservative neoliberalism. That is, while morality can and does inflect neoliberal discourses, deregulating the marketplace serves less an ethics and more an ethos. And in making that distinction

I mean to suggest a neoliberal disposition that need not rely on goodwill or virtue to gain ground or legitimacy. Why? Because deregulation describes not only the removal of restrictions fixing industry practices and prices but also the letting go of a certain capacity to care, giving license to conceiving all interactions with others as if they were marketplace exchanges—in an environment where fair exchanges are not the point (where the point is, very often, just the opposite). In adopting the language of deregulation to think about teenagers and teenage authors, then, we are compelled to recognize not only everyday consciousness inflected with materialism, and not only a sense of life media-saturated and commercialized, but a reckoning of purpose, along with the development of a narrative identity, marked by gains and losses in a realm of deliberately uneven exchanges. The difference, finally, between Swarup on the one hand and Guène and Yousafzai on the other, is the difference between either reading the narrative of young identity as a done deal, according to which the garden of childhood (a phrase alluding to Rousseau's depiction of Émile in their sequestered garden and the narrator's ensuing reflections on cultivation, autonomy, and property) is indistinguishable from the marketplace; or reading the narrative of young identity as a work in progress, according to which the garden of childhood, though encroached upon, might yet be turned over and put to some radically other use.

NOTES

1. The classic example of the neoliberal individualist creed is Margaret Thatcher's claim, in a 1987 interview for *Women's Own* magazine, that there is no society, only individuals: "We have gone through a period when too many children and people have been given to understand 'I have a problem, it is the Government's job to cope with it!' or 'I have a problem, I will go and get a grant to cope with it!' 'I am homeless, the Government must house me!' and so they are casting their problems on society and who is society? There is no such thing! There are individual men and women and there are families and no government can do anything except through people and people look to themselves first."

2. See, for example, A. W. Hastings; and Mendelsohn.

3. Almost but not quite: as David Sadler notes, for a spell in the early twentieth century "child authors became almost a fad," with "at least eighteen books by eleven young authors—most of them American" published by the end of the 1920s (24).

4. Between 2018 and 2019, I reached out to a number of writers who had published as teenagers to ask about that experience. I framed my query along the following lines: "I'm a scholar researching the rise of teenage novelists, and I'm wondering if you're able to comment on your experience as a teenager contracting to write and publish? I'm especially interested in two things: how much autonomy or independence you felt in negotiating or signing your contracts; and whether it changed your sense of being a youth." My intention was to synthesize qualitative claims about the intersection of young identity, cultural

production, and the contractual marketplace. As it turned out, Hinton and Korman were the only two to reply (Hinton in January 2018 by email; Korman in January 2019 through the Readers Forum on his website).

5. The Golden Age of children's literature conventionally refers to a period in the late nineteenth/early twentieth century when popular children's writers such as Lewis Carroll dispensed with the moral and evangelical imperatives of earlier generations in favor of more romantic understandings of childhood that emphasized innocence, imagination, and play.

WORKS CITED

Abrams, Douglas E., and Sarah H. Ramsey. *Children and the Law: Doctrine, Policy, and Practice*. West/Thomson, 2010.
Adams, Gillian. "Speaking for Lions." *Children's Literature Association Quarterly*, vol. 17, no. 4, 1992, pp. 2–3, *Project MUSE*. Accessed 1 Mar. 2019.
Adorno, Theodor. 1962. "Commitment." *Marxist Literary Theory: A Reader*, edited by Terry Eagleton and Drew Milne, Wiley-Blackwell, 1996.
Aitchison, David. "Lost Causes, Affective Affinities: Radical Chronotope in the Age of Liberal Narrative." *JNT Journal of Narrative Theory*, vol. 45, no. 3, 2015, pp. 395–418.
Alexander, Christine. "Nineteenth-Century Juvenilia: A Survey." *The Child Writer from Austen to Woolf*, edited by Christine Alexander and Juliet McMaster. Cambridge University Press, 2005, pp. 11–30.
Alexander, Christine, and Juliet McMaster, editors. *The Child Writer from Austen to Woolf*. Cambridge University Press, 2005.
Arizpe, Evelyn, and Morag Styles with Abigail Rokison. "Sidelines: Some Neglected Dimensions of Children's Literature and Its Scholarship." *Routledge Companion to Children's Literature*, edited by David Rudd, Routledge, 2010, pp. 125–38.
Brown, Wendy. *Undoing the Demos: Neoliberalism's Stealth Revolution*. Zone Books, 2015.
Butcher, Kasey. "I Am Malala: Comparing the Young Readers Edition to the 'Original.'" *Ph.D.s and Pigtails: Girlhoods, Grad School, and Popular Culture*. 12 Mar. 2015, www.phdsandpigtails.com/2015/03/12/i-am-malala-comparing-the-young-reader-edition-to-the-original. Accessed 10 Sep. 2020.
Cadden, Mike. *Telling Children's Stories: Narrative Theory and Children's Literature*. University of Nebraska Press, 2010.
Chakrabarti, Ajachi. "The Sanctification of Malala Yousafzai." *Tehelka*, 23 Oct. 2013, *Anant Media Pvt Ltd.*, www.tehelka.com/the-sanctification-of-malala-yousafzai. Accessed 21 Mar. 2019.
Cook, Daniel Thomas. *The Commodification of Childhood: The Children's Clothing Industry and the Rise of the Child Consumer*. Duke University Press, 2004.
DeHart, Jonathan. "Why Did the Taliban Shoot Malala?" *The Diplomat*, 18 Jul. 2013, *James Pach*, www.thediplomat.com/2013/07/why-did-the-taliban-shoot-malala. Accessed 21 Mar. 2019.
Flanagan, Constance. *Teenage Citizens: The Political Theories of the Young*. Harvard University Press, 2013.
Genette, Gérard. *Narrative Discourse: An Essay in Method*. Translated by Jane E. Lewin, Cornell University Press, 1980.

Ghosh, Palash. "Malala Yousafzai Gets $3 Million Book Deal: Has a Backlash Started?" *International Business Times*, 28 Mar. 2013, *IBT Media Inc.*, www.ibtimes.com/malala-yousafzai-gets-3-million-book-deal-has-backlash-started-1158261. Accessed 21 Mar. 2019.

Gubar, Marah. *Artful Dodgers: Reconceiving the Golden Age of Children's Literature*. Oxford University Press, 2009.

Guène, Faiza. *Kiffe Kiffe Tomorrow*. Translated by Sarah Adams, Harcourt, 2006.

Harvey, David. *A Brief History of Neoliberalism*. Oxford University Press, 2005.

Harvey, David. "Contradictions of Neo-Liberalism." *David Harvey's Anti-Capitalist Chronicles*, Nov. 2018, *Reading Marx's Capital with David Harvey*, davidharvey.org/2018/11/new-podcast-david-harveys-anti-capitalist-chronicles. Accessed 22 Dec. 2019.

Hastings, A. Waller, "Science Fiction." *Keywords for Children's Literature*, edited by Philip Nel and Lissa Paul, New York University Press, 2011, pp. 202–7.

Howlett, Caitlyn. "Neoliberalism, Critical Pedagogy, and the Child." *Philosophical Studies in Education*, vol. 48, 2017, pp. 65–73, *EBSCOhost*. Accessed 1 Dec. 2018.

Huehls, Mitchum, and Rachel Greenwald Smith. "Four Phases of Neoliberalism and Literature." *Neoliberalism and Contemporary Literature*, Johns Hopkins University Press, 2017, pp. 1–18.

Ioannou, Filipa. "Group of Pakistan Schools Disses Nobel Peace Prize Winner With 'I Am Not Malala Day,'" *Slate*, 11 Nov. 2014, *The Slate Group*, www.slate.com/news-and-politics/2014/11/i-am-not-malala-day-anti-yousafzai-backlash-from-pakistan-schools.html. Accessed 21 Mar. 2019.

Irr, Caren. "Neoliberal Childhoods: The Orphan as Entrepreneur in Contemporary Anglophone Fiction." *Neoliberalism and Contemporary Literature*, edited by Mitchum Huehls and Rachel Greenwald Smith, Johns Hopkins University Press, 2017, pp. 220–36.

Jameson, Fredric. *The Political Unconscious: Narrative as a Socially Symbolic Act*. Cornell University Press, 1981.

Karim, Fariha. "Malala Makes Millions on Her Life Story." *The Times*, 29 Jun. 2016, *Times Newspapers Limited*, www.thetimes.co.uk/article/malala-makes-millions-from-her-life-story-3msfjvp99. Accessed 21 Mar. 2019.

Klein, Naomi. *The Shock Doctrine: The Rise of Disaster Capitalism*. Random House, 2007.

Kugelman, Michael. "Why Pakistan Hates Malala." *Foreign Policy*, 15 Aug. 2017, *The FP Group*, www.foreignpolicy.com/2017/08/15/why-pakistan-hates-malala. Accessed 21 Mar. 2019.

Lamb, Christina. "My Year with Malala." *Sunday Times*. 13 Oct. 2013. *Christina Lamb OBE*. www.christinalamb.net/articles/my-year-with-malala. Accessed 12 Sep. 2020.

Latour, Bruno. *Reassembling the Social: An Introduction to Actor-Network Theory*. Oxford University Press, 2005.

Levine, Caroline. *Forms: Whole, Rhythm, Hierarchy, Network*. Princeton University Press, 2015.

Locke, John. *Some Thoughts Concerning Education and of the Conduct of the Understanding*. 1693. Edited by Ruth W. Grant and Nathan Tarcov, Hacket Publishing Company, Inc., 1996.

Louv, Richard. *Last Child in the Woods: Saving Our Children from Nature-Deficit Disorder*. Algonquin Books, 2005.

Mackinnon, Mark. "One Year after Being Shot by the Taliban, Malala Yousafzai Is a Mighty Machine." *Globe and Mail*, 8 Oct. 2013, *The Globe and Mail Inc.*, www.theglobeandmail.com/news/world/malala-yousafzai-a-strong-message-a-mighty-machine/article14762416. Accessed 21 Mar. 2019.

"Malala Inc: Global Operation Surrounds Teenage Campaigner." *Dawn*, 11 Oct. 2013, *Pakistan Herald Publications*, www.dawn.com/news/1048971. Accessed 21 Mar. 2019.

Masood, Salman. "Malala Yousafzai, Nobel Laureate, Is Assailed by Schools Group in Pakistan." *New York Times*, 10 Nov. 2014, *The New York Times Company*, www.nytimes.com/2014/11/11/world/asia/malala-yousafzai-nobel-laureate-is-assailed-by-schools-group-in-pakistan.html. Accessed 21 Mar. 2019.

McCormick, Patricia. "I Am Malala FAQ." *Patricia McCormick*, www.patriciamccormick.com/i-am-malala. Accessed 12 Sep. 2020.

Meltzer, Marisa. "The Other Paris." *Salon*, 25 Sep. 2011, *Salon Media Group, Inc.*, www.salon.com/2006/07/26/guene. Accessed 27 Feb. 2019.

Mendelsohn, Farah. "Is There Any Such Thing as Children's Science Fiction?: A Position Piece." *The Lion and the Unicorn*, vol. 28, no. 2, 2004, pp. 284–313, *ProjectMUSE*. Accessed 1 Mar. 2019.

Michaels, Walter Benn. "Fifty Shades of Neoliberal Love." *Neoliberalism and Contemporary Literature*, edited by Mitchum Huehls and Rachel Greenwald Smith, Johns Hopkins University Press, 2017, pp. 21–33.

Moretti, Franco. "Network Theory, Plot Analysis." *New Left Review*, vol. 68, 2011, pp. 80–112, *The New Left Review Ltd.* Accessed 1 Mar. 2019.

"The Nobel Peace Prize 2014." *The Nobel Prize*, 2014, *Nobel Media AB*, www.nobelprize.org/prizes/peace/2014/summary/. Accessed 21 Mar. 2019.

Postman, Neil. *The Disappearance of Childhood*. Delacorte Press, 1983.

Randall, William J. "Composing a Good Strong Story: The Advantages of a Liberal Arts Environment for Experiencing and Exploring the Narrative Complexity of Human Life." *The Journal of General Education*, vol. 61, no. 3, 2012, pp. 277–93, *ProjectMUSE*. Accessed Jan. 2016.

Randall, William J. *The Narrative Complexity of Ordinary Life: Tales from the Coffee Shop*. Oxford University Press, 2015.

Randall, William J. *The Stories We Are: An Essay on Self-Creation, 2nd Edition*. University of Toronto Press, 2014.

Ricoeur, Paul. *Time and Narrative*, vol. 1. Translated by Kathleen McLaughlin and David Pellauer, University of Chicago Press, 1984.

"rip-off, n." *OED Online*, Mar. 2019, Oxford University Press, www.oed.com/view/Entry/166229. Accessed 4 Feb. 2019.

Rose, Jacqueline. *The Case of Peter Pan, or, The Impossibility of Children's Fiction*. University of Pennsylvania Press, 1984.

Rosenfeld, Lucinda. "Catcher in the Rue." *New York Times*, The New York Times Company, 23 Jul. 2006, www.nytimes.com/2006/07/23/books/review/23rosenfeld.html. Accessed 27 Feb. 2019.

Rousseau, Jean-Jacques. *Émile, or On Education*. 1762. Translated by Allan Bloom, Basic Books, 1979.

Sadler, David. "Innocent Hearts: The Child Authors of the 1920s." *Children's Literature Association Quarterly* vol. 17, no. 4, 1992, pp. 24–30, *ProjectMUSE*. Accessed 1 Jan. 2019.

Sanders, Barry. *A Is for Ox: Violence, Electronic Media, and the Silencing of the Written Word*. Pantheon Books, 1994.

Sartre, Jean-Paul. *"What Is Literature?" And Other Essays*. 1948. Harvard University Press, 1988.

Shah, Bina. "Malala Yousafzai: Pakistan's Divisive Figure." *Al Jazeera*, 19 Nov. 2015, Al Jazeera Media Group, www.aljazeera.com/indepth/opinion/2015/11/malala-yousafzai-pakistan-divisive-figure-151118085120135.html. Accessed 21 Mar. 2019.

Spolton, L. "The Secondary School in Post-War Fiction." *British Journal of Educational Studies* vol. 11, no. 2, 1963, pp. 125–41, *JSTOR*. Accessed 14 Aug. 2018.

Steinberg, Shirley R., and Joe L. Kincheloe, editors. *Kinderculture: The Corporate Construction of Childhood*. Westview Press, 1997.

Swarup, Vikas. *Q & A*. Doubleday, 2005.

Thatcher, Margaret. 1987. "Interview for *Woman's Own* ('no such thing as society')." *Margaret Thatcher Foundation*, 2019, www.margaretthatcher.org/document/106689. Accessed 30 Dec. 2019.

Withnall, Adam. "Pakistan Schools Denounce Nobel Peace Prize Winner Malala Yousafzai with 'I Am Not Malala' Day.'" *The Independent*, 12 Nov. 2014, Independent Print Ltd., www.independent.co.uk/news/world/asia/pakistan-schools-denounce-nobel-peace-prize-winner-malala-yousafzai-with-i-am-not-malala-day-9855642.html. Accessed 21 Mar. 2019.

Worden, Daniel. "The Memoir in the Age of Neoliberal Individualism." *Neoliberalism and Contemporary Literature*, edited by Mitchum Huehls and Rachel Greenwald Smith, Johns Hopkins University Press, 2017, pp. 160–77.

Yousafzai, Malala, and Patricia McCormick. *I Am Malala: How One Girl Stood up for Education and Changed the World*. Little, Brown and Company, 2014.

AFTERWORD

The school story gives powerful expression to a critical nexus of young identity, education, and growth, underpinned by a complex of pedagogical, cultural, political, and economic forces. And the nature of the experience recounted in the school story lends itself well to a formalist reading—of spaces, rhythms, hierarchies, and networks. Helpful for disclosing contemporary renegotiations of education and authority, whether in the classroom, the curriculum, or the wider world of work and culture, are the binary and hierarchical forms depicted in *Frindle* and *Charlie Joe Jackson's Guide to Not Reading*. Not only does entrepreneurship trump education in both stories, it does so with gusto and charm, suggesting that the classroom is best understood as a gateway to the marketplace—nothing more and nothing less. Network forms matter, too, in both stories (in the increasing circulation of the new word and in the ripple effects of the position paper), but the real conflict comes down to hierarchies competing with hierarchies, the traditional authority of the classroom having to compete with the rise to power of marketplace interests. As for *Push* and *Speak*, if rhythmic form is indeed *the* critical form for understanding the rationality shaping our education systems, of all the works discussed in this project, these two offer especially powerful reflections on the rhythms and routines of school life. Weaving through distinct spaces—apartments, classrooms, closets—as well as clashing with peer networks and institutional hierarchies, the damaged rhythms of such protagonists' lives invite serious reflection on the well-being of students and teachers alike, and on the extent to which the school as an institution is a reliable locus of health and promise.

Just as thought-provoking are the spatial forms underwriting the teacher/student conflicts in *Battle Royale* and *Cooties*, films worlds apart in their tenor and territory yet converging remarkably in their misgivings about formal education, which collapses irremediably in both stories. Whether thinking of the hallways in the Japanese junior high where students run riot, or the library and basement in the US elementary school where teachers hole up to reflect on flagging careers, the school spaces in these works figure as punishing enclosures: intimately bound up with hierarchical and network forms, they certainly play on fears easily exploited by horror, but more importantly they tease out the difficult emotions informing student and teacher experience burdened by precarity and vulnerability. It is just as eye opening to find teenage authors like Guène and Yousafzai theorizing social relations and showing the young mind to be shrewdly analytical in its grasp of how individuals, cultures, and institutions intersect in terms of agency and power. Colliding with spatial enclosures ghettoized and occupied, and with cultural hierarchies premised on ethnic, gender, and religious divisions, the network forms in both of their books compel us to reevaluate the social role and marketplace possibilities of the child author in the neoliberal era.

Because the ranks of school story authors now include writers of school age, it seems that we are at a privileged moment in the development of a genre with potential to help us make sense of such a strange institution: a realm ostensibly governed by adults bent on imagining the world that will be, albeit adults often beleaguered by the system they serve, and whose students are more often than not compelled to question, resist, and at times unsettle the order of things. Considered together, the school stories discussed in this book reveal a critical juncture in contemporary life for countries around the world, an extended field of conflict in which antidemocratic and anti-intellectual forces compete for control over the meaning and purpose of formal education. As I have argued, there is profound uncertainty in most if not all of these works, with authors moving seamlessly between leftist and rightist impulses, as if suspicious of neoliberal reality yet unable to imagine a radical alternative. Still, at the very least, the bounded wholes, temporal rhythms, structured hierarchies, and evolving networks informing the contemporary school story lay bare a staggering complex of power—whether institutional or individual, discriminatory or inclusive, self-interested or civic minded, punishing or forgiving, pathological or healthful. But that our youngest authors are cognizant of marketplace encroachments on democratic freedoms—even if the word "neoliberal" is not in their lexicon—and that they are ready to speak of protest and social revolution in the name of justice for all, confirms the school story as a genre to be reckoned with for its politics and ethics as much as aesthetics.

ACKNOWLEDGMENTS

Sincere thanks to everyone who has guided, encouraged, and helped me in thinking and writing about school fiction:

To Jennifer Berner, my first reader, who with characteristic care helped knock each chapter into shape; to my anonymous reviewers on the first full draft, whose wisdom and insights helped me further refine the manuscript; to Elizabeth A. Marshall and Lissa Paul, who helped me ready the early version of "Bookish Boys" for publication in *Children's Literature in Education*, and to that journal's publisher, Springer; and to Katie Keene and everyone at University Press of Mississippi and the Children's Literature Association for their interest in and commitment to publishing this work.

To my fellow scholars at the annual conventions of the Children's Literature Association and the Modern Language Association, especially Michelle Ann Abate, Clare Echterling, and Derritt Mason for organizing panels at MLA 2019, ChLA 2018, and MLA 2016, respectively, in which I made my first forays into thinking about children's literature and education; to my fellow educators and scholars in online communities including the Syllabus Swap: Children's and YA Literature group on Facebook and the child_lit and children-literature-UK listservs, collectively the hive brain on which I have long depended for building and refining my archive; to my students, for being such good sports in engaging with so many of the materials I had in mind for this project, and for daring to collaborate in discussions, surveys, and papers that continue to influence my understanding of pedagogy and education; and to all my friends, colleagues, and comrades on campuses around the world who still believe in democracy in education.

To all the novelists, filmmakers, and critics who have crafted such powerful and provocative stories of students and teachers, including those who took the time to correspond with me and share their experiences as young writers.

Finally, to my son, Theodor, whose birth in 2012 compelled me to reflect more purposefully on the meaning and value of children's literature and public education (helped further when, at three months, he gifted me Julia Mickenberg and Philip Nel's *Tales for Little Rebels*), and whose words and deeds endlessly inspire.

Onward, my friends.

INDEX

adolescence, 33–34, 38, 41, 57, 113, 134, 146
Adorno, Theodor, 60, 173
adult chauvinism, 33–34, 39–40, 52
Alcott, Louisa May, 50
Alexander, Christine, 174–75
Alexiadou, Nafsika, 3, 8
Alington, Adrian, 33–34
Amalgamated Press, 34, 42
Anderson, Laurie Halse, 9, 14, 71, 92–100, 109–15, 148n7, 183. See also *Speak*
Arnold, Thomas, 22–24, 37
art, 95–99, 112–13, 116n5
Auchmuty, Rosemary, 4, 49–53, 58
autobiography, 22, 35, 111, 164, 167
Avery, Gillian, 25, 40–41, 44

Baker, Rita Anthony, 25
Bakhtin, Mikhail, 69–72, 78, 111
Banks, James A., 4, 11
Barkan, Ross, 16n2
Battle Royale/Batoru Rowaiaru, 9, 14, 123, 127–37, 143–47, 183–84
Bildungsroman, 69–71
Billy Bunter stories, 34–35, 43, 45
Blackwood's Edinburgh Magazine, 22
Blyton, Enid, 37, 41, 49–50, 54, 55
Book Scavenger series (Bertman), 71–72
Boys of England, 124
Boy's Own Paper, 19, 34–35, 43, 45, 48
Braithwaite, E. R., 38, 48–49
Brazil, Angela, 31, 37, 39, 41–43
Brent-Dyer, Elinor, 31–32, 37, 39, 41–42, 49–51

British Empire, 19–21, 27, 30, 35–37, 43, 45, 58, 62, 73
Brock, Colin, 3, 8
Brown, Wendy, 5–6, 21, 56, 74, 162, 177
Bruce, Dorita Fairlie, 31–32, 37, 39, 42, 49–51
bullying, 123, 130–31, 139–40, 148n6

Cadogan, Mary, 41, 42, 45, 49
capital: cultural, 159; human, 6, 7, 21, 56, 64n3, 98
capitalism: and childhood, 154; and commercialization, 115; commodity, 76, 83; consumer, 143; and exchange, 5, 113–14, 177; free-market, 6; global, 15, 78, 173; *laissez-faire*, 105; and production, 173
Chakrabarti, Ajachi, 169–70, 172
Charlie Joe Jackson's Guide to Not Reading (Greenwald), 9, 13, 71–72, 79–86, 183
Child, Harold, 27
Chocolate War, The (Cormier), 46, 53, 61, 123, 125, 132–34, 148n1
cinema, 9, 14, 54, 123, 126–27, 135–36, 138
citizenship, 4, 7, 10, 14–15, 56–57, 62, 102, 127, 133–34, 135
Clabaugh, Gary, 46
Clare, Hilary, 51
Clark, Beverly Lyon, 4, 10, 50–51
class politics, 9–11, 14, 23, 28, 34–36, 38–39, 45, 56, 57, 62, 102, 160–62
Clements, Andrew, 71, 74–79, 82, 84–86
coalitional consciousness, 110–11
Coke, Desmond, 28, 33, 36

college, 23, 25–26, 44, 46, 56, 76–77, 84–85, 103, 109, 132, 136, 164, 175, 15n2
Common Core State Standards, 7–8, 16n4, 84–85
common school narratives, 4, 20, 58, 60
competitiveness in education, 14, 62, 76, 79, 125–26, 128, 130–32, 134–35, 145–46
contracts, 155, 164–66, 172–73, 178n4
Coolidge, Susan, 31, 51
Cooties, 9, 14, 123, 126, 137–47, 183–84
Cormier, Robert, 125. See also *Chocolate War, The*
corporal punishment, 124–25, 130
Craig, Patricia, 41–42, 45, 49
Croft, Michael, 38, 48, 49
Crouch, Marcus, 39–40, 49, 52
cultural studies, 44, 49, 54

D. C. Thomson & Co., 34, 44
Dance of the Dead, 137–38
Day, Thomas, 19, 22
democracy, 4, 7, 11, 21, 36, 40, 50, 56, 63, 72, 74–77, 80, 86, 97, 102, 115, 133–34, 145, 147, 154, 161–63, 167–69, 173, 176–77, 184
democratization of education, 32, 36, 37, 48, 53, 56, 86n3
deregulation, 4, 5, 64n3, 72; of childhood, 165–66, 173, 176–78
Detention of the Dead, 137, 138
Dickens, Charles, 19, 32, 39, 70, 155–56
didactic-pedagogical novel, 69–72, 78–79, 85–86
domestic sphere, 26, 40–42, 47, 50, 58, 160

Edgeworth, Maria, 19, 22, 26, 32
Edinburgh Review, 22
Émile, or On Education (Rousseau), 3, 38, 70, 176, 178
entrepreneurialism, 21, 56, 76, 80–82, 153–55, 163, 172–73
Eric, or Little by Little (Farrar), 19, 23, 27, 36, 47, 124
Escape from Mr. Lemoncello's Library (Grabenstein), 71–72
Eyre, Frank, 37, 52

Farrar, Frederic, 19, 23, 27, 39, 43, 47, 57

feminist criticism, 40–42, 44, 46–47, 49–52, 63, 110
Fielding, Sarah, 10, 25, 53
Fisher, Margery, 37–38, 40
Flanagan, Constance, 10, 126–27, 133, 145–47
Forest, Antonia, 38, 40, 51
forms: hierarchical, 12–13, 21, 73–74, 75–79, 80, 82, 85, 94, 97, 104, 112, 133, 183, 184; network, 12, 14, 155–56, 167–68, 183–84; spatial, 12, 14, 93–94, 101, 104, 125–27, 129–30, 133, 140–41, 167–68, 183–84; temporal, 12, 14, 92–95, 97, 100–101, 104, 108, 111–12, 114, 140, 183–84
free market principles: 5–7, 64n3, 144, 155, 169, 173, 177; and children, 165–66, 173; and education, 7–8, 12–13, 62, 75, 81, 85, 142, 144, 146, 183; and government, 5
freedom, 4, 6, 26, 42, 56, 64n3, 74, 97, 103, 106, 109, 115, 161, 165–66, 173, 176, 184
Freire, Paulo, 81–82, 87n9, 105–6, 117n13, 154
Friedman, Milton, 5–6, 144, 177
Frindle (Clements), 13, 72, 74–79, 82, 84–86, 183
Frith, Gill, 44, 57
Fukasaku, Kinji, 127, 130–32, 134–35. See also *Battle Royale/Batoru Rowaiaru*

Gem, The, 34
gender politics, 11, 21, 23, 25–27, 30–31, 37, 42, 44–47, 49–53, 59, 72, 109–10, 160
Gibson, Rich, 7
Giroux, Henry, 6, 21, 146, 154, 162
Greaux, Candice, 16n2
Greenwald, Tommy, 79–86. See also *Charlie Joe Jackson's Guide to Not Reading*
Grenby, M. O., 53–54, 86n3, 125, 127
Gruner, Elisabeth, 10, 55, 82
Gubar, Marah, 163, 166
Guène, Faïza, 14, 154–55, 157–62, 166, 176, 178, 184
Gurdon, Meghan Cox, 91–92

Harry Potter series, 10, 53–56, 62, 87n10
Hastings, Matt, 7, 97–98
Hay, Ian, 27–28
Hayek, Friedrich, 5–6, 177
Hechinger, Fred M., 130–31

Hemyng, Samuel Bracebridge, 124
Hicks, W. R., 4, 32–33, 52
Holt, Jenny, 57–58, 62–63
hooks, bell, 154
Hopkins, Lisa, 10, 54–55
horror, 9, 12, 14, 94, 124–27, 135–41, 144, 147, 148n2, 184
Howlett, Caitlyn, 154
Hubler, Angela, 110–13
Huehls, Mitchum, 5–6, 64n3, 163
Hughes, Thomas, 19, 22–24, 27, 33, 36–37, 39, 43, 45, 47–48, 54, 57
Humphrey, Judith, 57–59
Hunger Games, The, 127–28, 148n4

I Am Malala (Yousafzai), 14, 154–58, 163, 166–77, 178, 184
Immordino-Yang, Mary Helen, 127, 133, 144, 146–47
individualism, 9, 21, 44, 55, 62, 71–72, 79, 85–86, 102–3, 110, 114, 116n9, 127–28, 155–56, 163, 171, 173, 178n1
Irr, Caren, 116n8, 153–54, 158–59, 169, 172

Jackie, 44
Japan: cinema, 135, 137, 148n2; education system, 8, 131, 148n6; school stories, 14, 126–28, 183; youth violence, 130, 144, 148n5
justice, 5, 153, 159, 172, 184
juvenile audience, 8, 19, 24–25, 28–29, 33–35, 37, 43, 52
juvenilia, 164, 174–76

Katanski, Amelia V., 4, 58–60, 63
Kiffe Kiffe Tomorrow/Kiffe Kiffe Demain (Guène), 14, 154–63, 166, 173, 176, 178, 184
Kingsley, Charles, 22
Kipling, Rudyard, 24, 27–28, 31, 33, 35–37, 39, 42–43, 47, 52, 57
Kirkpatrick, Robert J., 48, 51–52, 124–25, 127
Klein, Ezra, 5
Klein, Naomi, 162, 177
Kobe child murders, 131, 144–45
Kreighbaum, Andrew, 15n2
Krinsky, John, 103–4, 116n9

Lamb, Christina, 156–57, 163, 171
Lamb, Felicia, 25, 40–41, 125
language arts, 74, 85, 112
Latour, Bruno, 155, 168
Levine, Caroline, 9–10, 12, 73–74, 92–93, 126, 129, 132–33, 142, 155–56
liberal arts, 56, 175
literacy, 10, 12, 13, 52, 55, 63, 71–72, 77–85, 100–101, 103, 106, 109, 117n13, 158
literary marketplace, 81, 162–64, 172, 174
Locke, John, 3, 176
Loom of Youth, The (Waugh), 28–29, 33, 47, 164

Mack, Edward C., 35–37, 52
Magnet, The, 34, 43
marketplace: consciousness, 46, 64n3, 72, 76–77, 79, 81–82, 93, 125, 134, 153–55, 158–60, 163, 175–76; rationality, 6, 21, 56, 162, 167; readiness, 13, 79, 103, 142, 175; skepticism, 154, 158; success, 84, 86
Marshall, Elizabeth, 10
masculinity, 19, 22–23, 31, 62
Mathieson, M., 38, 40
McCormick, Patricia, 14, 156–57, 163
McMaster, Juliet, 174
McRoy, Jay, 135–36
Meade, L. T., 26, 44, 47
Meltzer, Marisa, 160, 162–63
mental illness, 11, 92, 94, 116n5, 159
Mickenberg, Julia, 10
Moretti, Franco, 69, 155–56
Mr. Lemoncello series (Grabenstein), 71–72
muscular Christianity, 22–23, 27
Musgrave, P. W., 43–46, 52

Nelson, Claudia, 47–48, 63
neoliberal child, 102, 116n8, 153, 158–59, 169, 172
neoliberalism: assault on education, 4, 16n2, 45–46, 56, 77, 81, 86, 97–100, 105, 155; policies, 4–5, 72, 103–4; stages of, 5–6, 21, 153; tenets of, 4–5, 56, 105

Orwell, George, 8, 20, 34–36, 37, 52, 57, 63, 76, 125, 133–35
Oxenham, Elsie J., 32, 37, 42, 49–51

Pakistan: anti-Malala backlash, 170–71; girls' schools, 154; Taliban invasion of, 167–68; war correspondence, 157
pathological fiction, 12, 14, 91, 92, 94, 100, 108, 113, 114
penny dreadful, 124–25, 134
Perks of Being a Wallflower, The, 71, 92, 148n7
Pinsent, Pat, 4, 53–54, 86n3
Pinsker, Joe, 15n2
Pitofsky, Alexander, 58–60
politics of silence, 109
protest: anti-Malala, 170; in fiction, 38–39, 184; student, 160
Push (Sapphire), 14, 92–94, 100–110, 114, 115n1, 183

Quigly, Isabel, 4, 27, 30, 42–43, 45–46, 52, 73, 125

racism, 4, 7, 11, 14, 58–59, 94, 101–4, 109
Randall, William, 155, 175–76
rape, 11, 14, 91, 94–96, 99–100, 107, 114, 116n6, 118n18
rape novel, 14, 110–12
Ray, Sheila, 53, 86n3
Reagan, Ronald, 5–6, 7, 44, 46, 64n3, 80, 101–2, 105, 117n12
Reed, John, 39–40
Reed, Talbot Baines, 19, 28, 34, 36–37, 39, 42–43, 45, 48, 52
Religious Tract Society, 19, 34
revolution: cultural, 46; and literature, 156, 161, 175, 184; social, 61
Reynolds, Kimberly, 10
Richards, Frank (aka Charles Hamilton, aka Hilda Richards), 34–35, 42–43, 45
Richards, Jeffrey, 4, 45–46, 48, 52
Roosevelt, Theodore, 24
Rose, Jacqueline, 164, 173
Rosenfeld, Lucinda, 161, 170
Ross, E. Wayne, 7
Rousseau, Jean-Jacques, 3, 38, 70, 176–78
Rowbotham, Judith, 46–47
Rowling, J. K., 10, 53–56, 62, 87n10
Roy, Ravi, 5

Salmon, Edward, 23
Sapphire, 14, 92–93, 105–9, 117n14. See also *Push*
Sartre, Jean-Paul, 111, 173
School Friend, The, 42
school story: American, 8, 12–13, 20, 24–25, 50, 54, 58–60, 71–72, 74, 78–79, 84–86, 108, 136, 138; boys', 19, 23–24, 27, 32, 35–37, 39, 45; decline of, 37, 40, 43–44, 49, 51–52, 63; genre of, 3–4, 8, 10, 13, 19, 22–23, 25, 28, 32–33, 38–39, 43, 45, 48, 69, 82, 86n3, 92, 101, 127, 155, 184; girls', 20, 23, 25, 30–32, 37, 39–44, 49, 51, 57; Native American, 20–21, 58
schoolboys, 22–24, 27–31, 47–48, 52, 72–73, 76, 79, 81, 84–85, 125, 131
schoolgirls, 25–26, 30–32, 40–42, 94, 108, 158, 163, 167, 169, 172
Schoolgirls' Own, The, 42
Schoolgirls' Weekly, 42
schools: alternative, 101, 103, 105; boarding, 4, 8, 10, 19–20, 25, 33, 37–38, 40, 50, 54, 58–59, 61–63, 64n1, 73, 125; charter, 4, 63, 98; coeducational, 25, 50–51, 61; comprehensive, 20, 36, 40, 43, 48, 51, 63; public (UK), 19, 20, 22–23, 27–30, 32–33, 35, 37, 39, 40, 43–45, 48, 51–52, 57, 59, 61–62, 64n4; public (US), 4, 60, 63, 77, 99–100
self-harm, 91–92, 94, 100
Simon, Caroline, 15n2
Sims, Sue, 48, 51
Singmaster, Elsie, 25
Smith, Rachel Greenwald, 5–6, 64n3, 163
social emotional development, 127–33, 144–45
social work, 101, 103–5, 158, 161
Spectator, The, 23–24, 26, 28–29, 31
Speak (Anderson), 9, 14, 71, 92–100, 109–15, 148n7, 183
Speicher, Allison, 4, 58, 60
Spolton, L., 38, 40, 176
Springhall, John, 124
Stalky & Co., 24, 27, 31–33, 45, 47, 125
Steger, Manfred, 5
Swarup, Vikas, 153, 172, 178

Takami, Koushon, 127–28, 132, 134
teachers, representations of, 28, 38, 41, 54, 60, 71, 74–78, 81, 86n3, 95–106, 113–14, 125–29, 137, 139–47, 184
teenage authors, 14, 28–29, 154–57, 162–66, 171, 173–76, 178, 184
tests, 7–8, 77, 98, 103, 106, 131–32
Thackeray, William Makepeace, 19, 22, 39
Thatcher, Margaret, 5–7, 44, 46, 64n3, 178n1
therapy, 113–14, 117n15, 158–59, 162; through art, 96, 113, 116n5
Tom Brown's School Days (Hughes), 9–10, 19, 21–25, 27, 32–37, 43, 45 47, 50, 52, 54–55, 57, 60–61, 123–24, 125
Townsend, John Rowe, 39–40, 43, 52
Trease, Geoffrey, 37, 52
Twain, Mark, 72, 81

Vachell, Horace Annesley, 33, 36, 57
Vipont, Elfrida, 39

war: correspondence, 156–57; First World War, 29, 40–41; in schoolgirl fiction, 30–31; Second World War, 32, 35, 40–41, 49, 131; Taliban occupation of Pakistan, 167–70
Watson, Benjamin, 48
Waugh, Alec, 28–30, 33, 35, 38–39, 43, 47, 57, 164
welfare, 4–6, 93–94, 101–5, 109, 114, 158
Wells, H. G., 33, 36, 39
Westman, Karin, 10, 55, 87n10
Whiteside, M. T., 38, 40
Whitney, Jason, 78
Wilby, Peter, 46
women's education rights, 25–26, 40
writing: child development and, 56, 77, 81, 84–85, 101, 103, 106–7, 111, 117n13, 163, 174–76; commercialization of, 81–82, 163; politics of, 111

Yogerst, Chris, 137–39
Yonge, Charlotte M., 23, 40
Yousafzai, Malala, 14, 154–55, 163, 166, 168–72, 174, 176, 178, 184

youth violence, 128–35, 139–41, 144–45, 148n3, 148nn5–6, 149n9

zombies, 126, 135, 137–43, 146–47

ABOUT THE AUTHOR

Photo courtesy of the author

A graduate of the writing programs at the University of Glasgow and Boston University, David Aitchison earned his PhD in American literature and history from the University of Wisconsin–Madison in 2012. He is an independent scholar based in Chicago, where he teaches for Chicago Public Schools.